MOTOR LEARNING

from theory to practice

MOTOR LEARNING
from theory to practice

LORETTA M. STALLINGS, Ed.D.

Professor, Department of Human Kinetics and Leisure Studies,
School of Education and Human Development,
The George Washington University,
Washington, D.C.

with 51 illustrations

The C. V. Mosby Company

ST. LOUIS • TORONTO • LONDON   1982

MOSBY

A TRADITION OF PUBLISHING EXCELLENCE

Editor: Charles K. Hirsch
Assistant editor: Michelle Turenne
Editing supervisor: Elaine Steinborn
Manuscript editor: Elizabeth O'Brien
Book design: Susan Trail
Cover design: Diane Beasley
Production: Barbara Merritt

Cover photograph by **James E. Bryant**

The C.V. Mosby Company
11830 Westline Industrial Drive, St. Louis, Missouri 63141

Library of Congress Cataloging in Publication Data

Stallings, Loretta M.
  Motor learning.

  Bibliography: p.
  Includes index.
  1. Motor learning. 2. Motor learning—Study
and teaching. I. Title.
BF295.S76   152.3′34   81-14118
ISBN 0-8016-4768-1   AACR2

AC/D/D 9 8 7 6 5 4 3 2 1   02/A/243

With thanks
to my students—past, present, and future

PREFACE

Information applicable to the learning of motor skills comes from a variety of sources, including psychology, neurology, physiology, physical education, physical and occupational therapy, engineering and communications, and system development. As a result, many theories and concepts are available, which, if applied selectively, can contribute to the improvement of instruction. Unfortunately, application of this information to the practice of physical education has been lacking. The purpose of this book is to help bridge this gap by providing the practitioner in the field and the future teacher with practical implications of these theories and concepts and a framework for applying them systematically.

Although directed primarily to undergraduate physical education majors and to teachers and coaches in the field, this book is equally pertinent to graduate students whose objective is the application of learning concepts in the field setting. In addition, this book should be of value to others interested in motor skills, whether they be in the dance studio, on the playground, in the classroom, or in the clinic.

Part One deals with the practical implications of various learning theories so that students can see recurring, as well as conflicting, implications. This gives students a more valid basis for evaluating their present instructional practices or beliefs and a sounder base for accepting new approaches. Part Two provides what students have called the ABC's of the job. Here three variables affecting motor learning are discussed in separate sections dealing with (1) the state of the learner, (2) the nature of the skill, and (3) the methods of instruction. A major feature of this book, in addition to its practical orientation, is its flexibility for meeting the needs of different instructors and of different groups of students. As one example, instructors may choose to begin with Part Two and pick up specific learning theories from Part One as their objectives and their students' needs dictate. However, many other arrangements have also proved useful.

Each chapter concludes with a sample thought sheet, which is deemed a major tool in meeting the theory-to-practice objective of the book. These thought sheets have been useful in stimulating active participation by students before class sessions. As a result, class time can be devoted to clarification and application of the theories and concepts. However, the thought sheets should be considered samples only. Instructors may desire to design their own thought sheets specifically relevant to the needs of their own students.

An appendix to the book suggests a sequence of practice opportunities that can help the student acquire a higher level of ability to apply the theories and concepts to instruction. This particular sequence of experiences has evolved from use in motor learning classes at The George Washington University. However, not all of the opportunities described will be feasible in all situations. In addition, I would be grateful for comments from those using the book so that both the text and the practice opportunities can be made more useful to a variety of students and instructors.

This book is not intended to be a compendium in the area of motor learning or a reference manual to research in the field. Only those theories, concepts, and models that are deemed to be applicable to teaching motor skills are included. Motor development has not been included as a separate topic, since it has an extensive body of knowledge in its own right. Fortunately, motor development courses are becoming a recognized part of physical education curricula, and a number of motor development texts are now available.

An attempt has been made to delete sexist language in this text; however, this has not always been possible. Therefore, for expediency and clarity, the third person, masculine gender, is used in reference to any person. Of course, pronouns in quoted material have not been changed.

I wish to extend thanks to my reviewers: Mike Allison of Fort Lewis College at Durango, Colorado; Dr. Charles Daniel of Western Kentucky University at Bowling Green; Patricia Del Rey, Ed.D., of the University of Georgia at Athens; Douglas D. Larish, Ph.D., of the University of Iowa at Iowa City; and Richard A. Miller, M.S., of Tennessee State University at Nashville.

I am particularly indebted to Dr. James L. Breen, Professor and Chairman of the Department of Human Kinetics and Leisure Studies at The George Washington University, for his consideration during the preparation of the manuscript. Special thanks is due Mr. Charles K. Hirsch for his constructive criticism. To the editor and contributors to the journal *Motor Skills: Theory into Practice*, appreciation is extended for helping me "bridge the gap." I am also grateful to Judy Mermelstein, my typist, not only for interpreting my handwriting but also for her interest in the topic. Finally, I want to thank Ann Williams for her editing help and her humor.

Loretta M. Stallings

CONTENTS

1 INTRODUCTION

Recently, increasing attention has been devoted to the study of motor learning and performance. As a result, many theories and concepts are available that, if applied selectively, can increase not only the rate at which individuals learn skills, but also the proficiency they attain. The sad fact is, however, that there is little indication that this knowledge is having any appreciable effect on what is taking place in physical education. This problem has been voiced repeatedly of late both at professional meetings and in the journals (e.g., Bain & Poindexter, 1981; Locke, 1979; Rothstein, 1981; Templin, 1980).

There is no question that knowledge regarding motor performance has increased enormously in recent years. However, it is questionable whether this growth of information is the major cause of the gap between the knowledge and instructional practices. For example, there are principles of learning that have been known for many years that have yet to find their way into most gymnasia, dance studios, playfields, or swimming pools.

A major problem appears to lie in how this knowledge has been imparted and the lack of opportunities for guided practice. Knowledge by itself is not sufficient to bring about changes in practice. Indeed a basic tenet of any learning theory is that we do not become adept at a skill until we practice it. This is no less true for a new teaching skill than it is for a new motor skill.

The purpose of this book is to help bridge this gap between theories and concepts of motor learning and performance and the practice of teaching and coaching. First, however, it is necessary to clarify the value of theories and concepts to instructional practice, the dimensions of motor skill development, and the specific terminology used in this book.

Theories and concepts: a basis for practice

One of the traditional quests of psychology has been to attempt to explain how learning comes about. Unfortunately, theories of learning have not for the most part provided practitioners directly with information on how to teach. As a result, an all-too-common assumption among teachers is that theories and concepts of learning are unnecessary and irrelevant to effective teaching. Nothing could be further from the truth. If ever any subject has demanded a theoretical approach, it is learning. If a construction engineer attempted to build a house without the necessary blueprints, we would not expect an effective job; indeed only one or a few of the specifications need be in error for the long-term stability of the structure to be in doubt. We can certainly give no less rigorous attention to human learning.

Theories provide us with blueprints or guidelines that can help ensure that our methods of teaching are consistent with scientific evidence. Theories, if based on a scientific approach, must meet several criteria (Singer, 1975):

1. Material is presented in a systematic and orderly fashion.
2. Material is essentially based on the most accurate scientific information present at the time.
3. Material is such that it allows us to understand behavior better.
4. Material is offered in a conceptual form.
5. Material is of such a nature that it encourages further research.
6. Material is applicable to practical situations (p. 55).

There is no question that this last criterion, practical application, has been the most difficult to achieve. The cliché "It sounds great in theory but it doesn't work in practice" is not as nonsensical as is sometimes assumed. The statement reflects some critical limitations of theories in general and of learning theories in particular. Since a basic assumption of this book is that theories and concepts of learning are essential tools of our profession, we need to be clear as to their limitations as well as to their contributions.

FACT AND FICTION

Theories are mixtures of fact and fiction. At best, they begin with the facts observable at the time of their formulation, but beyond that they must infer, conceptualize, or hypothesize what is not known. Learning theories are close to the low end of the disciplinary totem pole in their ratio of knowns to unknowns; this is one of the reasons there are so many of them. However, many of the theories are not as different as they may seem at first glance. In Part One of this book you will note recurring theoretical concepts of learning. These are the concepts that would appear to have the greatest import for the practitioner.

GROWTH OF THEORIES

Theories are not static; they grow or die. If they are to grow, they must be tested. But the question is not Do they work? but rather Under what conditions do they work or not work and why? The answers to these questions generate new knowledge on which the theory may be revised or refined. However, the most valid theories and concepts are those that have been subjected to verification beyond our own individual experience. This is one of the reasons we find conflicting results in our research publications. No matter how carefully planned and conducted, a single research study seldom lends itself to generalization beyond the particular conditions of the study. I hope that my selection of theories and concepts discussed in this book lifts us beyond the confines of our own experiences.

THEORETICAL CONCEPTS

Any single theory is composed of logically constructed or compatible concepts. When the theory is subjected to practical verification or testing, some of these concepts may be confirmed; others may not be or may be confirmed within certain limitations. Therefore we can accept a certain concept without accepting the theory in its entirety. One of the purposes of this book is to encourage the use of concepts from many different theories. However, theoretical concepts are practical and useful only to the extent that the conditions of their operation are explicitly understood by the person using them. The practitioner who praises an individual following a good performance is applying one concept of learning, but is it the best concept for that situation? The practitioner who praises an individual immediately following a poor performance to provide encouragement is applying incompatible concepts of motivation and reinforcement to the detriment of the individual. The problem, then, is not one of theory versus practice, but of practicing the proper theoretical concept in the proper situation.

TEACHING AND THEORIES OF LEARNING

Learning theorists attempt to explain how human beings learn; teachers are concerned with how to influence individuals to learn. Thus teachers often maintain that what they need are procedures rather than explanations. While such a viewpoint is understandable, it indicates a failure to recognize the relationship of theory to application (Jones, 1967, p. 19). Hilgard (1964) points out that there may be as many as six steps from pure research on learning to the development of an instructional technology and its application. Fig. 1-1 emphasizes that regardless of their expressed attitudes toward learning theory, teachers *do* operate on the basis of theories. For example, teachers who encourage learners to concentrate on the feel of their movement during performance are applying one theory of motor learning whether they know it or not, and as we shall see, it is not a very good theory for many situations. One of the purposes of studying learning theories is to force us to examine the underlying theoretical concepts on which our practices and beliefs are based.

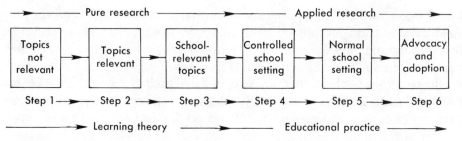

FIG. 1-1. Relationship between learning theory and educational practice. (Modified from Hilgard, E. A perspective on the relationship between learning theory and educational practices. In E. Hilgard [Ed.], *Theories of learning and instruction*. Chicago: University of Chicago Press, 1964.)

THEORIES OF INSTRUCTION

The fact remains, however, that learning theorists themselves have been negligent in their attention to the concerns of the practitioner. While this situation is by no means limited to motor learning theorists, the urgent need for more attention to applied research in motor learning and performance (Fig. 1-1) has been voiced frequently in recent years (e.g., Gowan, Botterill, and Blimkie, 1980; Martens, 1980; Salmela, 1980; Whiting, 1976). Until the conflict between the practitioner's need to solve practical problems and the theorist's desire to build theories is resolved, practitioners must rely on their study of learning theories to design an up-to-date, systematic theory of instruction. It is the purpose of this book to assist you in doing this. I hope you will also be encouraged to participate in some much needed field-based research in the future.

Using theories and concepts

The purpose of this section is to suggest some of the ways in which the practitioner can use theories and concepts in practice: as a barometer of acceptability of instructional methods, as a basis for generalization, and as a model for instruction. Brief examples are given to show not only that theories and concepts are used in these ways, but also that their use requires in-depth knowledge.

AS A BAROMETER OF ACCEPTABILITY

Such common sense beliefs as "practice makes perfect" or "the more motivation, the better" have probably been more detrimental to learning than if we had left learners to their own devices. Practice will "set" whatever one practices, including inefficient movement patterns, and each skill has its own optimal level of arousal that is conducive to peak performance.

Unfortunately, such misleading generalities abound in the field of learning, and everyone appears to be a self-appointed expert in the area of teaching. Although the structure of our knowledge regarding learning is not yet sufficient to provide us with a true science of teaching, it is certainly now sufficient to dictate that we go beyond the art of teaching. To accomplish this, however, we must subject our beliefs and practices to the light of current knowledge to determine the extent of their acceptability.

The problem of determining the acceptability of learning concepts, however, is more subtle than the "practice makes perfect" example reveals. Consider the following exerpts, one taken from a newspaper article and the other from a physical education newsletter:

> We should learn to play better tennis the way we learned to walk by moving our arms this way and our legs that way. . . . We watched them, made a few mistakes and did what came naturally. That's how we should learn to play tennis (Gallwey, 1976, p. H-9).

> Perhaps in learning some skills, the best approach is not to practice at all in the early stages of development, or perhaps to practice only minimally. It may be more fruitful to watch, listen to, or passively move with a model for extensive periods of time until the model becomes firmly fixed in memory (McGrath, 1977, p. 10).

Are you willing to accept these statements as valid learning concepts? On what basis? Let's glance at just some of the facts relative to the statement by Gallwey.

There is considerable neurological evidence (e.g., Eccles, 1977, p. 121-144) that the cerebellum of the brain is involved in the smooth and reliable control of movement and therefore can free the cerebrum to concentrate on the objective of the act (e.g., picking up the glass or intercepting the ball). However, as Basmajiian (1978) emphasizes, cerebral concentration together with proper biofeedback techniques can activate individual groups of muscle cells; such motor unit training has been useful in at least partial rehabilitation of certain stroke victims. In addition, it appears that the cerebellum may need to *learn* to carry out its task (Eccles, 1977, p. 124). This suggests that in the early stages of learning a skill there may need to be an interplay between cerebral concentration on movement and a release to the automatic control mechanisms of the cerebellum and more peripheral structures. Certainly, concentration on movement is usually needed in learning to inhibit certain neuromuscular reflexes when these reflexes are detrimental to performance (e.g., the head-righting reflex in diving).

More will be said later about some of the neurological mechanisms involved in movement control. The point being made here is that while the concept of concentrating on the objective of the skill rather than the movements involved may be extremely useful, it may not be the most effective in all situations.

Should we limit physical practice in the early stages of learning as McGrath suggests? She bases her suggestion on well-documented evidence that questions the traditional chaining concept of skill development, that is, that the kinesthetic feedback from one segment of a movement is necessary to initiate the next segment. A more recent view that movements can be controlled by motor programs (stored in memory) suggests, as McGrath notes, a different approach to skill learning. One would limit practice until the pattern of the skill becomes sufficiently fixed in memory so as to provide an internalized picture of the skill. This model could then be used by the learner as a basis for comparison when practice begins. McGrath suggests as alternatives to physical practice, techniques of mental practice, loop films, demonstrations, and manual guidance.

McGrath's suggestion has merit. It is true that continued practice of the inefficient movement patterns typical of the beginner will "set" those inefficient patterns. However, information theory tells us that what individuals see in a demonstration or film is not necessarily what we show them. It is more often filtered by or pooled with their own background of experience. What, then, are beginners rehearsing when they engage in mental practice? Probably not what we want them to. Manual guidance, in turn, while a useful technique in certain situations, has some inherent limitations, especially if it produces passive movement. This is not to say that McGrath's suggestion is not useful. She has provided a needed and too seldom taken step in applying theory to practice. It is now up to us to determine the particular conditions of its applicability.

I hope these examples have helped convince you of the value of theoretical concepts to practical concerns and of the need to proceed with some caution in accepting a learning concept as valid. This does not mean that we should not experiment; indeed we must. But let's do it with the understanding that there is no guarantee that a specific concept will work in every situation.

AS A BASIS FOR GENERALIZATION

Once a concept has been established, through repeated testing, as having general applicability, it allows us within the limits of its operation to solve problems with which we have previously had no experience or to solve problems more efficiently.

For example, Fisher and Motta (1977) suggest some applications of the inverted U concept of arousal to coaching procedures. Basically, this concept states that proficiency increases with increases in arousal level up to a certain optimal point beyond which further increases in arousal will have detrimental effects on performance. The authors note that too often coaches employ strategies aimed at infecting team members with high levels of arousal. They ask some cogent questions:

Is this arousal necessary? If so, is high activation necessary for all team members irrespective of position? Are high levels of arousal equally effective for all sports (p. 98)?

They go on to say the following:

The subject of activation would seem to be a major concern for coaches of all sports. . . . As evidence of this, almost every book on coaching and sport psychology deals with the activation/performance relationship to some degree. Why such an interest? Very simply, if activation and its control can lead to greater success, then coaches want a "handle" on it (p. 98).

The desire of coaches to get a "handle on it" is reflected in the recent sprouting of what may become a whole new industry—commercial sports psychology. Although the rash of current books dealing with sports "psyching" is one indication of this, more recently there have emerged several commercial enterprises that specialize in packaging mental training programs. Coaches contract with these firms for their services, which can run anywhere from a day to a week or longer. For the most part, the training personnel work directly with the team members. Although the package may be individualized depending on whether the sport is swimming, tennis, or diving, basically the techniques are similar and usually involve such considerations as arousal control, mental imagery, concentration, and relaxation. What makes these programs possible, of course, is that there is a general concept of arousal that can be applied to most sports.

Arousal control is the subject of Chapter 6. The point here is that theories can provide us with concepts applicable to a wide range of skills. However, as research tells us, this transfer is not automatic. Not only must the concept be thoroughly understood by the practitioner, but practice is required to ensure its application.

AS A MODEL FOR INSTRUCTION

The next four chapters of this book are devoted to theories of learning: traditional learning theories, neurological theories, information-processing models, and theories of motor control. Any one or all of these theories can be a basis for designing instruction. For example, Rushall and Siedentop (1972) have developed a systematic plan for instruction in motor skills based on Skinner's operant conditioning (behavior modification), Sage (1977) has done the same using a neuropsychological approach, and Marteniuk (1976) uses an information-processing model.

However, the viewpoint taken in this book is that all of these theories offer the practitioner applicable concepts and therefore need to be included. The desirability of such a multitheoretical approach to learning and teaching should become obvious as we proceed.

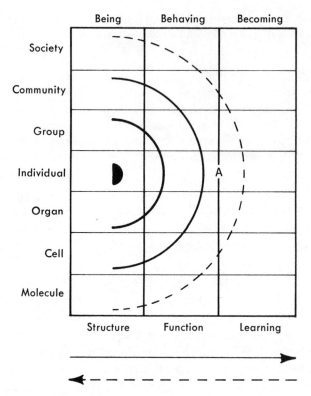

FIG. 1-2. Dimensions of human development. (Modified from Gerard, R.W. Neurophysiology: an integration [molecules, neurons, and behavior]. In J. Field [Ed.], *Handbook of physiology: section 1, neurophysiology, vol. 3*. Washington, D.C.: American Physiological Society, 1960.)

Dimensions of motor skill development

No single book can hope to encompass all the dimensions of motor skill development. The limitations are due partly to our lack of knowledge and partly to the inability of any single person to interpret all the information we have. However, this does not relieve an author of the obligation to clarify the dimensions of the field under consideration and the limitations imposed.

Gerard (1960, p. 1923) presents a conceptual model of the "Architecture of Knowledge," which, because of its versatility, can be used to clarify these dimensions and, in general, the limits of our knowledge (Fig. 1-2). Thus our knowledge regarding human development started with the individual and in the descriptive or structural area. Consideration has spread (as shown by the expanding semicircles in Fig. 1-2) horizontally to encompass function and learning, and vertically to encompass internal constituents and external factors. As Gerard notes, the impressive phenomenon of all living systems is that they depend on learning for growth and development.

PHASES OF DEVELOPMENT

The phases of human development are shown horizontally at the top and bottom of Fig. 1-2 and constitute a cycle of development from being (structure), to behaving (function), to becoming (learning). Learning in turn impresses new functional and structural intricacies on the individual (arrows), and the cycle of progressive change is thus assured.

For example, the earliest patterns of motor behavior appear to be genetically coded in the species. That is, there is some initial organization or template that guides the pattern of new formations (structure). In addition, there are some operational rules that lead to patterns of behavior (function) in which variable changes are accounted for by the particular conditions of individual experience (learning). Learning in turn modifies function and structure, thus continuing the cycle of development.

The study of motor skill development, therefore, is concerned with the factors that influence motor behavior, with the design of experiences that will result in desirable changes in this behavior, and with the potential for this learning to increase the individual's capacity for future development. However, until we know more about the way in which learning interacts with structure and function, theories of human development will remain fragmented. The limits of knowledge in this cycle are indicated by the dotted lines in Fig. 1-2; for the most part, we can only theorize regarding the nature of these relationships.

LEVELS OF DEVELOPMENT

The levels of organization that concern human development are shown vertically on the left side of Fig. 1-2. These include not only internal constituents (organ, cell, molecule), but also external components (group, community, society).

Each of these levels interact to influence individual motor skill development. For example, motor performance (individual behavior) is influenced both by physiological condition (organic behavior) and by the dynamics of the student-teacher and intergroup relationships (group behavior). The organic reactions to environmental stress are another example of the interdependency of these levels. We are just beginning to study the influence of socioeconomic class and family background on motor skill development, and the effects appear to be on the kinds of activity engaged in and the extent of participation.

The roles of societal and molecular development in behavior and learning, however, are far from being understood. That societal changes contribute to changes in individual behavior, including life-styles, can hardly be argued, but the details of the interactions remain obscure. In addition, although there is some experimental support and logical rationale for the concept that learning has a molecular correlate, these molecular theories are not sufficiently refined to aid us in understanding individual learning.

LIMITATIONS

The limitations of our knowledge regarding human development have been broadly outlined in the preceding sections. However, you should also be aware of the limitations imposed by the author.

The primary concern of the practitioner is to design instruction to facilitate learning. Therefore the emphasis in this book is on theories and concepts of individual motor performance and learning (point A in Fig. 1-2) and their systematic application to instruction. In addition, Fig. 1-2 should make obvious the fact that information relating to motor skill development is derived from a variety of disciplines, each approaching the topic from a different point of view. Many of the disciplines represented use a specialized language. While I have tried to interpret and present information to facilitate its application, some effort on your part will be required to learn some new and essential terminology.

Terminology

Andrews (1976), speaking on the topic "Motor Learning Theory and the Practice of Teaching," highlighted a major problem in moving from theory to practice.

> At a very basic stage of theorizing, that of *definition,* motor learning has a great deal of work to do. Whilst sharing the practitioner's irritation with much of the jargon used in so-called scientific discourse, I realise that the situation is by no means a simple one. . . . I would only plead that each of us in trying to communicate . . . should attempt to make as clear as possible what we mean when we use certain terms (p. 4).

Throughout this book numerous terms are used, which, to convey the meanings intended, require operational definitions. Unfortunately, definitions vary considerably, and even subtle differences in meanings, if undetected, can lead to misunderstandings not only of the intent but also of the implications of the discussion for instructional practice. For example, the term *skill* is used variously by different authors to mean a specific act (such as throwing a ball), a particular level of performance of an individual (one is at such and such a skill level), or a high proficiency (one has skill). Therefore we as authors are obligated to define our terms operationally, that is, to ascribe to each term a meaning that you as a reader are asked to accept, temporarily at least, to properly interpret what is being said. An operational definition does not assume that it is the one correct definition or even that it is the best one, only that it is the definition essential to understanding the material presented.

Examples of the variability that exists in the use of terms will be found in any supplementary reading you may do, and you are cautioned to determine the meanings ascribed to terms by each author. In the following section, operational definitions are in italics. Other terms will be defined later as needed.

SKILLS AND ABILITIES

Variously called sensorimotor and perceptual motor skills, the shortened term *motor skills* is used here with the assumption that all motor skills have a perceptual component. One of the concepts emphasized in this book is that motor skills need to be analyzed in terms of both their perceptual and their motor prerequisites.

For present purposes, *motor skill* is used to denote *any muscular activity that is directed toward a specific objective*. This activity may be viewed along a continuum extending from that of large movement (gross motor skill) to that of small movement (fine motor skill). Thus motor skills run the gamut from broad jumping to driving a car and even to speaking.

Notice, however, that this definition does not require that a motor skill involve movement. Thus it does not exclude purposeful activity resulting from static contraction as in stationary balancing. In fact, this definition does not even require that the muscular activity be one of contraction. Inhibition of muscular contraction is essential not only in gradually refining movements of the body during learning but also in achieving the benefits of relaxation exercises.

In this book a critical distinction is made between *skills* and *abilities* similar to that proposed by Fleishman (1964). Skills are directed toward a specific objective; abilities are more general. Abilities are attributes that can facilitate performance in a variety of skills. *Motor skill abilities, therefore, are those attributes that can contribute to proficiency in a number of motor skills*. For example, leg strength (power) is a motor skill ability that contributes to proficiency in such skills as broad jumping and sprinting. Dynamic visual acuity is a perceptual ability required in such skills as batting, catching a fly ball, and skeet shooting. Some examples of abilities are muscular power, balance, and perceptual speed; examples of skills are the 100-meter dash, walking a balance beam, and a tennis volley, respectively.

OPEN AND CLOSED SKILLS

Poulton (1957), in an attempt to define and classify motor skills, introduced a concept that has gained wide acceptance and that has direct relevance to instruction in motor skills. He classified skills according to the type of environment in which they were performed. Skills performed in an environment in which conditions are always changing he termed *open skills;* those skills performed in a static or unchanging environment he called *closed skills.* Examples of open skills are a tennis drive, intercepting a ball, and skiing. Examples of closed skills are bowling, a free throw in basketball, and target archery.

In addition, as learning progresses in a closed skill, the performer evidences increasing consistency in movement patterns, whereas increasing proficiency in an open skill requires diversification of movement patterns to meet the demands of the particular situation (Higgins & Spaeth, 1972). It seems desirable to incorporate both the environmental considerations and the movement considerations into our definitions. *Open skills,* therefore, are *skills in which the stimuli for the action are variable and which require a flexibility of movement response.* Conversely, *closed skills* are *skills in which the stimuli are fixed and which require a consistency of movement response.*

However, such a classification is relative and is best placed on a continuum rather than on an either-or basis. Chapter 8 emphasizes the importance of determining both the closed and open elements of a skill. The important point being made here is that the open-closed concept has critical implications for instruction. For example, in the case of closed skills (such as diving) instruction would focus on increasing the movement consistency of the skill; in the case of open skills (such as intercepting a ball) the instructor would want to encourage flexibility of movement to meet the exigencies of the particular moment.

LEARNING AND PERFORMANCE

Another important distinction is that between *learning* and *performance.* Learning occurs within the individual and therefore is never directly observable. What we mean when we say we "have seen a person learning" is that we have seen a change in behavior. That is, we infer learning when we observe an improvement in the level of performance over a period of time. In the individual learning curve shown in Fig. 1-3, each trial represents a performance, while the difference between the final and initial performance trials ($T_2 - T_1$) represents the amount of improvement or learning.

Motor performance, in relation to the more lengthy course of learning, *is a one-trial or temporary expression of motor skill behavior. Proficiency* is the *level of performance* at any specific point in time. Note in Fig. 1-3 that the level of performance is variable from trial to trial. This is accounted for by the fact that day-to-day proficiency is influenced by a number of temporary conditions, including motivational and physiological fluctuations. This is one reason that single-trial scores (e.g., $T_2 - T_1$) are seldom reliable indicators of learning. Reliability is increased by combining (averaging) scores on three or more sequential trials.

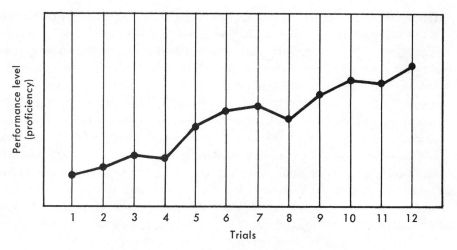

FIG. 1-3. Individual learning curve.

Traditional definitions of learning generally include three criteria: (1) there must be a *change* in behavior, (2) this change must be relatively *stable,* and (3) the change must be the result of *practice* or experience. To clarify the definition of motor learning used in this book, a brief discussion of these criteria follows.

Learning as a change in behavior—As shown in Fig. 1-3, individual learning curves reveal increments, plateaus, and occasional decrements. Although these day-to-day fluctuations in motor performance are useful in describing the course of learning and often in clarifying individual learning problems, few practitioners would view a steady decrement as learning. Despite the fact that both decremental and maladaptive changes in behavior obviously occur, the criterion of *improvement* in proficiency would seem to be a more useful one for our purposes.

Learning as being relatively stable—The criterion of relative stability excludes from the definition of learning the changes in proficiency that are not long lasting. For example, whether practice is massed or distributed (interspersed with rest periods) appears to have an immediate effect on performance level but not on the final proficiency attained. The stability of learning is usually determined by measuring retention, that is, the amount of proficiency remaining after a no-practice interval. If the curve in Fig. 1-3, for example, indicates an increase in the number of sit-ups accomplished, this would not be considered learning, since the increase is brought about by strength and endurance development that would fall off rapidly without continued practice.

Learning as a result of practice—The criterion of learning as a result of practice excludes from the definition of learning the changes in behavior that are due to growth and maturation. This exclusion presents some thorny problems, and these are discussed in the next section on motor skill development. However, it also seems desirable to differentiate between the terms *practice* and *experience*. Although practice is more commonly used in definitions of learning, it is the quality of an individual's experiences that is crucial to learning. The *conditions of experience* (including practice), not repetitions, are what practitioners must be concerned with.

For the purpose of this book, *motor learning* is defined as *improvement in proficiency on a motor skill that is due to experiential or practice conditions rather than to maturational processes or temporary motivational and physiological fluctuations*. It should be noted, however, that learning is not always demonstrated in overt performance. For example, an individual can learn much about a skill or game, yet may not have the necessary perceptual or motor abilities (or motivation) to perform. Dunham (1971), among others, notes this weakness in defining learning in terms of performance changes. However, while recognizing that much learning may be covert, a major assumption in this book is that optimal performance at each stage of learning motor skills increases the probability of attaining a higher level of final proficiency.

MOTOR SKILL DEVELOPMENT

The exclusion from the traditional definition of learning of changes in proficiency due to maturation has been a limiting factor for both the practitioner and the researcher. The problem of distinguishing what proportion of improvement is due to learning and what proportion is due to maturation appears to the practitioner to be only academic. In addition, few learning studies are conducted with infants and children because of the problem of isolating maturational factors. The unfortunate result is that we know very little about the learning capabilities of children.

The numerous different concepts of growth, maturation, and development only further confound the problem. However, the dimensions of human development diagrammed in Fig. 1-2 may help to clarify the distinction. Changes in behavior (point A in Fig. 1-2) that are a result of structural patterns and functional rules genetically coded in the species can be considered maturation. Changes that are a result of experience or practice should be considered learning. For example, maturation provides the potential for walking; opportunity is needed to elicit walking behavior; and practice is required to perfect it, that is, to change it adaptively (Eckert & Espenshade, 1980, p. 92).

While early studies tended to emphasize the role of maturation in the development of motor skills, the trend now seems to be toward recognition of the critical role of opportunity and experience. However, as Thompson (1962) concludes, the influences of maturation and learning are so inextricably interwoven that it is futile to try to delineate the influence of each. Hunt (1961) suggests that the maturation-learning dichotomy may well be artificial and has proposed an interaction approach to development. This is consistent with the concept diagrammed in Fig.1-2 in which learning is seen to influence structure and function, thus increasing the capacity of the individual for further development. Therefore *motor skill development,* as used in this book, refers to *changes in proficiency on a motor skill that are the result of maturation and learning.* Note, however, that this definition does not necessarily imply an improvement in proficiency. Maturation is a continuous process, albeit accelerated during infancy, youth, and old age. At any point, Hunt (1971) suggests, proficiency is the result of the interaction between the competencies individuals have available and the situational demands made on them.

The conceptual framework

This book is organized around a specific conceptual framework, and this organization is deemed as important as the content if the objective of moving from theory to practice is to be achieved. This framework assumes that motor skill development is influenced by three major factors: (1) the state of the learner, (2) the nature of the skill, and (3) the methods of instruction.

Specifically, this organization was designed not merely to help you recall the factors involved in motor skill development but also to encourage you to view learning and instructional problems systematically. No matter how much we may like to think of ourselves as intuitive teachers or coaches, the problem-solving approach, while less expedient than intuition, may also be less subject to error. Error on our part, if avoidable, is in the long run a disservice to students. The practitioner with a framework for viewing the variables of motor skill development systematically should be better equipped to plan instruction in such a way as to facilitate learning and to identify and solve individual learning problems.

PRINCIPLE OF FUNCTIONAL DEPENDENCE

One way of visualizing this conceptual framework is to draw on the principle of functional dependence. Thus the equation $X = f(y)$ is read "X is a function of y" and means that the value of X will change systematically with changes in the value of y. Applying this principle to our conceptual framework, we would write $L = f(a/b/c)$, where L is the level of skill development, a the state of the learner, b the nature of the skill, and c the instructional methods. Translated, the equation $L = f(a/b/c)$ means that the level of skill development will change with changes in the state of the learner, changes in the requirements of the skill, or changes in the methods of instruction.

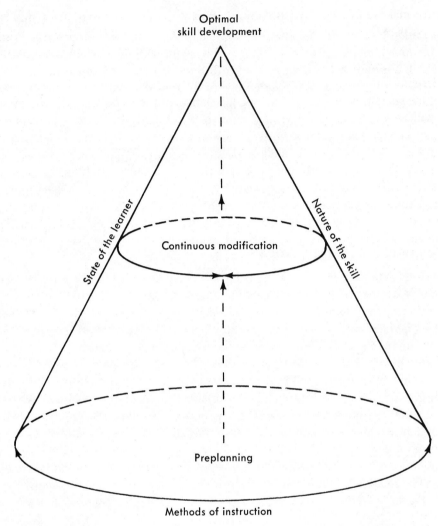

FIG. 1-4. Learning variables: state of the learner, nature of the skill, and methods of instruction. (See text for further explanation.)

In Fig. 1-4 the methods of instruction are shown as forming both the base and interior of a cone, the curved surface of which represents the other two learning variables: the state of the learner and the nature of the skill, which interact (arrows) both with each other and with the methods of instruction. The goal (apex) is optimal skill development. The fact that the surface of a cone is curved emphasizes the interaction between the learner and the demands of the skill to be learned. In addition, the peaking of a cone to an apex suggests that as the level of individual performance increases, the requirements of the skill change, and this in turn makes new demands both on the learner and on instructional planning. The purpose of visualizing instruction as forming the base and interior of the cone is to highlight two major instructional operations: preplanning and continuous modification.

Preplanning—As practitioners we do not need to be reminded that in planning instruction we need to consider the nature of the individual and the group we will be teaching. Thus we have always been concerned with maturational level, past experience, and so on. What we often fail to consider, however, are the requirements of the specific skill or skills to be learned. While Chapter 8 deals with skill analysis, it is important to state here that every motor skill is seen to require certain perceptual motor abilities and certain specifics. Effective preplanning requires that we estimate whether the prospective learners have the abilities required by the skill and, if not, how they might be developed or enhanced. However, we also need to plan for the development of the skill specifics, that is, practice in the skill that emphasizes its unique characteristics. For example, a teacher who asks an individual to do a forward roll when he has insufficient arm strength to support his own body weight is expecting the impossible. Conversely, to learn to do a forward roll requires more than the development of the basic abilities involved. It requires a timing, for example, that can be achieved only by practicing the forward roll.

Continuous modification—Let's assume that we have preplanned instruction in such a way as to ensure, to the greatest degree possible, the learning of a skill by a specific group of individuals. Obviously, individuals will differ in their ability to profit from such instruction, and modification of instruction for individual differences is an accepted facet of the practitioner's responsibility. Again, what is not so obvious is that modification of instruction must be continuous. As individuals increase their proficiency in a specific skill, new demands are made on them, not only in mastering the skill specifics but also in terms of basic ability requirements. As we shall see, individual performance level and learning rate in the early stages of learning are not necessarily predictive of later learning or the final level of proficiency that the individual attains. This is not to underestimate the importance of preplanning or the solution of early learning problems. It merely emphasizes that the interaction between the learner and the skill changes as proficiency increases and that the instructional format that is the most useful in the later stages of learning is not likely to be the same as the one that was effective in the early learning period.

The assumption is, of course, that the changes effected in these variables should be such as to result in the highest possible level of individual skill development. To the extent that any of these factors is assumed fixed or unchangeable, a priori, the probability of achieving maximal skill development is decreased. Consider the following two examples.

A 15-year-old girl born without a left forearm or hand was assigned to scoring when her class began learning archery. Not content with this, she asked to experiment with drawing the bow. She did so by pushing against the grip with her elbow stump. After releasing the arrow, she lifted her left arm, allowing the bow to drop over her shoulder. This awakened her instructor (me) who then fitted her with a heavier weight bow to offset the necessarily short draw and adjusted her arrow length. The idea that the requirements of a skill are more a matter of the objective of skill than its form finally dawned on me.

When the practice of physical fitness testing collided with the concept of special education, the result in many cases was the assignment of low-skilled students to special physical education classes. A teacher took issue with the prescribed curriculum of recreational games and proceeded to spend part of each session on developing basic perceptual motor abilities (balance, strength, flexibility, relaxation) and fundamental skills (running, jumping, throwing). By the end of the following semester, all of her low-skilled students (and most of her special education students) were deemed ready to profit from regular classes.

The important question is not How do we teach the low-skilled? but rather What does the learner need to do? and How can we help? An unfortunate and spurious interpretation of the important concept of individual differences has been that these differences are necessarily fixed. When an individual has a fixed limitation, as did the girl in the archery class, there are implications for modification of either the skill or the methods of instruction or both. However, a limitation should not be assumed before the fact nor should it be abetted by labels such as low-skilled and slow learner. Special education has used a nonclassification approach that emphasizes functional diagnosis and treatment and that we would do well to emulate.

MOVING FROM THEORY TO PRACTICE

It's obvious that if practitioners are to achieve the goal of planning instruction in such a way as to facilitate learning, and that if they are to be capable of identifying and solving learning problems systematically, they need specific information that will aid them in analyzing the state of the learner, the nature of the skill, and instructional tasks. The purpose of this book is, in fact, to provide such information.

However, as has been emphasized previously, knowledge does not transfer to practice automatically. The extent to which you can expect to be able to apply the concepts will depend on the depth of your understanding of them. Such understanding will probably occur in a stepwise fashion: (1) you can *recall* the concept, (2) you can *restate* it in your own words, (3) you can *give an example* of it, and (4) you can *use it to solve* a problem.

This book, including the thought sheets at the end of each chapter and the

Opportunities for Practice in the Appendix, is designed to help carry you through these stages. However, you must be willing to endure some "learning pains" in the process. We do not become adept at a skill by trying it once, and this is as true of instructional skills as it is of motor skills. I hope that the journey will be an exciting one as you confirm or reject old beliefs, discover new alternatives, and share with your students the benefits of your new knowledge.

Sample thought sheet

Answer the following questions in your own words.
1. What is the relationship between learning and development? Give an example.
2. What is the difference between skills and abilities? Give an example of each.
3. What do the terms *motor learning* and *motor performance* mean to you? What is the difference?
4. What is the difference between *open* and *closed* skills? Give an example of each.

References

Andrews, J.C. *Motor learning theory and the practice of teaching.* Opening address presented at the International Congress of Psycho-Motor Learning, The Free University of Brussels, Belgium, November 1976.

Bain, L.L., & Poindexter, H.B.W. Applying disciplinary knowledge in professional preparation. *Journal of Physical Education and Recreation,* February 1981, pp. 40-41.

Basmajiian, J.V. *Progress report on motor unit work.* Paper presented at Department of Anatomy Seminar, The George Washington University School of Medicine, Washington, D.C., December 1978.

Dunham, P., Jr. Learning and performance. *Research Quarterly,* 1971, 42, 334-337.

Eccles, J.C. *The understanding of the brain* (2nd ed.). New York: McGraw-Hill, 1977.

Eckert, H.M., & Espenshade, A.S. *Motor development* (2nd ed.). Columbus, Ohio: Merrill, 1980.

Fisher, A.C., & Motta, M.A. Activation and sport performance: some coaching guidelines. *Motor Skills: Theory into Practice,* 1977, 1(2), 98-103.

Fleishman, E.A. *The structure and measurement of physical fitness.* Englewood Cliffs, N.J.: Prentice-Hall, 1964.

Gallwey, T. Quoted in N. Seitz, A new way to learn tennis: stop trying. *The Sunday Star-Bulletin and Advertiser,* Honolulu, July 25, 1976, p. H-9.

Gerard, R.W. Neurophysiology: an integration (molecules, neurons and behavior). In J. Field (Ed.), *Handbook of physiology: section 1, neurophysiology, vol. 3.* Washington, D.C.: American Physiological Society, 1960.

Gowan, G.R., Botterill, C.B., & Blimkie, C.J.R. Bridging the gap between sport science and sport practice. In P. Klavora & J.V. Daniels (Eds.), *Coach, athlete and sport psychologist.* Toronto: University of Toronto, School of Physical and Health Education, 1979.

Higgins, J.R., & Spaeth, R.K. Relationship between consistency of movement and environmental condition. *Quest,* January 1972, 15, 61-69.

Hilgard, E. A perspective on the relationship between learning theory and educational practice. In E. Hilgard (Ed.), *Theories of learning and instruction.* Chicago: University of Chicago Press, 1964.

Hunt, J.M. *Intelligence and experience.* New York: Ronald Press, 1961.

Hunt, J.M. *Informational interaction and early development.* Paper presented at the AAHPER Region East Perceptual-Motor Conference, Clearwater, Florida, October 1971.

Jones, J.C. *Learning.* New York: Harcourt Brace Javonovich, 1967.

Locke, L. *Supervision, schools, and student teaching: why things stay the same.* Paper presented at the American Academy of Physical Education, New Orleans, March 1979.

Marteniuk, R.G. *Information-processing in motor skills.* New York: Holt, Rinehart and Winston, 1976.

Martens, R. From smocks to jocks: a new adventure for sport psychologists. In P. Klavora and J.V. Daniels (Eds.), *Coach, athlete and the sport psychologist.* Toronto: University of Toronto, School of Physical and Health Education, 1979.

McGrath, S.M. Concepts of information-processing and motor programs. *Learning and Physical Education Newsletter,* 1977, *1,* Division of Health and Physical Education, University of Toledo, Toledo, Ohio. (Mimeographed).

Poulton, E.C. On prediction in skilled movement. *Psychological Bulletin,* 1957, 54, 467-478.

Rothstein, A. Basic Stuff-Series I. *Journal of Physical Education and Recreation,* February 1981, pp. 35-37, 46.

Rushall, B.S., & Siedentop, D. *The development and control of behavior in sport and physical education.* Philadelphia: Lea & Febiger, 1972.

Sage, G.H. *Introduction to motor behavior: a neuropsychological approach* (2nd ed.). Reading, Mass.: Addison-Wesley, 1977.

Salmela, J.H. Psychology and sport: fear of applying. In P. Klavora and J.V. Daniel (Eds.), *Coach, athlete and the sport psychologist.* Toronto: University of Toronto, School of Physical and Health Education, 1979.

Singer, R.N. *Motor learning and human performance* (2nd ed.). New York: Macmillan, 1975.

Singer, R.N. *Motor learning and human performance* (3rd ed.). New York: Macmillan, 1980.

Templin, T.J. Issues in professional preparation: It's just too theoretical. *Journal of Physical Education and Recreation,* November-December 1980, pp. 64-66.

Thompson, G.G. *Child psychology.* Boston: Houghton Mifflin, 1962.

Whiting, H.T.A. *Skill is specific?* Paper presented at International Symposium on Motor Learning, Wingate Institute, Israel, April 1976.

PART ONE

Practical implications of learning theories

2 TRADITIONAL LEARNING THEORIES

The purpose of this chapter is not to give a historical review of learning theory; rather, it is an attempt to encourage you to examine the underlying bases of your present instructional practices. Even if you have not taught formally, it is probable that you have concepts about teaching that have been conditioned by how you were taught. The question is whether the concepts have been carefully considered or whether they have remained unexamined.

The learning theories described in this chapter remain the predominant bases for instructional practice today. This is not surprising, since they include valid concepts, that is, concepts that work. However, the question is not whether a concept works, but which concept works best in which situation. Individuals appear to learn by many different means, and our concern as practitioners is to select the most effective means for a given situation. This requires that specific concepts within each theory be analyzed for their contributions and for their limitations. In fact, one of the purposes of this book is to discourage the use of instructional methods based on a single theory. The advantages of a multiconceptual approach to learning and instruction are clarified further in the next three chapters.

Basic differences

Historically, theories of behavior, including learning, have been dichotomized into two broad categories or schools of psychology: (1) connectionist or stimulus-response theories and (2) cognitive or field theories. This dichotomization has been unfortunate in that it has often led to accepting either one or the other as *the* basis for instructional practice rather than profiting from the contributions of both.

The fundamental difference between connectionist and cognitive theories is illustrated below where *s* represents the environmental stimuli, *r* the response or behavior, and *o* the organism or individual learner. The capitalizations indicate the different points of emphasis in the two theories.

Connectionist theories	Cognitive theories
S–o–R	s–O–r

Thus the connectionist considers the environment the primary source for explaining, predicting, and controlling behavior (and therefore learning), while the cognitive theorist emphasizes the individual's interpretation of the environmental situation as the critical factor. This fundamental difference is reflected in the relative importance each school assigns to three interrelated aspects of learning: repetition or practice, perception and cognition, and reinforcement.

In general, connectionists conceive of behavior as the result of a connection, association, or bond. Learning occurs when these connections are strengthened by repetition or when new connections are formed. The individual is then said to be conditioned. Perception, while not negated, is considered a hypothetical factor within the individual, which is unobservable and therefore cannot be manipulated to control behavior. Reinforcement generally consists of either rewarding individuals when they elicit the desired response or, less often, punishing them when they do not.

The cognitive theorist is concerned with the individual's perception of the total learning situation, and this perception is seen to be affected by a multitude of stimuli, including both present and past experiences. Thus what goes on within the individual becomes a critical variable intervening between stimulus and response and in fact is deemed a major determinant of the response the individual will make to any specific set of environmental stimuli. Learning, to the cognitive theorist, is more a product of the individual's efforts to analyze the situation, perceive relationships, and solve problems than it is a product of conditioning. Therefore perception rather than repetition is stressed. Reinforcement occurs when individuals discover relationships, solve the problem, or achieve their goal.

Some specific theories within each category have been selected for mention in the following sections. The only reason for this particular selection is that these seem to be the theories that continue to dominate educational practice. The theories are not discussed in their totality; rather, those concepts in each theory that seem to have had the greatest influence on instructional practice are analyzed for both their contributions and their limitations. The reader who desires a more comprehensive description of the theories can find it in some of the readings listed at the end of this chapter, especially Henry (1942) and Grant (1964).

Connectionist theories

Behaviorism, associationism, and *connectionism* are terms often used synonymously despite the fact that each has different origins. These theories are usually classified together as stimulus-response (S-R) theories. *Connectionist* is used here to emphasize the concept on which the theories agree: that learning consists of a connection or bond between stimuli (S-S), between stimulus and response (S-R), or between response and reinforcement (R-R).

PAVLOV'S CLASSICAL CONDITIONING

Pavlov's salivation experiment is familiar to anyone who has taken an introductory psychology course. It is mentioned here primarily to distinguish classical conditioning from Skinner's operant or instrumental conditioning described later in this chapter. In the original Pavlovian experiment the stimulus for salivation was food placed in the mouth of a dog. However, when a second stimulus, such as the sound of a bell, was repeatedly presented just prior to each feeding, eventually the sound of the bell alone elicited salivation. The essential elements of classical conditioning are diagrammed below. *UCS* and *UCR* refer to the unconditioned stimulus and response; *CS* and *CR* refer to the conditioning stimulus and conditioned response.

INNATE REFLEX:	UCS $\longrightarrow$	UCR
	(meat)	*(salivation)*
CONDITIONING PROCESS:	CS with UCS $\longrightarrow$	UCR
	(bell) *(meat)*	*(salivation)*
CONDITIONED REFLEX:	CS $\longrightarrow$	CR
	(bell)	*(salivation)*

Rapone (1978) has advocated the use of such conditioning techniques in the control of anxiety in sport. For example, he suggests that a player, by continually repeating the phrase "breathe easy" while practicing muscular relaxation, can then induce a decrease in muscular tension by calling forth the phrase during the actual performance of a skill.

However, such conditioning can, and most often does, occur without our being aware of it. The individual who has developed a fear of the water, for example, will suffer the fear in the presence of almost anything associated with the circumstance that elicited the fear; just entering a locker room may signal the fear reaction. Practitioners should be aware that individuals bring with them to the learning situation a multitude of preconditioned responses that can limit their ability to profit from group instruction. Deconditioning in humans is a relatively slow process, and patience combined with individual instruction is often required.

GUTHRIE'S CONTIGUOUS CONDITIONING

There have been many criticisms of the simplistic nature of classical conditioning as an explanation for learning, one of the most explicit being that of Edwin Guthrie (1942). Guthrie took issue with the importance given to repetition in the Pavlovian conditioning experiments in which as many as 50 pairings of stimuli were required to elicit the conditioned response. He viewed a skill as being the result not of a single association (habit), but of a large collection of associations that connect *specific movements with specific situations*. Any one of these associations is fully established or learned in one trial. The purpose of practice, therefore, is not to strengthen an association by repetition but to provide the opportunity for establishing the additional associations required for performance in a variety of situations. For example, an individual learns to depress the brake pedal of a car in one trial, but to learn to depress it at the proper times required in driving depends on his practicing the movement under all the numerous environmental conditions that might be encountered.

The major contribution of Guthrie's theory is this emphasis on the situational specificity of skills. Thus to master tennis, the learner must practice under differing wind, sun, and court conditions; the aspiring concert pianist needs practice not only at the keyboard but also before audiences; football and basketball scrimmages provide learning opportunities that can be achieved by no other means.

Despite this obvious contribution to learning theory, Guthrie's insistence on one-trial learning formed the basis of his concept of specificity and therefore needs to be analyzed in more detail. That he differentiated between learning an association in one trial and developing a skill through practice is evident in his example of braking a car. However, pressing a foot pedal is a relatively simple act that can be seen to be learned in one attempt. The example does not explain how more complex movements are learned. To understand the extreme specificity of Guthrie's theory we must realize that to him the stimuli for learning were movement produced. In fact, his contiguous conditioning might as aptly be called kinesthetic connectionism—the first stage of a movement determines the next stage, and so on, throughout the movement. Although highly simplified, the diagram below may clarify this concept. A specific stimulus (S_1) initiates the first stage of movement, which elicits its own kinesthetic stimuli (R_{K1}), which determine the following stimulus (S_2) and movement response (R_{K2}).

$$S_1 \rightarrow R_{K1} \rightarrow S_2 \rightarrow R_{K2}$$

Therefore once a movement is begun, it sustains itself throughout its course unless some new external stimulus occurs to interrupt it. Any specific stimulus elicits a whole chain of internal stimuli, and all of these must be identical to elicit the same response. Guthrie's (1942) concept of the implications of his theory for learning and teaching motor skills is best stated in his own words.

A lucky drive to the green, a first arrow on the target or the first strike at bowling does not make a man a golfer, an archer or a bowler. The fortunate outcome was an accident. But is out of accidents that skills are made. The next try is likely to be from a different stance and to have less fortunate results. The very fact that it is a second try rather than the first means that the action has a different beginning. . . . The problem of teaching skills is largely the problem of breaking up wrong action and encouraging practice in which there is eventually a chance of success. The track coach or orchestra leader may correct many obviously wrong methods by interrupting the activities and suggesting new behavior to replace wrong methods. His method is to interrupt in order to discourage wrong movements and to leave undisturbed the right movements when they appear. *They will remain unless something happens to cause other behavior to be established in their place* (p. 36).

According to Guthrie, then, each trial is significant, since it results in learning an association whether or not the attempt is successful. Therefore it would be more effective to prevent or interrupt improper movements than to correct them after the fact. It is essential to note that Guthrie's concept assumes that the function of the teacher is to determine the specific movement that will achieve the desired result and then, preferably, to lead the individual into that movement. In fact, Guthrie was quite explicit in this belief regarding the desirability of errorless learning.

Obviously, Guthrie could give little credence to the concepts of transfer and reinforcement, and it is in this respect that his theory is most limiting. Transfer of a response to a new situation could only result from practice in that situation. Reinforcement, in the sense of reward, could only aid skill development by keeping the learner active and thereby increasing the possibility that a successful movement would occur. However, the limitations of any theory should not blind us to its contributions. Guthrie was one of the few traditional learning theorists to focus on motor skills, and his emphasis on the specificity of skills and the limitations of transfer, together with that of Thorndike (identical elements), led to the initiation of on-the-job training and the use of simulated or realistic practice conditions. It remains for present-day investigators to establish the limits of skill specificity and transfer.

THORNDIKE'S CONNECTIONISM

The influence of Edward L. Thorndike on educational practice in this century is probably even greater than that of John Dewey. However, connectionism has so many facets and interpretations that any selection becomes somewhat arbitrary. Probably the most influential of Thorndike's contributions, however, are his three major Laws of Learning (Law of Readiness, Law of Effect, and Law of Exercise), most significantly his Law of Effect. However, as with Dewey's "learn by doing," misinterpretation has often led to misapplication. That this should occur is not surprising, since Thorndike continually revised his theory, as did his students.

While Thorndike was primarily interested in the practical application of his theory, he was profoundly influenced by the developing field of neuropsychology. He believed that behavior, both innate and learned, was the result of connections (bonds) between stimulus and response and that these bonds were produced by changes in nerve cells and their synapses. Gates (1942), in an effort to harmonize Thorndike's connectionist theory with the cognitive theories, denied the importance of Thorndike's neurological orientation. The fact remains, however, that Thorndike conceived of the connection between stimulus and response as resulting from neuron modifications, and this orientation needs at least some consideration in any analysis of his theory, since it formed the basis for his part method approach to the teaching of skills. Sandiford (1942) gave an example of the application of Thorndike's bonding concept to coaching.

> From careful analysis, observation and experiment, the football coach has discovered the elements that enter into successful drop-kicking. . . . One by one, each of these elements is imparted to the learner and endless practice insisted upon. In this way, and apparently only in this way, can the good "footballer" be made. Similarly, the good pole-vaulter is made by teaching him the elements, one at a time, and insisting on concentrated practice . . . (p. 102).

Law of readiness—Since Thorndike conceived of connectionism in terms of neuron behavior, he recognized that nerve cells must mature to a certain point before conduction is possible. Briefly, the Law of Readiness states that when a pathway is ready to operate, to do so is satisfying; conversely, annoyance results when a conduction unit is called on to act and cannot do so. Interpretations of this law, however, have been much broader with Thorndike's. The concept of readiness has been extended to include other maturational conditions and also experience or prerequisite learning. Thus we hear such terms as *reading readiness* and *learning readiness*. More recently the term *prereadiness skills* has been used to denote the fundamental skills or abilities that are prerequisite to the learning of more complex skills (e.g., Kephart, 1971). For example, readiness to learn to play baseball may be seen to require the prereadiness skills of running, batting, and fielding. Even running can be viewed in terms of such prerequisite abilities as leg strength and endurance. While the concept of readiness is a useful one for the practitioner, establishing an age of readiness for any skill is a difficult procedure. Most of our ideas of skill readiness have come from normative studies (that is, the ages at which most children master specific skills) without consideration of motivation, opportunity, or prerequisite skills. As examples of the need for an altered view of readiness, the practitioner should consider these facts: (1) we are now teaching infants 3 to 9 months of age to swim and (2) foreign languages are now being taught in the elementary school. It may be that our readiness to teach is as important a concept as an individual's readiness to learn.

Law of effect—Of Thorndike's three major Laws of Learning, the Law of Effect came to be regarded by Thorndike and other connectionists as the fundamental law of learning. Briefly paraphrased, this law states that when a response to a given situation is accompanied by satisfaction, the probability is increased that the same response will occur when the situation recurs. Originally, Thorndike conceived annoyance as being just as effective in "stamping out" a connection as was satisfaction in "stamping it in;" however, he later modified his position regarding the potency of annoyers. The influence of an annoying aftereffect (punishment, failure, etc.) could only work indirectly, that is, by leading the individual to try a different response. Thorndike's modification was important not only in emphasizing reward rather than punishment as the more reliable force in learning, but also in describing the mechanism by which the law was seen to operate. A satisfying aftereffect arouses a confirming reaction that strengthens the S-R connection that elicited it. Thorndike's explanation of the operation of the confirming reaction was given by Sandiford (1942, p. 118).

The confirming reaction is at first an aftereffect of the S-R situation, thus

$$S \rightarrow R \rightarrow \text{Confirming reaction}$$

Afterward it functions as a force connecting and binding S to R, thus

$$S \rightarrow \text{Confirming reaction} \rightarrow R$$

The influence of both rewards and punishment, therefore, depends on what they cause the individual to do. Rewards are more dependable because they arouse this confirming reaction, a kind of neuronal reinforcement, which becomes tied to and strengthens the S-R bond. However, as Sandiford (1942) noted, there are other connectionist explanations of how the confirming reaction operates.

> I play a golf stroke; the action is completed; if the stroke is of the right length and in the right direction it tends to be stamped in; if it is hooked or sliced or foozled in any way it is stamped out. The selection of stamping in or stamping out has to await knowledge as to whether the stroke was a good one or not (p. 119).

Sandiford concluded: "Which explanation is the more satisfactory must be left to the reader and to time." However, whether learning proceeds more readily from the action of rewards (satisfaction) or from the knowledge of the results of an action is of critical concern to the practitioner who is charged with application. For example, the golfer, instead of relying solely on satisfaction (the stroke was a good one), may profit more from knowledge as to *how* good the stroke was (the shot was slightly short and to the right of the target). Knowledge of results is discussed in more detail later. Suffice it to note here that while both reward (satisfaction) and knowledge of results are potentially useful learning tools, they are not synonymous.

Law of exercise—According to Thorndike, repetition works to make the connection between situation and response more permanent by strengthening connections between nerves, that is, by decreasing synaptic resistance. Conversely, he conceived lack of use as weakening the connections and therefore the probability of the recurrence of the response. However, Thorndike (1932) was quite explicit when he said that mere repetition had little, if any, effect on learning.

> If a certain state of affairs acts upon a man a thousand times a week for a year, he will, so far as mere repetition of that state of affairs is concerned, probably respond no better the last week than the first (p. 62).

As Sandiford (1942) stated: "The law of effect has to be invoked to explain why practice does not necessarily and invariably lead to improvement" (p. 123). While this concept helped to put the "practice makes perfect" misconception to rest, it is misleading to imply that if the Law of Effect operates, this will necessarily lead to a change in response. It is important to note that Thorndike measured improvement in terms of an increase (or decrease) in the *frequency* of a response, not a change in the response itself.

Although Thorndike described learning as a trial-and-error process, he gave little attention to it in his writings. Woodworth (1940), however, listed the "minimum essentials" of trial-and-error learning:

1. A *set* to reach a certain goal
2. Inability to see any way clear to the goal
3. Exploring the situation
4. Seeing or somehow finding leads, possible ways to reach the goal
5. Trying these leads
6. Backing off when blocked in one lead and trying another
7. Finally finding a good lead and reaching a goal

However, Thorndike (1940, p. 6) said that new habits come about gradually as the Law of Effect acts to decrease the frequency of the old habit and increase the frequency of a new response. The concept of programming (establishing a sequential series of steps leading to a new response) to *direct* learning was made explicit by B.F. Skinner.

SKINNER'S OPERANT CONDITIONING

Whereas Thorndike emphasized reinforcement of the total S-R situation, Skinner in his theory of operant conditioning is concerned only with reinforcement of the response (R-R). Skinner (1974, p. 44) describes operant behavior as behavior emitted by an individual without reference to any specific stimulus. Those actions that are reinforced are strengthened; those that are not reinforced are weakened. For example, an animal deprived of food will emit a variety of responses; those responses that are followed by feeding will become more frequent, and vice versa. The connection or association is not between a specific stimulus situation and its response, but rather between an action and its consequences.

Skinner believes that most behavior is of an operant or emitted type and that learning can most predictably proceed through reinforcement of the correct response. The function of the teacher, then, is to determine the desired behavior or action and then to condition students by rewarding them when they elicit this action. However, should the student not emit the desired response, the teacher can proceed to shape the action (rather than waiting for it to occur) by rewarding successive approximations of the desired act. However, reinforcement must occur immediately (before another response intervenes), and this is part of Skinner's rationale for teaching machines. Since the teacher cannot reinforce all students immediately, programmed instruction is seen to make operant conditioning in the classroom feasible (Skinner, 1961).

Prior to 1960, the use of operant techniques was limited primarily to clinical settings. Since then, however, the application of the principles in school settings has developed at an extremely rapid pace (Brown, 1976). This is occurring not only in the classroom but in physical education as well (Rushall and Siedentop, 1972). Therefore the practitioner needs to examine the techniques in more depth to weigh their potential contributions and limitations.

Goldiamond (1967), speaking on the concept of programming, diagrammed a linear program as shown in Fig. 2-1. Goldiamond emphasized several points: (1) although the desired terminal behavior needs to be specified in advance to determine the program, it may need to be changed and should always be adaptive for the individual; (2) after determining the terminal behavior needed, the practitioner must assess those behaviors that the individual currently has available, *which are relevant to the terminal behaviors desired;* (3) the practitioner must then build on these available responses a program of successive approximations of the final performance; (4) these steps need to be ordered psychologically (for the learner) rather than logically (for the teacher); (5) each step in the program must be defined in specific and observable terms; and (6) *positive reinforcement must be made contingent on performance of the prescribed behavior at each step.*

To clarify these principles for the practitioner seeking application to the design of instruction, guidelines are described briefly below. These guidelines have been drawn from several sources (Goldiamond, 1967; Reese, 1966; Rushall & Siedentop, 1972, p. 175), and the reader desiring more detailed information should refer to these sources.

1. SPECIFY THE DESIRED TERMINAL BEHAVIOR IN SPECIFIC AND MEASURABLE TERMS. The instructor must specify in advance the desired proficiency in measurable terms. For example, we too often cite physical fitness as a desired goal, but until we specify what students are expected to do to *demonstrate* physical fitness, it has no

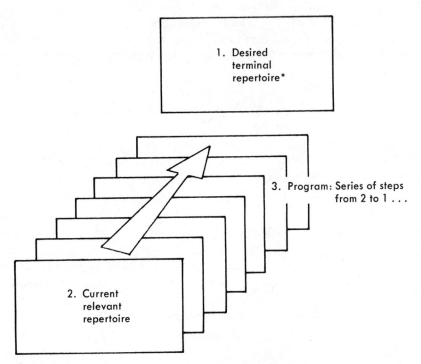

FIG. 2-1. A linear program (Slightly modified from Goldiamond, I. *The concept of programming and its relevance to the treatment of children with learning problems*. Paper presented at Postgraduate Course on the Diagnostic Evaluation of Children with Learning Problems, Children's Hospital of Washington, D.C., May 1967.) *Dr. Goldiamond (1972) notes, "The reason for the term 'repertoire' instead of 'behavior' is that often what we change of significance is not the behavior, but the variables which control it. For example, in reading, the behavior changed is eye movements, but the significant change is in fact that textual *stimuli* now control behavior, whereas formerly they did not."

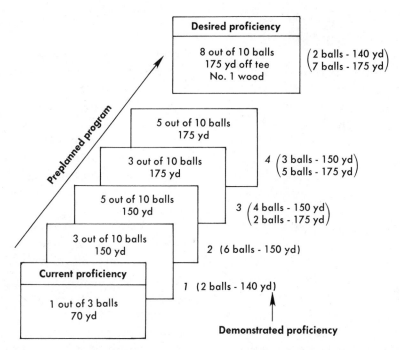

FIG. 2-2. An individualized program for a golf drive. (Modified from unpublished data by Gordon, S. *Teaching project for motor learning course.* Washington, D.C.: The George Washington University, 1974.)

meaning. As Rushall and Siedentop (1972) note, it is necessary to describe the desired behavior as, for example, "A mile run in less than seven minutes" (p. 175).

2. DETERMINE THE CURRENT CAPACITY OF THE INDIVIDUAL. Most practitioners are familiar with pretesting in motor skills. However, we usually use these measurements (together with posttest scores) to determine improvement rather than to give direction to program content. Specifying final proficiency tells us where we want to go; assessing current proficiency tells us where we must begin. Since current capacities depend on past experience and since individuals differ in their backgrounds of experience, the desirability of individualized programs seems obvious. Fig. 2-2 is an individualized program for a golf drive designed by a student for her teaching project in a motor learning class (Gordon, 1974). She began by determining what she felt to be a realistic proficiency goal for an individual who had no experience in golf. She then assessed the individual's proficiency after a single demonstration and preplanned the program in accordance with the five sessions available to her (45 minutes a day for 5 days). Obviously,

the sequencing of the steps to desired proficiency will depend on the current capacity of the individual, as well as on the nature of the skill.

3. SELECT AND CLARIFY THE MOTIVATING REINFORCER. In terms of operant conditioning, reinforcement *is* motivation. Therefore it is essential to locate reinforcers that are effective. Reese (1966) defines an adequate reinforcer as "one that can be presented immediately following a response, one that can be presented repeatedly without satiation, and—as a practical measure—one that is in reasonable supply" (p. 51). The most effective reinforcers are individualized. Therefore it is important to get to know your students, talk with them, and find out what they do in their spare time. However, it is possible to make use of general reinforcers such as praise and extrinsic rewards. Rushall and Siedentop (1972) contend that we must make clear to the individuals what the reinforcement is. For example, contingent on achieving a specified proficiency in a skill, they may have "two minutes of trampoline time" (p. 175). The essential procedure, once adequate reinforcers have been identified, is that they be made contingent on the performance of the desired behavior *only*. In the example noted above, individuals would not be allowed on the trampoline under any circumstances unless they had achieved the specified proficiency.

4. SHAPE THE DESIRED BEHAVIOR. Shaping consists primarily of reinforcing successive approximations of the desired behavior. However, it is no simple task. It requires that we select the most effective reinforcer, that we select the right response to reinforce, and that we determine how long to reinforce each approximation. Obviously, the task becomes more feasible if the practitioner establishes in advance the acceptable response for each approximation and states it in specific, observable terms (Fig. 2-2).

5. USE STIMULUS CONTROL. The task of shaping can become more effective if the practitioner makes judicious use of various types of guidance procedures. Rushall and Siedentop (1972) list four such general methods: (a) physical restriction, such as taping a body part to prevent movement, which limits the possibility of making errors; (b) manipulation, such as lifting a beginning diver's feet to prevent a bellyflop; (c) visual guidance, which may be by way of imitation or modeling; and (d) verbal guidance. However, such methods should be dispensed with as soon as possible, since they limit the extent to which individuals learn to control their own movements.

6. REINFORCE INTERMITTENTLY. While continuous reinforcement (reinforcing each occurrence of the response) is the fastest method of establishing a response, intermittent reinforcement is more practical, since it is not usually possible to observe each action. In addition, the practitioner needs to establish schedules of reinforcement for each step in the shaping process as well as for the terminal behavior. Readers desiring more detail regarding the various types of reinforcement schedules should refer to Reese (1966) or Rushall and Siedentop (1972).

7. KEEP CONTINUOUS OBJECTIVE RECORDS. A program, including the steps or approximations to final proficiency, should be adaptive for the individual. When response changes are not in the desired direction or to the desired extent, the prescribed program, procedures, or reinforcement may need to be changed. It is doubtful that this will occur unless performance records are maintained. Checklists and videotapes are examples of forms that might be used to record stepwise changes in proficiency in motor skills. With creative advanced planning, techniques can be set up by which learners can chart their own progress. Most practice regimens can be designed to include self-testing situations. In practicing the tennis drive, for example, if the desired goal is to execute the drive so that the ball crosses the net within 2 feet of the top, a rope stretched the length of the net at this height allows the learner to determine (and so record) the number of successful executions. Obviously, if learners know the expected proficiency, the task is made more feasible. In Fig. 2-2 the demonstrated proficiency recorded by the learner is shown on the right. If the discrepancy between the preplanned program and the demonstrated proficiency had been greater than shown, changes in the program, the final proficiency expectation, or the methods of instruction would have been indicated. Notice that the discrepancy might be in either direction; the learner may be performing higher or lower than expected.

Certainly Skinner's concept of specific advanced programming is a useful one and appears applicable to instruction *whether or not one chooses to apply reinforcement techniques*. However, because of the rapid growth of operant conditioning (behavior modification) techniques in the schools (Brown, 1976), it seems desirable to point out some of the limitations of the techniques as well.

One of the major problems associated with behavior modification techniques is their misuse. As Dunn (1975, p. 67) notes, teachers all too often use positive reinforcement following poor or undesirable performance. For example, we often praise a student following a poor performance to provide encouragement, thereby increasing the probability of a repeat performance. The timing of reinforcement is critical; it will affect whatever performance it follows.

Another problem lies in the difficulty of weaning the individual from extrinsic rewards (tokens, candy, praise) toward intrinsic (self-generated) motivation (MacMillan & Forness, 1974). We *can* become conditioned to rewards, that is, we may learn to withhold desired behavior conditional to promises of extrinsic rewards. Skinner himself (1977) emphasizes the desirability of avoiding contrived reinforcers.

> But behavior is most expeditiously shaped and maintained by its natural consequences. The behavior of the production line worker, which has no important consequence except a weekly wage, suffers in comparison with the behavior of a craftsman, which is reinforced by the things produced (p. 86).

The fact remains that although control can be returned to the individual (Lovitt, 1974b), it is questionable how often this occurs, and little appears to be written about the procedures for doing so. In addition, rigid behaviorists tend to ignore the fact that there are motivational sources other than reinforcement (MacMillan & Forness, 1974).

> The point to be made with regard to motivation is that the behavioristic viewpoint is not the only framework within which one can consider motivation. . . . One is unable to observe the consequences for behaviors that result from exploration, cognitive dissonance [discrepency or doubt], curiosity, and competence as motives. Yet these sources of motivation must not be ignored or discounted. . .(p. 84).

One of the most persistent criticisms of behavior modification programs is that they are too often designed for the convenience and benefit of teachers and administrators rather than for the best interests of the students they are supposed to help (Brown, 1976; MacMillan & Forness, 1974). For example, as teachers we are often accused of using these techniques, knowingly or otherwise, to achieve discipline at the expense of education. It is probably true that we are prone to reinforce those behaviors on the part of students that make us, as teachers, feel good about ourselves (the Law of Effect operating on us). Conversely, we tend to discourage (if only by failing to reinforce) behaviors that appear to call into question our knowledge and competence. The questioning student may thus inadvertently be "taught" not to question. However, these are tendencies that we, understanding that the Law of Effect operates on us as well as our students, can dispense with. We need to find in the thoughtful, questioning student an affirmation of our competence.

Operant conditioning has also been accused of fostering conformity. The desired terminal behavior is too often a specific performance expected of all. However, this is a misuse of the technique that need not occur. As Reese (1966, p. 62) notes, we can do just the opposite. We can enlarge an individual's capacities by making reinforcement contingent on a greater variety of responses. Thus with proper planning, behavior modification in the schools can be aimed at expanding students' skills, abilities, and independence (Brown, 1976, p. 69). Movement education programs in our elementary schools have done much to foster creativity, problem-solving ability, and self-confidence by posing such questions as How many ways can you move from here to there? However, we still have a long way to go toward fostering these capacities in the higher grades.

Behavior modification techniques have been used successfully by a variety of school-based personnel, including audiologists, speech therapists, and remedial, regular, and head start teachers, and by teacher consultants (Lovitt, 1974b). However, an operant program is, at its best, individualized at all levels (Lovitt, 1974a): specification of final performance, available repertoire (past experience), program steps, and reinforcement. The conditions under which behavior modification can or should be the method of choice in traditional school settings remain to be determined. The one thing we can be certain of, however, is that those who use it must be qualified to use it properly and for the benefit of the student.

Cognitive theories

The cognitive theories had their origin in the field theories of physics (Hartmann, 1942). According to these theories, all events (or objects) in nature are seen to be governed more by their relations to other events occurring with them (the field) than by their own inherent structure. (Einstein's theory of relativity is an example of this.) Thus the field theories maintain that we must perceive the relationships between all of the events occurring in the field before we can properly interpret the details of one event or a single object.

One of the most influential of the field theories in psychology was that of the gestaltists. (*Gestalt* is the German word for configuration or pattern.) The gestaltists emphasized the total pattern of the stimulus field and, in particular, the figure-ground concept. Hartmann (1942) gave an example of the operation of these concepts in learning to swim.

> In man the mastery of the necessary motor controls in swimming is like a delayed perceptual insight where the figure is hidden in the "ground," for it takes some time to grasp the "pattern" of the swimming performance and to translate this into the appropriate sequence of separate movements. It is not enough, as everyone knows who recalls his own first efforts to swim, to breathe correctly, to hold the head and body in the right position, to kick properly, and to swing the arms in the desired fashion, if all these things are done without reference to one another (p. 185).

Thus it would presumably be more productive to teach the whole stroke rather than break it down into parts.

Much of the experimental work of the gestaltists involved the study of insight, that is, a relatively slow acquisition of skill in the early stages of learning followed by a point of rapid progress. Insightful learning was assumed to be the result of the perceptual or cognitive organization and reorganization of the stimulus field until the individual perceived or discovered the relationships required to solve the problem.

KOFFKA'S LAWS OF PERCEPTION

Kurt Koffka was instrumental in introducing gestalt psychology to the United States and in translating gestalt theories of perception into principles applicable to learning. He defined several laws of perception, two of which are discussed here.

Law of similarity—According to the law of similarity, individuals tend to group patterns that are alike in size, shape, or other structural properties. Hartmann (1942, p. 197) defined structural similarities as "insights into common features." Neither abstraction nor generalization would be possible without the ability to discern similarities. However, such "insights into common features" may appear at different levels of completeness. For example, the beginner sees many likenesses between tennis and badminton; however, some of these are false, illusory, or incomplete insights and therefore hinder transfer from one game to another. The smash in badminton looks like the smash in tennis, and the learner assumes they are the same. The result is that the effective performance of the badminton smash is hindered. Not until learners discern the differences can proficiency with the badminton smash be expected. As Hartmann (1942) noted, learners will probably need several exposures before they are able to differentiate: "The first reproduction will probably catch the *general outline* with amusing errors and omission of details" (p. 201). Later, more of the parts will be filled in. However, the teacher can assist in this process.

> Educationally, one task of teaching that assumes greater significance in the light of this discussion is the function of enabling pupils to see differences where formerly they saw only likeness or to perceive likenesses where others discern naught but differences (Hartmann, 1942, p. 203).

The important point is that the gestaltists conceived of the perception of similarities as occurring at different levels of completeness, and they considered differentiation, as well as generalization, to be an important aspect of this.

Law of closure—The law of closure describes the tendency of an individual to complete patterns only partially given. An example often cited is a series of curved lines that the individual perceptually "closes" to form a circle. However, this is a relatively limited example of the concept.

Hartmann (1942) related closure to the phenomenon of insight. "Insight is really a kind of sight. . . . It is the internally apprehended correlate of the 'closing' of an incomplete configuration" (pp. 191-192). Hartmann gave an example of such internal closure in learning to swim. In his first attempts the learner "splashes about in a frightened and *ineffectively organized* way, which, to the observer, may appear as complete *disorganization*" (p. 187). However, as soon as the learner can swim a few yards (even if this is done clumsily and with intense exertion), the learner has achieved closure as far as the fundamental pattern of the skill is concerned. "The rest is a matter of smoothing off the rough spots in the performance. *This last apparently is the only real function that drill or practice in the narrow pedagogical sense actually has*" (p. 187).

LEWIN'S FIELD THEORY

Kurt Lewin developed a field theoretical approach to learning that emphasized the importance of individual differences. He felt that gestalt theory had overemphasized the physical nature of stimuli (structural similarities) to the exclusion of the inner psychological forces acting on the individual. To Lewin (1942), the field that influences an individual's behavior included internal forces (not only past experience but also future expectations, hopes, and desires) and external or environmental forces (including other people). Since these internal and external forces interact with each other, the problems of learning were seen by Lewin to require a psychological theory that would help bridge the gap between general laws of learning and individual differences.

The method Lewin developed to accomplish this was basically to differentiate between different types of learning.

> The term *learning*, in the broad sense of "doing something better than before," is a "practical" term, referring to a variety of processes which the psychologist will have to group and treat according to their psychological nature (p. 220).

Thus Lewin distinguished between four types of learning: (1) learning as a change in cognitive structure, (2) learning as a change in motivation, (3) learning as a change in ideology, and (4) learning as a change in motor control. Unfortunately, his disinclination to deal with motor learning in his writings, either as a type of learning or in relationship to the other types of learning, precludes our making direct applications of his theory to motor performance. However, since motor learning obviously involves both cognitive learning and motivation, these aspects of his theory are discussed briefly here.

Learning as a change in knowledge—Changes in cognitive structure occur by the processes of differentiation and restructurization. Lewin (1942, pp. 224-231) gave the example of a person moving to a new town. At first a large part of the city remains unstructured (undifferentiated). Gradually as the individual moves about, areas become more structured (differentiated) and at times restructured until finally the individual has a relatively complete knowledge of the city. While "moving about" might be construed as learning by repetition, Lewin emphasized that it is the change in cognitive structure that is essential to learning. "If the newcomer has a map of the city, the number of trips from the individual's home to his place of work which is necessary for the creation of an adequate cognitive structure may be reduced to a few cases" (p. 229). Such differentiation occurs in other areas as well.

> From all that we know, the newborn cannot distinguish between himself and his environment; slowly certain areas, for instance, those connected with eating, take on a specific character, become more and more differentiated; the parts of his own body become differentiated from each other and from the rest of the world; social

relationships develop and become differentiated; needs, emotion, language go through similar processes of differentiation (p. 226).

This process continues throughout the individual's life. Again and again a previously vague and unstructured area becomes cognitively structured, differentiated, and specific.

Learning as a change in motivation—To Lewin, motivation was a primary force influencing the acquisition of knowledge. However, he distinguished between the personal goals of an individual (needs, values, hopes) and extrinsic rewards as motivating forces in learning. He deemed the use of external rewards and general incentives to be inferior because they limit the avenues by which the individual can achieve a goal. That is, the learner can only reach the goal by performing the required (and often disliked) activity in the "correct" manner. Since motivation was considered to be so critical to the solution of tasks, the importance of motivational learning was stressed. Motivational learning occurs when individuals change a goal or change their method of satisfying a goal. Lewin later extended his theory into the field of social psychology, particularly in the area of group dynamics. However, his major contribution was his emphasis on the individuality of the learner.

> A teacher will never succeed in giving proper guidance to a child if he doesn't learn to understand the psychological world in which that individual child lives. . . . To substitute for that world of the individual, the world of the teacher, of the physicist, or of anybody else is to be, not objective, but wrong (Lewin, 1942, p. 217).

The major limitation of the traditional cognitive theories was that internal perceptual and cognitive functions had to be inferred from very little evidence. Knowledge of nervous system functioning was in its infancy, and the information-processing concepts that have proved to be so helpful in understanding perceptual and cognitive processes (and in designing instruction) had not yet appeared. Nevertheless, the emphasis given by the field theories to perception and problem solving was a major contribution to learning theory and was particularly useful in giving some balance to the view of learning then dominated by the connectionist theories.

Contributions and limitations

You might wonder how such divergent views of the nature of learning could occur. First, the experimenters set different tasks for their subjects to learn. An important concept that will be emphasized throughout this book is that the nature of the skill is a critical factor in learning. You need only to compare a simple task, such as pressing the brake pedal of a car, with a more difficult one, such as driving a golf ball, to appreciate the difference. Second, the experimenters were trying to prove a point. That is, for the most part, the experiments were designed to support the theory, not to test it. In addition, methods of instruction, another critical factor in learning, were not investigated. (Most of the earlier experiments were conducted with animals.)

One of the most unfortunate outcomes of these methodological problems was the dichotomy that resulted in terms of application. Thus connectionists emphasized integration of parts, drill and repetition, and reinforcement; proponents of the cognitive approach stressed whole learning, differentiation, and problem solving. As McConnell (1942, pp. 252-253) noted, this resulted in a shocking neglect of the parts (and of practice) by the cognitive theorists; and the connectionists, while giving lip service to the idea of purposeful learning, failed to emphasize it sufficiently to impress those who applied the principles to educational practice.

Despite the differences in the practical application of the theories, a great deal of agreement exists among the theories themselves (McConnell, 1942). The most pertinent points of agreement are the following:

1. Both the stimulus situation and the individual's response are complex and patterned.
2. During learning, responses are modified by their consequences.
3. Motivation is the selection, direction, and adjustment of behavior toward a goal.
4. Learning can be more appropriately described as a process of approximation and correction than as a trial-and-error process.
5. Differentiation, as well as generalization, is essential to effective learning.
6. Practice under the proper conditions, rather than repetition, is conducive to learning.

However, for the practitioner the most useful way to view the contribution of the traditional learning theories is to perceive them as representing a gradual accumulation of knowledge. Fig. 2-3 shows, in a stepwise fashion, the most significant concepts from each theory, resulting in a broad repertoire of concepts for consideration by the practitioner. This conceptual view of traditional learning theories should give you some appreciation of the limits of a single theory approach to learning. Recently, new neurological techniques and the refinement of information-processing models have led to the emergence of additional concepts of learning and teaching. These are the subjects of the next three chapters.

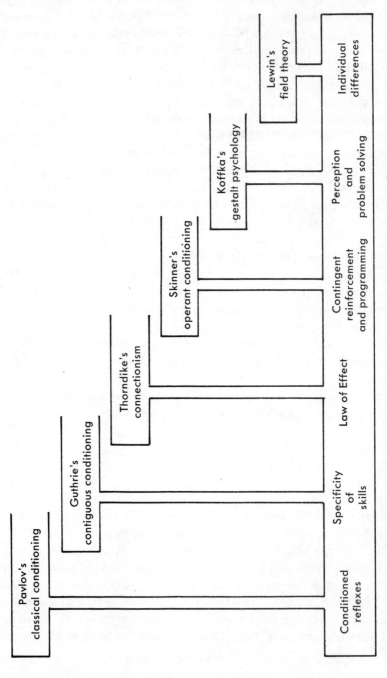

FIG. 2-3. Major conceptual contributions of traditional learning theories.

Sample thought sheet

1. Give an example (observed rather than hypothetical, if possible) of each of the following.
   a. Conditioned reflex (Pavlov)
   b. Specificity of skills (Guthrie)
   c. Law of Effect (Thorndike)
   d. Contingent reinforcement (Skinner)
2. Give an example of how you have applied, or might apply, each of the following concepts in teaching a specific motor skill.
   a. Specificity of skills (Guthrie)
   b. Law of Effect (Thorndike)
   c. Contingent reinforcement (Skinner)
3. Select a specific skill on which you wish to improve your own performance. Using Fig. 2-1,
   a. Define in measurable terms the terminal proficiency you wish to attain.
   b. Assess your current proficiency.
   c. Plan a series of steps from b to a, stating these in observable terms.
4. Without assistance, solve the following problem.
   a. Without lifting your pencil from the paper, connect all the dots below with no more than four straight lines.

```
        •     •     •


        •     •     •


        •     •     •
```

   b. Describe the process you went through in solving the problem.
   c. What did you learn that would help you in solving other problems?

References

Brown, B.S. Behavior modification: what it is—and isn't. *Today's Education*, January-February 1976, pp. 67-69.

Dunn, J.M. Behavior modification with emotionally disturbed children. *Journal of Physical Education and Recreation*, March 1975, pp. 67-70.

Gates, A.I. Connectionism: present concepts and interpretations. In N.B. Henry (Ed.), *Forty-first yearbook of the national society for the study of education. II. The psychology of learning.* Chicago: University of Chicago Press, 1942.

Goldiamond, I. *The concept of programming and its relevance to the treatment of children with learning problems.* Paper presented at Postgraduate Course on the Diagnostic Evaluation of Children with Learning Problems, Children's Hospital of Washington, D.C., May 1967.

Goldiamond, I. Personal communication, March 1972.

Gordon, S. *Teaching project for motor learning course.* Washington, D.C.: The George Washington University, 1974.

Grant, D.A. Classical and operant conditioning. In A.W. Melton (Ed.), *Categories of human learning.* New York: Academic Press, 1964, pp. 3-31.

Guthrie, E.R. Conditioning: a theory of learning in terms of stimulus, response, and association. In N.D. Henry (Ed.), *Forty-first yearbook of the national society for the study of education. II. The psychology of learning.* Chicago: University of Chicago Press, 1942.

Hartmann, G.W. The field theory of learning and its educational consequences. In N.B. Henry (Ed.), *Forty-first yearbook of the national society for the study of education. II. The psychology of learning.* Chicago: University of Chicago Press, 1942.

Henry, N.B. (Ed.). *Forty-first yearbook of the national society for the study of education. II. The psychology of learning.* Chicago: University of Chicago Press, 1942.

Kephart, N.C. *The slow learner in the classroom* (2nd ed.). Columbus, Ohio: Merrill, 1971.

Lewin, K. Field theory of learning. In N.B. Henry (Ed.), *Forty-first yearbook of the national society for the study of education. II. The psychology of learning.* Chicago: University of Chicago Press, 1942.

Lovitt, T. Behavior modification: the current scene. In A.R. Brown & C. Avery (Eds.), *Modifying children's behavior: a book of readings.* Springfield, Ill.: Charles C Thomas, 1974a.

Lovitt, T. Behavior modification: where do we go from here? In A.R. Brown & C. Avery (Eds.), *Modifying children's behavior: a book of readings.* Springfield, Ill.: Charles C Thomas, 1974b.

MacMillan, D.L., & Forness, S.R. Behavior modification: limitations and liabilities. In A.R. Brown & C. Avery (Eds.), *Modifying children's behavior: a book of readings.* Springfield, Ill.: Charles C Thomas, 1974.

McConnell, T.R. Reconciliation of learning theories. In N.B. Henry (Ed.), *Forty-first yearbook of the national society for the study of educaiton. II. The psychology of learning.* Chicago: University of Chicago Press, 1942.

Rapone, A.J. *A complete sports psyching program.* Unpublished manuscript, 1978.

Reese, E.P. *The analysis of human operant behavior.* Dubuque, Iowa: William C. Brown, 1966.

Rushall, B.S., & Siedentop, D. *The development and control of behavior in sport and physical education.* Philadelphia: Lea & Febiger, 1972.

Sandiford, P. Connectionism: its origins and major features. In N.B. Henry (Ed.), *Forty-first yearbook of the national society for the study of education. II. The psychology of learning.* Chicago: University of Chicago Press, 1942.

Skinner, B.F. Teaching machines. *Scientific American,* November 1961.

Skinner, B.F. *About behaviorism.* New York: Vintage Books, 1974.

Skinner, B.F. Between freedom and depotism. *Psychology Today,* September 1977, pp. 80-91.

Thorndike, E.L. *Fundamentals of learning.* New York: Columbia University Press, 1932.

Thorndike, E.L. *Human nature and the social order.* New York: Macmillan, 1940.

Woodworth, R.S. *Psychology.* New York: Holt, Rinehart, and Winston, 1940.

3 NEUROLOGICAL CONCEPTS

Although some of the traditional learning theories discussed in the previous chapter drew on what was then known about neurons for support, until recently most learning psychologists considered the nervous system a "black box," which, being inaccessible to observation, could not be expected to shed much light on the nature of learning. However, this situation is changing rapidly. While there is still much we do not know, we have at least some idea of the kinds of operations performed by the nervous system at the input (sensory) end and at the output (motor) end. It is fortunate, too, for those of us concerned with motor learning that neurophysiological research has given a major consideration to the output end. In fact, the purpose of this chapter is to consider these concepts of neuromotor control and their implications for motor learning and performance.

Information regarding neuromuscular control has accumulated over a period of time. Each of the stepwise gains in knowledge has had some influence on instructional practice, often without the practitioner being aware of it. Therefore this chapter focuses first on an analysis of those earlier theories of neuromotor development that had, and continue to have, the greatest influence on instructional practices. Second, a dual concept of neuromotor development is presented that appears to have special merit for the teacher of motor skills. Finally, some newer concepts of neuromotor control are organized into a framework that will give the practitioner some appreciation of the multiplicity of neural influences on movement. Examples of application of the theory or concept to motor performance and learning are also given.

Theories of prenatal neuromotor development

The dichotomy of the traditional learning theories is reflected in the reflex and integrated theories of prenatal neuromotor development. These theories warrant special attention because of their apparent conflicting implications for instruction and because they are currently being applied in practice, too often without explicit understanding of their assumptions or alternatives.

The reflex theory says that as behavior develops in the embryo, simple reflexes appear first, and only then are they combined into larger patterns of movement. The integrated theory maintains that only after the diffuse, gross movements of the embryo have been completed do the local reflexes appear. Hellebrandt's (1958) assessment of the two theories, while biased toward the integrated theory, is particularly relevant because of her focus on the application of the theories to motor learning and performance.

REFLEX THEORY

According to Hellebrandt, the reflex theory presupposes that "isolated reflexes, complete in themselves, are combined bit-by-bit into more and ever more complex chains and other circuits" (p. 12). Trial-and-error combinations of these reflexes lead to the development of movement patterns, which then become further modified by practice and experience.

> Most muscle training has been of this type. . . . Purity of movement has been the ideal, and many a physical therapist has visualized this as the achievement of the particular muscle to which treatment was being directed. There has been much careful suppression of overflow [movement], presumably because overflow is something indicative of decadence in coordination. Simple normal range movements have been added one to another like building blocks used to erect increasingly complex combinations of movement (p. 12).

The physical educator will recognize in these techniques a similarity to the strict *part* method of instruction in which detailed *steps* of a skill are added to each other and in which corrections at each step are aimed at preventing extraneous movement.

A primary limitation of the reflex theory is that while simple reflexes are obviously one part of a person's neurological endowment, there is no evidence that they necessarily precede the development of the diffuse patterns of innervation that are the basis for the mass movement characteristic of the infant. In addition, single-minded attention to purity of movement and to specific muscles can interfere with the capacity of the body to make its own adjustments to differing environments, including equipment, and to differences in body build. For example, a distance swimmer who has exceptionally long arms is going to use a different arm recovery than one who does not. We do not all use the same muscles or even the same movement to achieve the same result. We need to focus on the purpose of the movement.

INTEGRATED THEORY

According to Hellebrandt, the integrated theory assumes that living organisms are endowed with an ability to respond totally in ways most advantageous to them. This total body response is built into the organism, and it is only through neuromuscular inhibition that movements become refined. The total body response is characteristically seen in the beginner. Movement in one part of the body "overflows" to other parts so that the movement appears gross and uncoordinated. According to the integrated theory, this overflow movement is natural, and the learning of the motor skill can best proceed by starting with this total movement and gradually inhibiting unneeded portions of the movement.

Hellebrandt (1958) cites as evidence for the integrated theory the tendency of the individual to revert to overflow movement under stressful conditions.

> Anyone who has participated in sports or observed the muscle reeducation of the disabled has seen precise partial patterns of movement revert to total patterning under the exigencies of fatigue or emotional stress (p. 12).

She suggests that these gross body movements, which we usually interpret as a breakdown in performance, are never haphazard; rather, they are ordered and patterned and supposedly facilitate the execution of the skill.

> Overflow patterns may be manifestations of a stress too great to be coped with by discretely individuated partial patterns, but they are in no sense grossly disrupted skills (p. 13).

The integrated theory suggests a "whole" method approach to teaching motor skills. Instead of step-by-step chaining of movement parts (e.g., kicking, moving arms, and breathing in swimming), motor skills would be developed by gradually inhibiting unneeded portions of the initial gross movement (e.g., start with the total stroke and gradually refine it). Hellebrandt, among others, implies that we should concentrate on *what* to do (the objective of the skill) rather than *how* to do it (the specific movements). Conceivably, the how could be left to the automatic mechanisms of our highly integrated neuromuscular machinery.

> The physical therapist, shop foreman, physical educator or coach may wish to impose upon the human subject some precise and specific technique of movement, but an infinitely wise living machine, drawing upon the experience of centuries, makes its own autonomous adjustments. Instead of suppressing these we would do well to study them (p. 13).

Such an integrated theory has much to recommend it. There seems to be general agreement among neurophysiologists that the nervous system has built-in mechanisms that accommodate the routine adjustments required for coordinated muscle action and that neural inhibition plays a major role in the learning process. This is not to say, however, that the integrated theory should be the sole basis for instructional practice. Certainly, the assumption that primitive movement patterns facilitate the performance of motor skills needs to be qualified.

An intermediate and more practical view would seem to be that taken by

Waterland (1970). Continuing work begun with Hellebrandt, Waterland confirmed an integration of head and shoulder girdle activity that she termed a *natural linkage,* since it was invariable in all subjects systematically subjected to stress. That is, the subjects were unable under the stress conditions to move the shoulders independently of the head and vice versa. While such linkages can be considered complex reflexes, Waterland made a major contribution by emphasizing that, in terms of motor learning, some skills would require that a particular linkage be suppressed, while other skills might be facilitated by it. For example, an effective drive in golf requires that head movement be separated from shoulder movement, and practitioners who are aware of the head-shoulder linkage will employ techniques (e.g., antagonistic muscle action or mechanical means to prevent head movement) to inhibit the linkage. Conversely, effective performance in the standing broad jump appears to be facilitated by the head-shoulder linkage (Waterland, 1967).

Dual concept of neuromotor development

For the practitioner, the primary argument against adopting either the reflex theory or the integrated theory is that teaching effectiveness would be limited by doing so. If we accept the fact that much of the muscular integration required to meet a specific objective can be handled by automatic control mechanisms, and if we add to this the concept implied by Waterland that certain linkages or reflexes may need to be inhibited in certain skills while in others a reflex linkage may be facilitating, we come up with a dual concept of motor skill learning that should have special merit for the practitioner. The concept, diagrammed in Fig. 3-1, assumes that the most efficient learning of a motor skill occurs through differen-

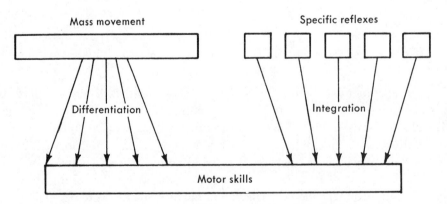

FIG. 3-1. Dual concept of neuromotor development.

tiation of the gross overflow movement characteristic of the beginner and by the integration (inhibition or activation) of those reflexes that operate in a specific skill.

DIFFERENTIATION OF GROSS MOVEMENT

Differentiation occurs as the individual attains the capacity for relatively isolated, independent movement of body parts. Observe, for example, the similarity between the total body response characteristic of an infant learning to swim and the gross body movement of the adult beginner. Each exhibits a lack of independent control of body parts. In accord with certain maturational principles, we accept the total body movement of the infant as natural and parallel this by gradually inhibiting unneeded portions of the movement and at the same time activating, through use, its functional components. In contrast, we generally view the gross movements of the adult beginner as a collection of errors and too often arbitrarily impose a strict part method of instruction.

It is possible and conceivably advantageous to view the gross movement of the adult beginner as natural, that is, as a matter of incomplete rather than erroneous development. Skill learning would then be best achieved by inhibiting the overflow movement characteristic of the beginner, that is, by gradually inhibiting those portions of the movement that do not contribute to performance efficiency (e.g., relaxing unneeded muscles) while leaving intact the nervous system's capacity to make autonomous adjustments.

Such a view appears to be tenable. As Gerard (1960, p. 1945) notes, the raw experiences of an individual are progressively differentiated by successive stages of patterning in the nervous system, with the larger categories being established first, followed by still finer and finer ones. Such a concept is implicit in the behavior of untaught learners. First attempts at imitation result in crude approximations of the skill. These gradually become more refined as the learners experience the results of their movements and are thereby motivated to reobserve the skill with increasing attention to its functional aspects. In fact, the suggestion has been made that our main job as practitioners is to speed up this natural process by providing (1) more effective models, (2) more functional cues, and (3) more usable feedback. While these three techniques will be elaborated on later, brief comments on them at this time may help to clarify the practical implications of the concept of differentiation.

Effective models—Our tendency as practitioners has been to assume that what learners see in a demonstration, for example, is what we show them. Not necessarily so. Individuals have different backgrounds of motor skill experience that are stored in memory and that influence what they perceive. Depending on the nature of their prior motor skill experience, which may be watching the skill on television, the learners will be at various levels of ability to differentiate with regard to memory as well as neuromuscular ability. This is all the more reason models need to be accurate without being rigid, even for the beginner.

Functional cues—Assuming that even the best demonstration will result in only an approximation of the movement by the beginner, we then need to begin to inhibit extraneous (overflow) movement. For example, in target archery the most functional aspect of the skill is the proper release of the arrow at full draw. This requires that the back muscles do the drawing with the forearm and hand muscles relaxed as much as possible. By touching the back muscles, the instructor can identify where the power comes from. This usually results in a relaxation of the hand and arm muscles, although in some cases conscious attention must be directed to the relaxation of these muscles. However, it should not be assumed that progressive differentiation is necessarily best achieved by movement cues. For example, to achieve opposition in a throwing movement, it may be more effective to require that the learner move farther from the target rather than direct attention to foot placement. Given the general direction to hit the target from the greater distance, the body will usually attempt to carry out the directive in the best way it can, opposition.

Usable feedback—A learner's instructional feedback does not necessarily need to answer his question How did I do? Many skills have a great deal of intrinsic feedback. That is, performance of the skill itself provides knowledge of the results of the movement (e.g., the ball was short and to the right of the basket). Nor must feedback necessarily answer the question What did I do wrong? What is needed is feedback that answers the question What do I need to do to improve on the next performance? This does not mean that there are not situations in which it is useful to answer How did I do? or What did I do wrong? but rather that the most useful feedback is whatever will best achieve an improvement or differentiation in the next performance.

INTEGRATION OF SPECIFIC REFLEXES

While differentiation is seen to involve the gradual and functional refinement of a skill, the integration of specific reflexes involves the inhibition of those reflexes that are detrimental to the performance of a particular skill and the activation of those reflexes that can facilitate its performance.

An example of the need for considering reflexes in teaching motor skills is the effect of the so-called head-righting reflex in diving. If the reflex is not inhibited, the head will automatically be lifted as soon as the body begins to fall forward and a belly flop ensues. Instructions such as "dig your chin into your chest" and "clamp your shoulders to your ears" help to neutralize the effects of the reflex; however, active contraction of the neck flexors is unnecessary later as inhibition becomes part of the learned pattern for the dive. O'Connell and Gardner (1972) note

> Teaching cues, based on understanding of neuromuscular mechanisms and reflex control, as well as on sound principles of biomechanics and applied anatomy, can be deliberately used to improve motor performance . . . and to shorten the time required to achieve optimal or maximal performance levels (p. 232).

There are many innate reflexes affecting movement, some of which are neither appropriate nor relevant to discuss here. Selections in this book have been limited to those reflexes that appear to have the most influence on the type of motor skills used in sports and dance. Since these reflexes have been assigned various names, the term most descriptive of the movement effects of the reflex is used in the following sections, with the anatomical name in parenthesis. In addition, it should be noted that the neural connections involved in these reflexes are extremely complex, and the final answers are not yet in. Readers interested in more detailed knowledge of the structure of the reflexes should refer to the sources listed at the end of this chapter, especially O'Connell and Gardner (1972, pp. 193-232), Powers (1976), and Sage (1977, pp. 88-108).

Stretch (muscle spindle) reflex—Muscle spindles are complex sensory receptors lying within muscles that are sensitive to the stretch of the muscle. When a muscle is stretched, the muscle spindle fires impulses into the spinal cord where these impulses in turn fire the motor nerves returning to that muscle, causing it to contract. The action of the muscle spindle can be likened to that of a door spring; the greater the stretch, the greater the force of the contraction. O'Connell and Gardner (1972, pp. 223-224) suggest some implications for techniques in motor skills. A common example is the use of a preparatory crouch to increase the force of a start of a jump. Conversely, in a tennis drop shot where force is not desired, the arm, instead of being taken back, is held in a ready position. Less common are the implications for activities involving a swing. Muscle spindles also respond to velocity of stretch (tonic response). When force is the main objective, the backswing should be long and fast with minimal hesitation prior to the forward swing. Conversely, if the primary objective is accuracy, as in golf approach shots, the backswing should be slower and shorter. In target throwing a short hesitation at the end of a backswing of optimal length would allow the phasic activity of the spindles to subside to a tonic level, resulting in greater precision. In addition, when force is the objective but a preparatory position must be held, the advantages of the stretch response is still available.

> In the case of a baseball batter awaiting a pitch, he can seek the advantages of the tonic spindle response to supplement his own muscle power by taking as long a backswing as possible within the limits of mechanical efficiency (O'Connell & Gardner, 1972, p. 224).

Safety (Golgi tendon organ) reflex—The tendon receptors sense tension in a muscle, and their activation leads to inhibition of contraction, not only in the muscle of origin, but also in the entire functional muscle group (deVries, 1980, p. 88). This safety reflex is evident when a contracting muscle suddenly gives out under a heavy load. It should be noted, however, that tendon organs have functions other than as protective devices. The tendon organs work together with the muscle spindles (deVries, 1980, p. 94; Evarts, 1979, p. 170). For example, in stretching exercises for flexibility or warm-up, phasic (active) stretching is accompanied by a decrease in the stimulation of the tendon organs with the result that the contraction elicited by the stretch reflex goes unabated and limits the stretching. Conversely, tonic (slow or passive) stretching increases the activity of the tendon organs, leading to inhibition of the stretch reflex, allowing the individual to obtain the maximal benefit from the stretch (deVries, 1980, p. 464). In addition, O'Connell and Gardner (1972, p. 109) suggest that maximal strength may be dependent on our ability to oppose the inhibition from our tendon organs. deVries (1980, p. 95) suggests that learning to disinhibit may be an important part of strength training.

Head-righting (utricular) reflex—Portions of the vestibular apparatus in the inner ear canal are stimulated by changes in the orientation of the head with gravity. This is accomplished mainly by contraction of neck muscles, although secondary effects occur in the trunk and limb muscles. In a backward dive, for example, this reflex "can cause flexion of the head so that the diver lands on his back or trunk flexion so that he sits in the water" (O'Connell & Gardner, 1972, p. 218). However, there are several righting reflexes, and one seldom acts alone; rather, they cooperate to help maintain vertical posture. Whenever skills involve movements in opposition to these reflexes, concentrated effort, together with antagonistic muscle action or mechanical techniques, is generally required to inhibit "doing what comes naturally."

Equilibrium (semicircular canal) reflex—Other portions of the vestibular apparatus in the ear also have reflex connections with the antigravity postural muscles and assist in maintaining or regaining body balance, either by adjusting the center of gravity over the base of support or by shifting the base of support to keep it under the center of gravity. For example, as the body begins to tilt to the side or fall forward, the extension muscles of the body are contracted by the equilibrum reflex to bring the body upright, or the individual may step sideward or forward to prevent a fall. O'Connell and Gardner (1972) observed the effect of this reflex on several motor skills. In a forward dive, for example, the diver may jump into the water feet first in response to the equilibrium reflex (p. 218).

In addition, since the semicircular canals are sensitive to rotary acceleration as well as to angular movement, whirling evokes extension of the limbs on the side rotated toward, and sudden deceleration results in extension in the opposite direction. The resulting head jerk can be offset, as in a figure-skating spin, through training aimed at voluntarily holding the head erect and immobile (O'Connell & Gardner, 1972, p. 216).

Head-shoulder (neck) linkages—Infants demonstrate a set of innate reflexes that tie head movement to limb movement. Although these tonic neck reflexes (TNR) and tonic labyrinthine reflexes (TLR) weaken early in the course of the infant's development, they are never completely obliterated. Even in the adult, anterior flexion of the head favors bilateral arm flexion (as in weight lifting), while posterior extension of the head favors extension of the arms (as in putting up a barbell). Similarly, anterior flexion of the head facilitates trunk and limb flexion for the forward somersault, and head extension facilitates arm extension for the layout backward somersault. Since rotation of the head to the side favors extension of the arm on that side and flexion movements on the opposite side, strong movements of the head can be used by the diver and tumbler to initiate spins (Gardner, 1969). However, when shoulder movement must be isolated from head movement, as in a golf drive, this tendency of the head and shoulders to work together must be inhibited.

Levels of neuromotor control

While a dual concept of neuromotor development should be extremely useful to the practitioner, it implies a separation of neuromotor control mechanisms that may limit the extent to which it can accommodate new knowledge. If we conceive of even relatively isolated reflexes, such as the knee jerk, as one level of motor control, and the complexity of mechanisms that must exist to account for the quantity and quality of voluntary movement as another level, then the dichotomy between specific reflexes and purposeful activity tends to resolve into a considera- tion of *levels* of motor control. For example, the message sent to muscles is influenced not only by the motor cortex of the brain and by simple spinal reflexes, but also by increasingly complex integrative centers in the cerebellum and basal ganglia.

However, as Hubel (1979) has emphasized, we know much less about neural connections in the brain than we know about simple reflex connections. Thus our knowledge regarding the various levels of motor control consists of a few facts, some hypotheses, and numerous speculations. Readers who want a more detailed discussion of these possibilities should refer to Eccles (1977), Evarts (1979), Kelso and Stelmach (1976), and Porter (1975).

Until recently, the main approach to investigating neuromotor control has been to study motor activity *following* specific sensory inputs. However, it is now possible to study activity in various parts of the nervous system *prior to* and *during* movement (Evarts, 1979; Lassen, Ingvar, & Skinhj, 1978). These new techniques show promise of allowing us to progress from a knowledge of relatively stereotyped sensorimotor interactions to how we might control our own movements.

For this reason, it is desirable to take Porter's (1975) suggestion that the best place to start when considering the nervous system's involvement in the control of movement is on the motor or output end and at the level of the final common pathway, that is, at the level of the motor units that begin in the spinal cord and end in the muscle. It is with these motor units that all levels of motor control must eventually connect if they are to have an influence, either excitatory or inhibitory, on muscular activity. As we shall see, each of these levels of motor control has implications for motor learning and performance.

MOTOR UNITS

Controlling muscle contraction involves much more than simply sending a signal from the brain to a muscle. Each of the motoneurons (nerve cells) that govern the contraction of muscle cells may have as many as 10,000 connections (synapses) on its surface. While not all of these connections are with separate neurons (neurons tend to make multiple synapses when they communicate with each other), the number does suggest that an incredibly large number of influences converge on the motoneurons (Nauta & Feirtag, 1979, p. 92).

We are far from understanding what all these connections mean in terms of movement control. For this reason and because many of the details we do know have at the present time little or no applicability to instruction in motor skills, the focus of this discussion is on highlighting those influences on the final common pathway that appear to have some implications for motor learning.

First, however, a brief review of the functional units of the final common pathway (the motor units) is desirable. It should be noted that even at this level of nervous system organization we do not have all the answers. Readers desiring more detailed information on motor units should refer to Buller (1975), Duncan (1975), and Henneman (1975).

ALPHA MOTOR UNITS

An individual muscle (e.g., the biceps) is supplied by many motoneurons, each supplying a specific number of muscle cells. We speak of an alpha motoneuron and the muscle cells it supplies as a motor unit. Since the motor unit behaves in an all-or-none fashion (that is, the muscle cells supplied contract to their fullest or they do not contract at all), it is mainly by increasing or decreasing the number of motor units in operation that we control the amount of force a muscle exerts. The greater the force desired, the more motor units (and therefore the more muscle cells) are activated.

However, muscles differ in the number of muscle cells supplied by a single

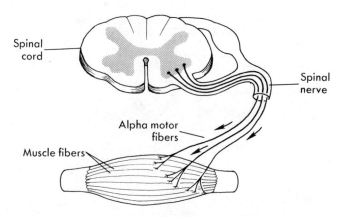

FIG. 3-2. Alpha motor units. Simplified diagram of three motor units to a muscle.

motor unit. In Fig. 3-2 you will note that each motor unit supplies only three muscle cells. Such a ratio (1:3) occurs only in the muscles that move the eye. Limb muscles, such as the biceps, have a ratio of one motoneuron to hundreds of muscle cells, and the manipulative muscles of the hand have an intermediate ratio. Obviously, the fewer muscle cells in a motor unit, the greater the degree of control possible. Thus we have more precise control of the manipulative muscles of the hand than we do of the muscles of the limbs.

However, gradations of force in a muscle are not only controlled by increasing or decreasing the number of motor units in operation, motor units also differ in contractile capability related to their size. The smaller units, while highly resistant to fatigue, generate little muscular tension; conversely, the larger units generate peak contraction, but fatigue rapidly. As Evarts (1979) notes,

> The difference between smaller and larger motor units is not trivial. For example, the largest motor unit in the human calf muscle develops 200 times more tension than the smallest (p. 166).

Therefore small degrees of muscle tension can be precisely controlled by activating varying numbers of small motor units; when force must be increased, larger motor units are activated (Evarts, 1979, p. 166). Duncan (1975) cites some evidence that suggests that brain centers may be capable of overriding the usual recruitment order in muscle contraction (low tension units first, followed by high tension units). That is, we may be able to select in advance the recruitment order that is most appropriate for the work intended. It is possible, as Jones (1974) suggests, that we may need to instill in the learner a mental "set" for the particular force requirements of the skill, and especially for ballistic actions that require a fast, forceful movement. As Evarts (1979, p. 166) notes, when maximal force is needed abruptly, almost all motor units can be fired simultaneously.

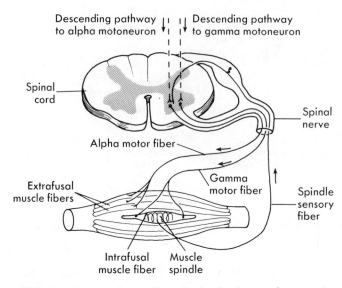

Descending pathway to alpha motoneuron   Descending pathway to gamma motoneuron

Spinal cord

Spinal nerve

Alpha motor fiber

Gamma motor fiber

Extrafusal muscle fibers

Spindle sensory fiber

Intrafusal muscle fiber   Muscle spindle

FIG. 3-3. Gamma loop. (See text for further explanation.)

GAMMA LOOP

In addition to the alpha motor units, there are smaller motoneurons called gamma motoneurons. Unlike the alpha motoneurons, which contract true muscle cells (called extrafusal fibers), the gamma motoneurons act on specialized small muscle cells (called intrafusal fibers), which regulate the sensitivity of the muscle spindle receptors (Evarts, 1979, p. 170). Impulses over the gamma motoneurons can, by maintaining contractile tension on the intrafusal fibers, set the muscle spindle at any prescribed firing level. This setting of spindle sensitivity over the gamma loop (Fig. 3-3) is known as *gamma bias,* and one of its main functions is to bring about the subtle adjustments in muscle contraction that help make possible smoothness and steadiness of movement.

Gamma bias can be set not only by local influences in the muscle and spinal cord, but also from higher centers according to expected load (O'Connell & Gardner, 1972, p. 205). A common example is when a person reaches to push open a door that previously had been stuck. If the door has been repaired and does not offer the expected resistance, the force is converted to the person's forward propulsion that results in his loss of balance. Similarly, the skier who has set his muscles for a "no ice" condition loses his balance on contacting ice, at least temporarily; the football runner who does not see the hole in the ground may end up with muscle trauma or tendon tear. Obviously, anticipatory setting of gamma bias, while useful, may be detrimental to performance and even dangerous when expectations do not coincide with reality.

The activation of skeletal muscle, therefore, can occur in two ways: (1) directly, by way of the alpha motor units or (2) indirectly, by way of the gamma loop. Although Merton (1972, p. 37) suggests that the gamma loop, acting at subconscious levels, coordinates all of our voluntary movement efforts, it now appears that most movement probably involves coactivation of both the alpha and the gamma motor units (Eccles, 1977, p. 120; Porter, 1975, p. 166). It is hoped that more definitive knowledge of the role of the gamma system will be forthcoming.

SPINAL CORD AND BRAIN STEM

We have already considered some of the spinal and brain stem reflexes that influence movement (e.g., the righting reflexes and the head-shoulder linkages). However, the effects of these and other spinal reflexes are seldom confined to a single muscle or even a single group of muscles. Since both reciprocal inhibition and proprioceptive facilitation have implications for motor performance, they are discussed briefly here.

Reciprocal inhibition—Lying entirely within the spinal cord are short intermediate neurons called Renshaw cells that function to inhibit (relax) those muscles having the opposite (antagonistic) action to a contracting muscle (Fig. 3-4). Any stimulus, from either spinal or supraspinal levels, that leads to contraction of a muscle usually also leads to inhibition of its antagonist. This is another example of the self-regulating capacity of motor unit organization. However, as we have seen, the effects of reflexes may be overridden by other influences coming to act on the motor units. For example, when stress is sufficiently high, relaxation of antagonistic muscles may be inhibited. That is, muscle tension remains high in, for example, both the flexors and extensors of a joint (cocontraction). When this occurs, movement appears stiff and conscious inhibition of contraction in the antagonistic muscles may be necessary. Anyone who has seen these cocontraction tension effects in a neophyte swimmer who is afraid of the water will recognize the problem.

Proprioceptive facilitation—The effects of reflexes are seldom confined to one level of the spinal cord or to one side of it. For example, if you prick your finger, you withdraw your hand (reflex effect); if you touch a hot stove, it is probable that you will not only withdraw your arm but also jump away from the stove (multisegmental and contralateral effect). However, this "spreading" of the effects of stimulation is not limited to specific reflexes such as the withdrawal reflex. O'Connell and Gardner (1972) note that stimulation of the joint receptors through movement has a widespread influence on the spinal cord. The upper

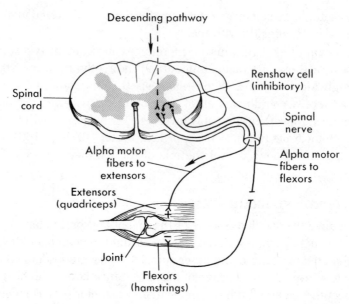

FIG. 3-4. Reciprocal inhibition. Alpha motor units to the extensors send collaterals to synapse with inhibitory Renshaw cells. This decreases excitability of the motor units to antagonistic flexor muscles, causing them to relax. The reverse would occur with flexor contraction.

extremities act powerfully on the lower extremities (e.g., clenching the fists increases the force and therefore the height of a jump) through both spinal and supraspinal circuits (p. 210). We speak of this as proprioceptive facilitation, that is, muscular activity or movement in one part of the body that facilitates activity in another part (Fig. 3-5). However, the spreading of proprioceptive impulses (from joint, muscle, and vestibular receptors) is not always facilitating. This is evident in the overflow movement of the beginning performer; inhibition is needed initially to prevent ineffective, extraneous movement and tension.

CEREBELLUM (AND BASAL GANGLIA)

By observing the effects on movement of damage to the cerebellum and basal ganglia of the brain, scientists have long known that these portions of the brain (Fig. 3-6) are intimately involved in the control of complex movements. The cerebellum, for example, is known to contribute to muscular coordination by correcting movements so that the movement is "on target" with respect to the position of the body. However, recent evidence (Eccles, 1977; Evarts, 1979; Kornhuber, 1975) suggests that, in addition to this correction function of the

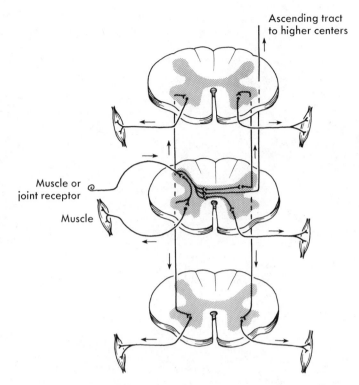

Ascending tract
to higher centers

Muscle or
joint receptor

Muscle

FIG. 3-5. Proprioceptive facilitation and overflow movement. Impulses from a receptor reach motoneurons at various levels of both sides of the spinal cord. This accounts for multisegmental, ipsilateral, and contralateral responses.

cerebellum, both the cerebellum and the basal ganglia have a primary function in designing voluntary movement, which only afterward is carried out by way of the motor cortex of the brain. Eccles (1977, pp. 134-135) uses the terms *updating* and *preprogramming* to differentiate between the correction and design functions of the cerebellum. While there are still many questions to be answered, a brief discussion of these functions should help to give you some appreciation of the interactive nature of higher brain centers in the design and control of movement.

Updating—The cerebellum receives information from almost all sensory modalities (e.g., proprioceptive) relative to the position of the body in space. In addition, it receives information from the motor cortex of the brain with the details of orders being given there, such as direction and amplitude of movement. The cerebellum thus has the information necessary to act as a comparator, and if the movement is "off target," it quickly adjusts the movement by sending

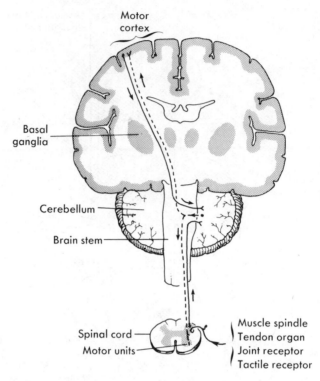

FIG. 3-6. Updating function of the cerebellum. Based on sensory input from the periphery and from the motor cortex *(solid lines),* the cerebellum updates ongoing movement by giving continuous corrections *(dotted lines)* to both the spinal cord and the motor cortex.

corrective messages back to the motor cortex as well as to the motor units in the spinal cord. The result is not a single correction, but a continuous updating throughout the duration of the movement (Eccles, 1977, pp. 131-137). Thus the cerebellum can be likened to the controlling system on a target-finding missile. Eccles (1977) concludes

> The more sub-conscious you are in a golf stroke, the better it is and the same with tennis, skiing, skating or any other skill. In all these performances we do not have any appreciation of the complexity of muscle contractions and joint movements. All that we are voluntarily conscious of is a general directive given by what we call our voluntary command system (p. 124).

Preprogramming—There seems to be a general consensus that the cerebellum, in addition to its role in correcting or updating an ongoing movement, is also involved in the generation of voluntary movements. The suggestion has been

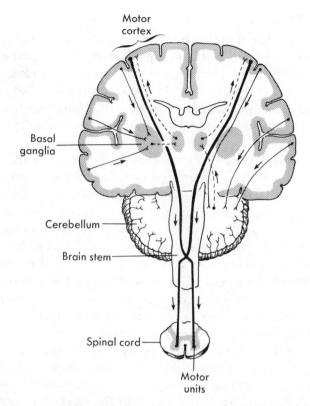

FIG. 3-7. Preprogramming function of the cerebellum and basal ganglia. Input *(solid lines)* to both the cerebellum *(right side)* and basal ganglia *(left side)* comes from wide areas of the cerebral cortex. Output *(dotted lines)* programs the motor cortex, which then executes the program by connections *(heavy lines)* with spinal cord motor units. (Modified from Evarts, E.V. Brain mechanisms and movement. *Scientific American*, 1973, 229(1), 96-103.)

made (DeLong, 1975; Evarts, 1973; Kornhuber, 1975) that the cerebellum may be responsible for fast, forceful ballistic movement, and the basal ganglia for slow movements. If this is true, we as practitioners may want to consider Jones's (1974) suggestion that we instill in learners a mental set for the type of movement involved in a particular skill. In any case, it is clear that there are numerous connections between the cerebral cortex and both the cerebellum and basal ganglia (Fig. 3-7). In addition, since neural activity in both the cerebellum and basal ganglia has been recorded prior to neural activity in the motor cortex of the brain, the concept of the motor cortex as being the highest center of voluntary movement controls needs to be qualified.

MOTOR CORTEX

The best way to understand the functions of the motor cortex of the cerebrum is to consider its interactions with other parts of the brain in the control of two types of movement: guided (or monitored) movement under closed-loop control and preprogrammed (or preselected) movement under open-loop control. It is unfortunate that these two concepts of motor control have been polarized, for as we shall see, it is probable that we use both at different times (goal-directed movement).

Guided movement (closed loop)—One of the most obvious examples of guided movement is walking a tightrope or balance beam, a feat that strongly depends on sensory feedback, especially tactile feedback, to maintain balance. This feedback continually flows into the primary sensory area of the cerebral cortex, which in turn sends messages directly to the adjacent motor cortex to regulate the motor commands being generated there (Eccles, 1977, p. 135). In Fig. 3-8 this sensorimotor or closed-loop control is represented by the dotted lines.

Preprogrammed movement (open loop)—The best way to understand the role of the motor cortex in preprogrammed movement is to consider what happens when an individual wants to make a movement that runs counter to a normal reflex response. In volleyball, for example, a receiver may need to dive forward to recover the ball before it hits the floor. This requires a continuation of movement past the point at which the equilibrium reflex would normally take over to keep the body upright. In this case the motor cortex must receive its orders, not from the sensory cortex, but from the cerebellum or basal ganglia (Evarts, 1979, p. 179) to benefit from their preprogramming functions. This preprogrammed or open-loop control is represented by the solid lines in Fig. 3-8.

Goal-directed movement—The controversy among motor learning theorists as to whether movement is controlled by feedback from the movement itself (closed loop) or by preprogramming movement (open loop) is, as Granit (1977, p. 166) notes, not apt to be very productive. Evarts (1979) suggests that we continually shift back and forth, depending on the goal or purpose of the movement, from peripherally guided movement by way of the closed sensorimotor loop (dotted lines in Fig. 3-8) to preprogrammed movement by way of the cerebellum and basal ganglia (solid lines in Fig. 3-8). Viewed in this manner, the problem is not one of peripheral versus central control of movement or of closed- versus open-loop control, but rather of determining which method of control can best achieve the desired purpose. For example, balancing activities may be seen to require feedback from proprioceptive receptors. However, when the performer wishes to carry out a maneuver, such as a flip dismount, a shift from guided closed-loop control to preprogrammed open-loop control would be necessary.

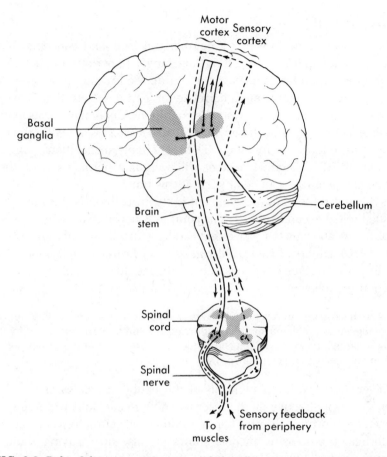

FIG. 3-8. Role of the motor cortex in guided and preprogrammed movement. Sensorimotor (closed) loop for peripherally guided movement is depicted by dotted lines. Preprogrammed movement (open loop) generated by cerebellum and basal ganglia is depicted by solid lines. (Modified from Evarts, E.V. Brain mechanisms of movement. *Scientific American,* 1979, *241*(3), 164-179.)

Viewed thus, what is voluntary about a movement is its purpose or goal. Given the goal, we can then presumably select the mode of movement control that will result in the most effective action to achieve that goal.

Learning and memory

As you have seen, there are many neurological facts and concepts that have implications for techniques of teaching, coaching, and performing motor skills. If applied properly, such techniques can speed up the learning process. However, we do not yet have a viable neural correlate for learning itself; that is, we do not know what changes in nervous system structure or function occur as learning is taking place, nor do we know how what we have learned is stored in the nervous system for future retrieval (memory). There are many speculations (e.g., Rosenweig & Bennett, 1976), and while some will eventually harmonize with the facts, there is no compelling evidence of such at this time.

Does this mean the light has gone out in the black box? No! It merely means we are still limited to candlelight at this point. It is hoped that research will in the very near future allow us to replace that candle with a light bulb. Rosenweig and Bennett (1976), editors of *Neural Mechanisms of Learning and Memory,* a volume dealing with various basic research approaches to the problem, state in their introduction the following:

> As such basic research is pursued, it may supply concepts and techniques that can be applied to problems such as improving teaching, alleviating the difficulties of the retarded, the aphasic and the senile, and fostering the fullest development of human intellectual potential (p. IX).

However, until we know more about the neural correlates of learning and memory, the most effective methods for teaching motor skills will remain somewhat arbitrary. Fortunately, the happy wedding of neurophysiological theories with information-processing models shows promise of clarifying some of the phenomena involved in both learning and memory. This is the subject of the next chapter.

Sample thought sheet

1. Select a specific motor skill. Describe how you would teach it by using each of the following theories of neuromotor development. Come prepared to demonstrate, if possible.
   a. The reflex theory
   b. The integrated theory
   c. The dual concept

2. For each of the following reflexes, name a skill that would require that the reflex be inhibited.
   a. Head-righting reflex
   b. Equilibrium reflex
   c. Safety reflex
   d. Head-shoulder linkage
3. Select a specific motor skill. Describe how you would make use of your knowledge of the stretch reflex to enhance performance.
4. Give an example of how you might apply your knowledge of each of the following in teaching or coaching.
   a. Gamma bias
   b. Proprioceptive facilitation

References

Buller, A.J. The physiology of skeletal muscle. In A.C. Guyton, & C.C. Hunt (Eds.), *Physiology: neurophysiology*, Series 1, Vol. 3. Baltimore: University Park Press, 1975.

DeLong, M.R. Motor functions of the basal ganglia. In E.V. Evarts (Ed.), *Central processing of sensory input leading to motor output*. Cambridge, Mass.: MIT Press, 1975.

deVries, H.A. *Physiology of exercise*. Dubuque, Iowa: William C. Brown, 1980.

Duncan, A.M. The size principle and motor unit recruitment. In W.W. Spirduso & J.D. King (Eds.), *Proceedings of the motor control symposium*. Austin, Tex.: University of Texas Printing Division, 1975.

Eccles, J.C. *The understanding of the brain* (2nd ed.). New York: McGraw-Hill, 1977.

Evarts, E.V. Brain mechanisms and movement. *Scientific American,* 1973, *229*(1), 96-103.

Evarts, E.V. Brain mechanisms of movement. *Scientific American,* 1979, *241*(3), 164-179.

Gardner, E.B. *Fundamentals of neurology* (4th ed.). Philadelphia: Saunders, 1963.

Gardner, E.B. Proprioceptive reflexes and their participation in motor skills. *Quest,* 1969, *12,* 1-25.

Gerard, R.W. Neurophysiology: an integration (molecules, neurons, and behavior). In J. Field (Ed.), *Handbook of physiology: section 1, neurophysiology, vol. 3*. Washington, D.C.: American Physiological Society, 1960.

Granit, R. *The purposive brain*. Cambridge, Mass.: MIT Press, 1977.

Hellebrandt, F.A. The physiology of motor learning. *Cerebral Palsy Review,* 1958, *19,* 9-14.

Henneman, E. Principles governing distribution of sensory input to motor neurons. In E.V. Evarts (Ed.), *Central processing of sensory input leading to motor output*. Cambridge, Mass.: MIT Press, 1975.

Hubel, D.H. The brain. *Scientific American,* 1979, *241*(3), 44-53.

Jones, R.E. Notes and comments: effector mechanisms of coordination. *Journal of Motor Behavior,* 1974, *6*(2), 77-79.

Kelso, J.A.S., & Stelmach, G.E. Central and peripheral mechanisms in motor control. In G.E. Stelmach (Ed.), *Motor control: issues and trends*. New York: Academic Press, 1976.

Kornhuber, H.H. Cerebral cortex, cerebellum, and basal ganglia: an introduction to their motor functions. In E.V. Evarts (Ed.), *Central processing of sensory input leading to motor output*. Cambridge, Mass.: MIT Press, 1975.

Lassen, N.A., Ingvar, D.H., & Skinhj, E. Brain function and blood flow. *Scientific American.* 1978, *239*(4), 62-71.

Merton, P.A. How we control the contraction of our muscles. *Scientific American,* 1972, *226*(5), 30-37.

Nauta, W.J.H., & Feirtag, M. The organization of the brain. *Scientific American,* 1979, *241*(3), 88-111.

O'Connell, A.L., & Gardner, E.B. *Understanding the scientific bases of human movement*. Baltimore: Williams & Wilkins, 1972.

Porter, R. The neurophysiology of movement performance. In A.C. Guyton & C.G. Hunt (Eds.), *Physiology: neurophysiology*, Series 1, Vol. 3. Baltimore: University Park Press, 1975.

Powers, W.R. Nervous system control of muscular activity. In H.G. Knuttgen, *Neuromuscular mechanisms for therapeutic and conditioning exercise*. Baltimore: University Park Press, 1976.

Rosenweig, M.R., & Bennett, E.L. (Eds.). *Neural mechanisms of learning and memory*. Cambridge, Mass.: MIT Press, 1976.

Sage, G.H. *Introduction to motor behavior: a neuropsychological approach* (2nd ed.). Reading, Mass.: Addison-Wesley, 1977.

Waterland, J. The effect of force gradation on motor patterning: standing broad jump. *Quest*, 1967, 8, 15-25.

Waterland, J. Aspects of motor learning: vision and natural linkages. In L.E. Smith (Ed.), *Psychology of motor learning*. Chicago: Athletic institute, 1970.

4 INFORMATION PROCESSING

The purpose of this chapter is to present a model of the processes that apparently underlie an individual's ability to handle information, not only instructional information, but also information from the actual performance situation that is needed to carry out a skill with proficiency.

As Galambos and Morgan (1960) note, learning may most profitably be thought of not as a single process, such as memory, located in a particular site in the nervous system, but rather as a series of events involving a number of information-handling processes that occur in a certain order (p. 1495). If this is true, then it is logical to assume that we should be able to faciliate learning more readily by applying information-processing concepts to teaching, coaching, and performing.

Let's take a simple information-processing model (Fig. 4-1) and apply it to the performance of a specific motor skill. This model assumes that between the information given to the individual (sensory input) and the actual performance of the skill (motor output) there are two major intervening processes; *perception* of the information given and the *decision* to take a particular course of action.

Marteniuk (1976) describes how consideration of these processes can assist the practitioner. If we observe only a batter's swing (motor output), for example, we can analyze only one third of the total performance.

> However, it may be that the pitch was missed because the batter was unable to recognize the type of pitch thrown (the perceptual mechanism) or that the pitch was identified but the wrong course of action was taken by the decision mechanism. . . . This leads to an important principle of motor performance: that observing the end result of a motor act is insufficient for determining the reasons for successful or unsuccessful performance (p. 7).

If the batter misses a pitch because of failure to identify it, Marteniuk suggests that the practitioner might proceed by filming different types of pitches from behind the plate and training the player to identify them or to decrease the time needed to identify them. Although we are cognizant of the need for muscular training, how often do we consider perceptual training?

67

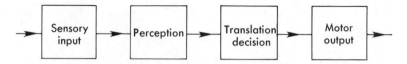

FIG. 4-1. A simplified information-processing model.

This is only one of a myriad of implications of information-processing concepts for instructional practice. In recent years there has been a decided shift in the study of motor learning and performance from the traditional stimulus-response theories to information processing. This is occurring not only in research (e.g., Stelmach, 1976, 1978) but also in application (e.g., Marteniuk, 1976; Welford, 1976; Whiting, 1970), and thus there is a growing body of knowledge that has implications for the practitioner. This is an exciting development. It allows us, for example, to consider the performance of individuals as manifestations of their perception of information received. In addition, it permits us to consider how instruction itself can influence an individual's capacity for handling information.

Information-processing concepts originated in part from communication theory and computer technology and therefore inherited much of their terminology: input, output, and so on. There has been some negative reaction to the use of such terminology in the field of education, presumably because of its mechanistic interpretations. It seems desirable to try to dispel the notion that the use of information-processing terminology is inhuman. One of the common problems appears to be in the use of the term *programming* when it refers to teaching.

Gervarter (1971), at a meeting of the American Society for Cybernetics, suggested that the goal of programming is to help individuals develop the capacity to mold themselves and exercise greater control over their lives.

> If we return to thinking of the human brain as a computer, we observe that the first thing required is to organize it through providing the infant with the proper care, love, exercise, and stimulation. Next it is important not to suppress any of its capacities by damping curiosity, attempts at explorations, or fouling up its judgment mechanism by producing feelings of inefficiency. . . . It is important for him to learn that any computer program is iterative, being updated, changed, and enlarged as more data and experience are obtained (p. 18-19).

This is hardly an attempt to compare humans to machines or to place computer limits on our capacities. In fact, communication techniques themselves emerged from observations of the human ability to handle information and solve problems (Meade, 1968). Later in this chapter consideration is given to how instruction itself can enhance the adaptive capacities of an individual.

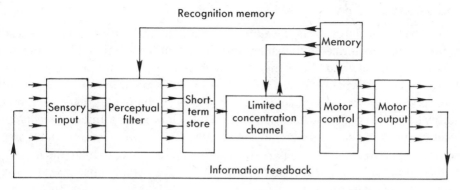

FIG. 4-2. A basic information-processing model for the use of practitioners.

A basic model

The emphasis in this chapter is on a relatively simple model of information processing that has proved useful to students in their initial attempts to apply information-processing concepts to skill analysis and instructional design. While a concerted effort has been made to ensure that the model is not inconsistent with research findings, the primary criterion for the inclusion of certain concepts and terminology (and the exclusion of others) has been their applicability to the needs of the practitioner who is relatively inexperienced in their use. Readers desiring additional, more sophisticated models should refer to the references listed at the end of this chapter, especially Marteniuk (1976) and Welford (1976).

The model used here is a modification of one developed earlier (Stallings, 1973, 1976) and has been pieced together from past conceptualizations from many sources. Certainly the works of Broadbent (1958), Fitts (1962, 1964), Gentile (1972), Gerard (1960), Marteniuk (1976), Welford (1960, 1968, 1976), and Whiting (1970, 1972) need to be cited. However, the model is not presented as a finished product; it continues to be revised as new research findings become viable and as critical comment from practitioners demands further clarification. Both the model and its component processes are referred to throughout the remainder of this book and are used specifically in the chapters on skill analysis (Chapter 8) and instructional tasks (Chapter 10).

The basic model (Fig. 4-2) is presented first with a brief comment on each of the processes to highlight its function. This is followed by an elaboration of the processes to clarify their nature and to point out some of the different implications.

SENSORY INPUT

Sensory input refers to the reception of stimuli by the sensory organs. These organs can be categorized into two groups: those that detect stimuli from outside the body (external) and those that detect changes occurring within the body (internal). The external receptors are probably more familiar to you. They consist of sensory organs in the skin (tactile/touch), eyes (visual/sight), ears (auditory/hearing), tongue (gustatory/taste), and nose (olfactory/smell). Internal receptors detect changes in the muscles (muscle spindle), tendons (Golgi tendon organ), and joints (joint receptors) and in portions of the inner ear (vestibular apparatus). Another group of internal receptors responds to other bodily changes, such as blood chemistry, blood pressure, and dehydration.

PERCEPTUAL FILTER (PF)

While the sensory organs are activated, in general, by any stimulus that affects them, what different individuals perceive is seen to be influenced in part by their own relatively unique background of past experience stored in memory. This means that we tend to hear what we are conditioned to hear and see what we are conditioned to see despite what our auditory and visual receptors tell us. This might be called a detection or recognition process; however, the critical concept for the practitioner is that people filter information (be it instructional or otherwise) so that what is "taken in" by the individual seldom coincides with the information given.

SHORT-TERM STORE (STS)

There is another limitation on what information "gets through" to the individual. Perceptual information can be stored for only a brief time; unless it is used immediately, it is lost. A common example is trying to remember a telephone number from the time you look it up until you dial the phone. In addition, STS is limited by the amount of information that it can handle. If you attempt to crowd it with too much information, some of it will inevitably be lost. Thus the practitioner must be concerned with both the amount of information the learner or performer is asked to handle and the time between the presentation of that information and its use.

LIMITED CONCENTRATION CHANNEL (LCC)

Note in Fig. 4-2 that the LCC is narrowed from top to bottom. This is to emphasize that at this point in processing information an individual can handle only one thing at a time. This process has been given various names: single channel, limited capacity channel, attention, concentration, and decision. Some of its probable functions will be elaborated on later. The important concept for the practitioner to understand is that interference or overload can occur if the learner is asked to concentrate on two or more things at once. If you've ever seen what an electrical storm can do to your television channel, you'll understand the problem. It either registers interference or blanks out entirely; in any case, the picture is lost.

MEMORY

Memory is the repository of learning, and as such it is often called long-term store. What exactly is stored here is a matter of controversy and often heated debate. Some of these hypotheses will be discussed later. However, here it is sufficient to note that memory influences not only our perception by way of the PF, but also the decisions and choices we make in the LCC and, in some concep- tualizations, the organization movement control. Thus each of us, on the basis of our own unique background of experiences, puts our own interpretation on the information we receive with resultant differences in the response (motor output) that we make.

MOTOR CONTROL

Neuromuscular mechanisms of motor control were discussed in some detail in the last chapter. Suffice it to note here that they have a profound influence on motor output. Thus I may know mentally what I want to do, but I need to take into account certain reflex mechanisms that might prevent my doing it effective- ly. However, there is more. Note in Fig. 4-2 that there is an arrow from memory to motor control. This means that even though I may know what I want to do and how to do it, prior conditioning (i.e., neuromuscular habits) may make it difficult to achieve the desired movement.

MOTOR OUTPUT

The foregoing description of the processes preceding a motor response should give you some appreciation of why individuals respond differently to the same instruction or to the same performance situation; individuals impose their own organization on the information they receive. The numerous sensory receptors have their motor counterpart in a single motor ending (motor end-plate) in each muscle cell. What takes place in the muscle cells (gradations of tension) must therefore be the result of not only the adequacy of the muscle (e.g., strength) but also prior processing.

INFORMATION FEEDBACK (IF)

Although an information-processing model may help us understand why indi- viduals perform the way they do, it does not tell us how they might improve their performance. This should be the function of IF. A separate section later in this chapter is devoted to IF. Suffice it to note here that this is one of the most important learning tools available to the practitioner.

I hope that the very short descriptions of the components of the model shown in Fig. 4-2 have helped you get an overall view of information processing. However, to see the direct relevance of the processes to learning, teaching, and performing, it is necessary to go into each of the processes in more depth. It will be helpful if you keep before you a copy of the model (Fig. 4-2) to refer to.

The processing components

An example of the implications of each process for motor skill learning, teaching, or performing is given in this section. However, you are encouraged to come up with your own examples so that the concept can be made specific to your situation. You will find as you do this that you will start with examples of things you have perhaps been doing all along intuitively. This does not make the concept any less useful. From this starting point of familiar examples, you can then expand (generalize) the concept to new techniques and procedures.

SENSORY INPUT

All stimuli of an adequate threshold that impinge on the sensory receptors activate those receptors. For example, if you look up a number in a telephone directory, not only the number you want but all the other information on the page of the directory is visually recorded for a second or so. At the same time, auditory receptors are picking up any sounds in the environment. If you add to these the input occurring through other receptors (touch, muscles and joints, etc.), you can perhaps appreciate the multitude of stimuli impinging on a person at any particular point in time. We are so accustomed, when performing a familiar skill, to filter out unessential stimuli that we forget that individuals to whom the skill is new have no background of experience to tell them what is essential and what is not. As Sage (1977) notes,

> Various stimuli impose upon the motor performer in sports: visual stimuli in the form of equipment, teammates, coaches, opponents; auditory stimuli such as the sound of balls being hit, voices of teammates, coaches, opponents, and starting signals. . . . There are of course many other stimuli that could be mentioned (p. 190).

Obviously, a beginner must make some choices from among this array of sensory input (Fig. 4-3), and these choices will be primarily on the basis of his past experience unless we as practitioners design instruction in such a way as to help ensure that the learner will absorb the relevant information. Fig. 4-3 suggests

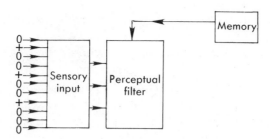

FIG. 4-3. Environmental stimuli. Relevant (+) and irrelevant (0).

several ways that this might be accomplished: (1) by gradually introducing the relevant stimuli, (2) by adapting the individual to irrelevant stimuli, and (3) by orienting the individual to the relevant stimuli. In Fig. 4-3 stimuli that are relevant to what is to be learned or performed are represented by the plus signs (+), and those that are irrelevant are indicated by zeros (0).

Gradually introduce relevant stimuli—The first thing we need to do is to determine what the relevant stimuli are for a particular skill, and this is no easy task. Gentile (1972) refers to such stimuli as "regulatory cues," that is, those stimuli that regulate what we do and when we do it. Gentile (p. 5) gives the example of a football player attempting an interception; the ball and its flight pattern determine the organization of the motor pattern that will be most effective. Gentile contends that "all of the regulatory stimuli must be evident during initial student attempts" (p. 16). However, as Whiting (1972) notes, "The relevant stimuli in a game situation will be different from those pertaining when a subskill is removed from the game" (p. 26). For example, the football player must also be aware of the position of opponents and the distance to the goal line or down marker; these become regulatory cues in a game situation. Obviously, to introduce all of these relevant stimuli at once can overload a beginner. Whiting (1972) cautions against the assumption that the beginner uses the same information as the expert: "The teacher and learner must be aware of what the regulatory cues are at various stages of learning a particular skill" (p. 26). These should then be introduced as rapidly as possible, consistent with the individual's information-processing capacity.

Adapt the individual to irrelevant stimuli—Although it might be assumed that the ideal situation would be one in which we could isolate the learner from irrelevant stimuli, there are two arguments against this. First, there are usually stimuli present in the game situation that the performer must learn to filter out, as, for example, the banter of a catcher who is trying to distract the batter. Second, it appears that judicious imposition of these inherent distractions during learning may lead to more rapid development of the PF (Stratton, 1978). Harrison and Reilly (1975), in fact, suggest that coaches include in their training regimen exercises designed to train the individual to ignore visual, tactile, and auditory distractions. For example, as players are practicing eye control, the coach should have someone walk back and forth in front of them; the player should continue to look through the distraction to the target. In the same manner, players can be trained to maintain concentration when touched or bumped and in spite of loud noise such as clapping. However, it would seem important to gradually introduce such distractions and to limit as much as possible the distracting stimuli that do not occur in the performance situation.

Orient the individual to the relevant stimuli—In catching or hitting a tennis ball, such admonitions as "keep your eye on the ball" or, conversely, in basketball dribbling, "keep your eye on the play" are obvious efforts to direct the player's attention to the regulatory cues for that skill. Arend (1980) suggests the possibility that having students observe the game prior to participation might speed up their learning of relevant information.

> We cannot take for granted that the learner knows the regulatory conditions in the environment nor that the learner has the ability to detect this information when needed. These are perceptual skills that develop through time and experience. . . . For example, contrast the observational ability of a casual spectator with that of an experienced spectator . . . (pp. 11-12).

Again, logically it would seem that directed observation might expedite the process, thereby not losing too much in the way of actual practice time.

Up to this point in the discussion of sensory input the emphasis has been on the perception of cues necessary for effective performance (versus learning). Therefore it seems desirable to emphasize that the learner may be receiving three types of input (Fig. 4-4): (1) performance or regulatory cues, such as the flight of the ball to be caught; (2) instructional information, such as a demonstration of the pattern of the skill; and (3) evaluation or corrective feedback regarding the actual performance of the skill. It is important that both the practitioner and the learner know what the purpose of the input is and where attention should be directed.

PERCEPTUAL FILTER (PF)

Perception is essentially an organizing process and has various functions: detection, discrimination, recognition, and identification. These terms should be familiar to you, and such perceptual abilities are obviously important in the performance of many skills, particularly open skills such as catching and batting that depend on perceptual cues for their successful execution. However, perception is always a highly critical factor in learning; instructional information, be it visual,

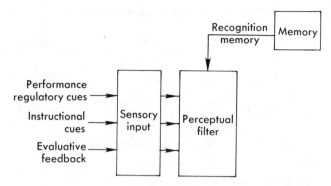

FIG. 4-4. Three sources of input. (See text for further explanation.)

verbal, or tactile, must be perceived by the individual if it is to be used. The point of emphasis in this section is therefore on the filter function of the process.

Fig. 4-2 shows that past experience in memory plays a leading role in determining what is perceived. Assuming that we, by appropriately designing the learning environment, have sufficiently emphasized the relevant stimuli (a large assumption), we might expect that the learner perceives the relevant information as given. Not necessarily so. Loftus and Loftus (1976) highlight the function of the PF by describing the process as essentially one of recognition: "The process essentially consists of 'recognizing' a raw physical pattern in sensory store as representing something meaningful" (p. 23). For example, if the visual sensory analyzers project the letter pattern A, this is recognized not necessarily as an A, but as (1) the first letter of the alphabet, (2) a vowel, or (3) a good grade. In the same manner, a Z may be recognized as (1) the last letter of the alphabet, (2) a consonant, or (3) the sound of a person snoring. What is of import to the practitioner is that it is not the letter A or Z that is passed on to short-term store but the meaning attached to it.

In Fig. 4-5 an attempt is made to show how we might transform raw sensory data through the filter process. Fig. 4-5 assumes that three things can happen to the sensory input: (1) it may get through to short-term store as given ($+$), (2) the information given may be pooled with the concept from memory (θ), or (3) it may be completely transformed by what would appear to the practitioner to be a completely unrelated concept from memory (0). Let's look at these possibilities.

Information untransformed—Information untransformed is the ideal but least likely event. The information given by the practitioner, for example, is seen, heard, or felt as was intended. The learner and the teacher are speaking the same language. This might occur for a couple of reasons: (1) the information was already known by the learner or (2) the practitioner knew the learner's back-

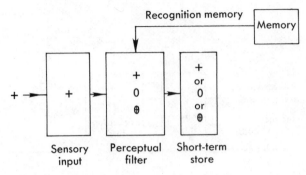

FIG. 4-5. Perceptual filter (recognition memory). Information untransformed (+), transformed (0), or pooled (θ).

ground of experience and provided sufficient information to make differentiation possible (e.g., "The smash is like the serve except. . . .").

Information pooled—An example of information pooled might occur in teaching an individual how to pitch. The practitioner's demonstration of the pitch is pooled perceptually with the individual's past experience with pitching, which may be how big brother throws. One of the interesting things that often occurs in pooling is the addition of extraneous parts. For example, the learner may add to the pitch the elements of style, such as rubbing the ball, taking an exaggerated windup, toeing the plate, and so on—a hangover from television perhaps. It should not be assumed that the learner is necessarily "fooling around." What background of experience exists to tell the learner that these are not essential aspects of the skill? If we as practitioners emphasize essential aspects and help individuals differentiate, we can speed up the learning process.

Information transformed—Information transformed appears to occur more often with verbal direction than with visual direction (visual direction tends to be pooled). For example, if you ask dancers to extend their foot, you will probably get plantar flexion; if you ask a child to extend his leg, you will get hip flexion. However, although we must take a great deal of care in the use of terminology that is specific to our profession, other transformations occur for which even the individual cannot divine the reason. Nevertheless, it is seldom stubbornness on the part of the learners; they are probably as frustrated at not getting it right as we are. Incidentally, the problem often exists in neuromuscular conditioning; the individual has perceived what is to be done but cannot carry it out because of prior conditioning. This occurs at the level of motor control rather than at the PF, and therefore the remedy to be taken will be different. More will be said of this later.

SHORT-TERM STORE (STS)

We often assume that once an individual has perceived the information given, the information can then be used to affect performance. This is not always the case. Even if we assume the learner has perceived the information given without transforming it (again, a large assumption), STS is limited both by the amount of information it can store (capacity) and by the length of time the information can be stored before it is lost. As with sensory input, once it is lost it cannot be recalled. These limitations of the STS are discussed here together with potential remedies.

Capacity-chunking—Information appears to be held in STS in "chunks." Miller (1956) suggests that the STS can handle only about seven chunks at any one time. Simon (1976, p. 83) suggests that the number is probably closer to four. This suggests that the practitioner must be extremely cautious in giving a number of directions to a student. Although the STS may be limited to a few chunks of information, it does not dictate the amount of information in each chunk. Miller (1956) gives an analogy: we have a purse that will hold a small number of coins whether they be pennies or dollars. Thus we can use our storage capacity more efficiently if we stock it with rich symbols such as models and goals than with minutely detailed steps. It would seem then that a major task of the practitioner is to "chunk" instruction in such a way as to help ensure that it will not be lost. In a tennis backhand, "Reach into your back pocket"; on a tennis serve, "Hammer the nail in at an angle." Be sure that the individual has the necessary background of experience. Not everyone knows how to hammer a nail.

Time-rehearsal—STS is limited not only by the amount of information it can handle but also by time; that is, unless it is used, information in STS is forgotten very rapidly. According to Loftus and Loftus (1976), this forgetting begins in about 2 seconds and is virtually complete by 15 seconds; "At intervals longer than 15 seconds, responses must be based on the (meager) information that has been transferred . . ." (p. 40). This suggests that for the learner instructional information should be short (as well as chunked) and that, if possible, practice should be immediate. If it is not possible for a student to practice immediately, mental rehearsal is possible. In this case, the contents of the STS are passed into the LCC and returned to the STS (Fig. 4-6). Note, however, that this process occupies both the STS and the LCC so that new input cannot get through. Mental rehearsal may be visual, verbal, and perhaps kinesthetic (feeling of movement); the advantages of each are discussed in Chapter 10. Suffice it to note here that there is a danger in mental rehearsal for beginners because they are more apt to transform or pool information while rehearsing, as shown in Fig. 4-6. Mental rehearsal not only maintains the information in STS, but also facilitates its transfer to memory (long-term store). We learn what we rehearse, right or wrong.

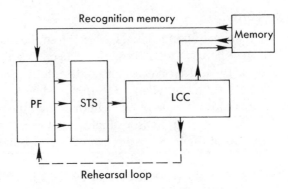

FIG. 4-6. Rehearsal loop. Information (*dotted lines*) passed from short-term store (*STS*) to limited concentration channel (*LCC*) back to STS by way of perceptual filter (*PF*).

LIMITED CONCENTRATION CHANNEL (LCC)

There is little consensus on the exact nature of the LCC, much less the terminology associated with it. Marteniuk (1976), for example, calls it the *decision mechanism*, while Welford (1976) uses the term *translation into action*. The assumption here is that it is concerned with the cognitive (thought) processes associated with performance. Obviously, this will be different for the learner and for the expert performer, since the latter has been able to relegate certain aspects of information processing to an automatic level.

The term *limited concentration channel* was selected to emphasize that we can only concentrate on one thing at a time. For the learner this would appear to have three aspects that can be seen to compete for concentration space: (1) uncertainty with regard to the perceptual data from STS, (2) choice of an action plan, and (3) conscious attention to movement control. These functions are shown in Fig. 4-7; they are separated with dotted lines to emphasize the fact that, as proficiency increases, the perceptual and motor components can be largely relegated to the PF and to the automatic motor control processes, thus freeing the LCC to deal with strategy problems. The critical point for the practitioner is that the novice cannot deal with all these tasks at once.

Perceptual analysis—Even assuming that, as practitioners, we have done our best to organize input in such a way as to ensure its assimilation untransformed, there is bound to be a great deal of ambiguity for the novice in the skill. Learners continue to try to decrease that uncertainty by thinking about it in relation to their past experience, that is, to attempt to resolve doubt. This suggests that, as practitioners, we might do well to try to determine where the individual's uncertainty or doubt lies. Thus we might speed up the perceptual learning pro-

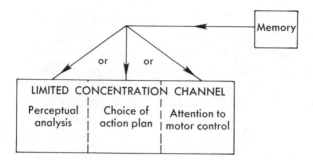

FIG. 4-7. Competing tasks in the LCC. As the skill becomes well learned, perceptual analysis and motor control tend to become automated.

cess, that is, start the learner on the road to perceptual anticipation. This might be accomplished by encouraging the learner to vocalize the doubt (e.g., "How can I tell which way my opponent is going to move?").

Choice of an action plan—Ideally, the choice of a particular plan of action is going to depend on the specific performance situation at any point in time, but this is obviously influenced by the individual's background of experience. Left to his own devices, a learner will choose that action which has been most successful in the past. However, as practitioners, we can manipulate this process by suggesting effective plans. This may be in terms of a specific form of movement (particularly for closed skills), or it may be in terms of strategy. It should be noted that decision time increases with the number of choices considered. We can aid by clarifying for the learner what conditions should determine a particular course of action (e.g., "When should I go to the net and when should I stay back?"). The question remains as to whether an action plan (be it form of movement or strategy) should be dictated by the practitioner or whether individuals should be encouraged to formulate their own action plan. There are several arguments for the latter view. First, individuals differ in both body build and motor abilities that determine the form of movement that will be most effective for them. Second, demands for a specific form of movement, beyond that required by principles of biomechanical efficiency, can considerably decrease an individual's capacity to adjust to the varying situational conditions in an open skill. Finally, the practitioner must consider how present instruction will influence future motor skills development through the building of a memory repertoire.

Attention to movement control—When learners must (or feel they must) concentrate on the neuromuscular carrying out of a skill, this blocks the LCC from attending to perceptual analysis or decision making. I hope that the discussion of neurological motor control mechanisms in the previous chapter convinced you that the human body has a number of automatic control mechanisms that should be allowed to operate without much interference from thought processes. Basically, it was suggested that there are two ways in which concentration might need to be brought into play: (1) inhibition of innate reflexes (or learned habits) when these are detrimental to performance and (2) refinement of initial gross movement by way of gradual inhibition of overflow. In addition, it is often desirable for us to evaluate our movement in relation to goal attainment. More will be said of this later. Nevertheless, it is not too out of line to suggest that traditional instructional methods have been overly involved with focusing the learner's concentration on movement control. This has resulted in our excluding, to a large extent, consideration of the perceptual and decision-making requirements of skills.

To reiterate, the LCC can handle only one task at a time. We must decide whether we want the individual to concentrate on high-level perceptual analysis, decision making, or control of movement.

In addition, concentration on instruction is part of the learner's task. Thus the limitations of the LCC suggest that instruction should not occur simultaneously with one of these other tasks. Also, if the learner is asked to concentrate on a demonstration of a skill, we should not expect his attention to a verbal description of it at the same time. The learner will filter out one or the other, or, in attempting to attend to both, overload may occur. We can either save our breath and not verbalize, or we can intersperse visual and verbal instruction. Incidentally, such overloading is not unique to teachers. The intrusion of television commentators on our viewing of sports events can be attested to by newspaper headlines such as "Sight versus Sound at the Olympics" and "Tennis—Without the Racket."

MEMORY

The importance of memory or past experience to performance and continued learning is obvious. Yet it is the process we know least about, which is why there are so many theories about it. The purpose of this section is not to present these theories, but rather to ask What does an individual need to know about a skill to optimize performance and learning? There is an obvious danger in this approach, since no one really knows the answers, but it would appear to be the most useful for the practitioner. This approach also assumes that memory, while it may have some intrinsic organizational properties of its own, is also flexible with regard to its adaptation to input.

We need to first look at memory in our information-processing model (Fig. 4-2) and note what it is deemed to contribute. Note the arrows to the PF, the LCC, and motor control. Thus as Marteniuk (1976) notes, we must assume (1) a perceptual memory that is capable of recognizing incoming information, (2) an integrative or relational memory that assists in decision making and problem solving, and (3) a movement memory that allows us not only to organize sequential movements into a skill but also to retain these over long periods of time (p. 156). This does not imply that these are separate memories; the weight of evidence is that they are intimately related.

Recognition memory—There seems to be a general consensus that there is a component of memory that functions as a PF of incoming information. However, this recognition memory does not contain all of our information store; rather, it is a tag, or label. Simon (1976) suggests that the relation of recognition memory to our information store is comparable to that between an index and a book. However, we index our own books. Perhaps one of the practitioner's tasks is to help individuals index motor skills more effectively. In any case, it appears that an important task of the practitioner is to aid learners in achieving an appropriate recognition tag. For example, the learner, seeing a demonstration of a badminton smash, may tag it as tennis if that is his background of experience. The practitioner can then aid the learner by pointing out differences.

Relational memory—Having tagged or recognized an object or pattern, we then call on information in memory related to that object or pattern. For example, having tagged the badminton smash as tennis, we are apt to use not only the neuromuscular patterning for the tennis smash, but also strategies related to tennis. This obviously biases us and may prevent, if inappropriate, the learning of badminton strategies. Such bias might be prevented if the practitioner emphasizes differences. Simon (1976) suggests that although relational memory is in no way a photograph of sensory input, it appears to be flexible in terms of the forms in which it stores information. If this is true, then it is possible that memory is capable of classifying input in a variety of ways.

Movement memory—Theories of movement memory abound. Henry (1960), for example, postulates a "neuromotor memory drum" in which the sensorimotor coordination pattern of each motor skill is stored, and the theory has been used to support the contention that there can be little, if any, transfer between skills. Pew (1970), however, suggests that what is stored as the result of a well-learned skill is not a fixed pattern of movements but a set of rules or procedures for the conduct of the skill (schema). He notes, for example, that no two tennis drives are performed in exactly the same way, although each may serve the same purpose. The schema approach to movement memory had a rebirth in the 1970s and is discussed in the next chapter on motor control theories. All of the motor control theories make inferences with regard to the memory representation of movement, and at this time research findings are equivocal.

The question for the practitioner remains: What is stored in memory? Sensory or motor patterns, goals in terms of the objective of the act, or strategy rules? What is proposed here is that each of these is important and that we need to program these into memory so that a *relational scheme* for each skill takes root in

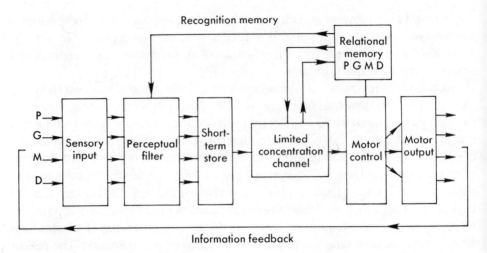

FIG. 4-8. A relational scheme for a motor skill. *P,* Perceptual or regulatory cues; *G,* goal or objective of the skill; *M,* patterning of the movement; *D,* conditions for decision making.

memory. Fig. 4-8 is an attempt to depict how this might be done, based on the following hypothesized essentials for motor skills: (1) the goal (objective of the skill), (2) the perceptual performance cues (regulatory cues), (3) the spatial-temporal patterning of the movement itself, and (4) the conditions for decision making. There are other relational schemes, some of which are discussed in the next chapter on motor control concepts. The point being made here is that until practitioners know more about how motor skills are, or can be, represented in memory, they must make some educated guesses.

This is nothing new, at least to learners. Observation suggests that much of their effort seems to go into devising some kind of relational scheme for a skill. However, we need to make it more systematic. In addition, practitioners can use such information to manipulate input in accord with (1) the nature of the skill, (2) the stage of learning, and (3) the phases of performance. For example, open and closed skills differ in the parameters that would be essential: open skills require emphasis on the goal of the movement and the perceptual cues and, conversely, closed skills require close attention to the form of movement. More is said on this in Chapter 8.

MOTOR CONTROL

At this point in our information-processing model, perceptual information from the environment has been perceived (as transformed or pooled), and an action plan (purpose of the act, its form, or a strategy) has been decided on. The motor control mechanisms must now organize a set of commands to the muscles so that the movements to achieve the action plan can be carried out in an effective fashion. We have already studied some of the neuromuscular mechanisms involved in the control of movement (Chapter 3), and the next chapter deals with some specific concepts of motor control. Suffice it to note here that there are three basic concepts of how movements are controlled: closed-loop control, open-loop control, and goal-directed control.

Closed-loop control—The role of feedback in the reflex control of movement has already been noted. Thus, as a person begins to fall forward, sensory stimuli (e.g., in the muscles and in the vestibular mechanisms of the ear) alert the central nervous system structures to return the body and head to an upright position. According to Adams (1976), all movements are controlled in a like manner. Peripheral feedback from an ongoing movement is compared to a sensory image of past movements stored in memory. When there is a mismatch between the present movement and the stored image, motor commands are generated to the muscles to correct the movement. The image, stored in memory, works basically as a recognition memory; when the movement "feels wrong," the correction is generated. Since learners have relatively poor movement images of a new skill, they make use of feedback from other sources (e.g., vision or hearing) to help refine the movement and, therefore, the movement image in memory (Adams, 1976).

Open-loop control—In an open-loop concept, movement is seen as being controlled by centrally stored motor programs planned by the individual prior to movement initiation and then carried out without recourse to peripheral feedback. The movement is said to have been preprogrammed or preselected (Kelso & Wallace, 1978), and peripheral feedback from the ongoing movement has no guiding or corrective function. One of the advantages is, of course, that by not having to monitor peripheral (e.g., kinesthetic) feedback the individual can free the LCC to attend to other tasks such as decision making.

Goal-directed control—Both the open-loop and the closed-loop control theories have major limitations, which will be discussed in the next chapter. Suffice it to note here that both the nature of the skill and the stage of learning appear to be important factors in determining which method is the more effective and when (Schmidt, 1980). A recent point of view (e.g., Evarts, 1979) is that we as performers might select the more appropriate control method depending on our purpose or goal. Thus in skills, the performance of which will profit from being under peripheral feedback control, we would use the feedback to guide our ongoing movement; conversely, we would use preprogrammed movement when peripheral feedback would be detrimental to performance. It is also possible that we may need to switch back and forth quickly between open- and closed-loop control during a single performance (e.g., a balance beam routine) or even during a single movement.

MOTOR OUTPUT

Motor output is the end result we are trying to influence. Prior processing is to no avail unless the motor response mechanisms (strength, flexibility, etc.) are adequate for the task. Although Chapter 7 deals with motor abilities, it is not within the purview of this book to present information on biomechanics or physiological training. Suffice it to note here that there is no substitute for a thorough understanding of, and competence in developing, the motor capacities of the individual. Unfortunately, the use of information-processing theory has tended to make us forget the critical importance of training the output end.

Information feedback (IF)

Although an information-processing model such as that just described may help us understand why individuals perform the way they do, it does not tell us how they might improve their performance. This should be the function of IF. In very general terms, *IF* is defined in this book as *sensory input that makes possible an improvement in proficiency*.

The importance of both excitatory and inhibitory neural feedback loops in the reflex control of movement has already been noted in Chapter 3. For example, the righting reflexes consist of the integration of a number of sensory impulses from muscles, joints, and vestibular organs that "feed back" to the muscles to help prevent loss of balance. Eccles (1977), among others, notes that similar feedback loops operate at the level of consciousness. The rehearsal loop described in the previous section (Fig. 4-5) is an example of conscious feedback.

There are many facets of feedback, some of which are not relevant to discuss here. The concern of the practitioner would appear to be feedback that can enhance learning and performance. Note that a distinction is made in this book between feedback and IF. Students are always receiving feedback about their performance from teachers and coaches, from parents, from other players, from themselves, and, as we shall see, even from the equipment they are using. Not all of this feedback is useful in improving their performance; in fact, it may be just the opposite. The concern of the practitioner, then, is not only to provide IF, which can improve performance, but also to eliminate or direct attention away from feedback that may be detrimental.

It should be emphasized, however, that providing IF does not ensure that the individual will make use of it to improve performance. For example, motivation or the lack of it is an obvious factor in learning. Moreover, there are many types of feedback that influence its effectiveness. Therefore, it seems desirable to discuss these briefly so that the practitioner will have a more valid and varied repertoire of techniques.

CATEGORIES OF FEEDBACK

There is little doubt that IF is critical to learning. The evidence is overwhelming. The question remains as to what type of feedback and when. Although we do not have all the answers, the following discussions are designed to clarify some of the possibilities.

Reinforcement and IF—Although a number of authors object to classifying reinforcement as IF, this would, from the practitioner's point of view, appear to be shortsighted. It should be noted, however, that such an objection has some basis. *Reinforcement* in the traditional sense (Law of Effect and operant conditioning) is generally used to refer to events following a response that increase or decrease the probability that the same response will recur. *IF* is generally used to refer to information the learner can use to make his next response different. However, when reinforcement provides information (right or wrong) that leads to an improvement in performance, it should be considered IF. The practitioner should note that reinforcement has limited informational content. It is an axiom of information theory that we can only control something to the extent that we have information about it.

Internal and external—It has already been noted that movement itself generates sensory feedback that influences motor control (e.g., balance). This is often termed *proprioceptive feedback,* a term that is used interchangeably with *internal feedback* in this book. *External feedback* is any feedback that is not produced by input from muscles and other proprioceptive organs. There is a major controversy at this time as to the relative value of proprioceptive feedback in motor performance and learning, and as of yet we do not have all the answers. This is discussed in the next chapter on motor control.

Intrinsic and supplementary—Some skills have considerable *intrinsic* IF; that is, performance of the skill itself provides feedback regarding the performance. This is particularly obvious in such skills as goal shooting in basketball, shooting in archery, and steering a car. Performance in other activities, such as diving and gymnastics, provides little if any IF, at least in the early stages of learning. *Supplementary* or added IF is obviously important in the early stages of learning. Supplementary IF can be provided directly by the teacher or coach or indirectly by such means as videotape. The potency of IF in learning suggests that a critical task of the practitioner is to determine the intrinsic IF provided by the skill, to supplement this by the most effective means, and to call the learner's attention to both sources, since providing IF does not ensure its use.

Concurrent and terminal—IF that occurs during performance is called *concurrent,* while that which occurs following a performance is called *terminal.* Most tracking skills, such as catching a ball and steering a car, are obviously enhanced by intrinsic concurrent IF; however, concurrent IF may also be supplementary as, for example, providing mirrors in dance. Some skills occur so quickly (e.g., a kip) that terminal IF is the only alternative. However, we have often relied on terminal IF as a crutch, since it is administratively more feasible. We should instead devise methods of providing concurrent IF in those skills that would profit from it.

Immediate and delayed—IF may occur immediately following performance or after varying periods of delay. Although a common assumption has been "the more immediate, the better," Gentile (1972) suggests that providing supplementary IF immediately after a performance might interfere with the individual's processing of and profiting from the intrinsic IF provided by the skill. "Teacher comments should be delayed for a brief interval of time so that the student can profit and encode information he obtained during and after the movement" (p. 19). Moreover, Adams (1971) suggests that the critical factor in learning rate is the time between responses rather than that between response and IF or between IF and the following response (p. 133). Provided there is sufficient time for the individual to process the IF and decide on an action, and not so much time that the IF and the plan of action are forgotten, there seems to be some latitude with regard to the timing of IF during the interval between performances.

Knowledge of results (KR) and knowledge of performance (KP)—Del Rey (1972) makes what appears to be a very useful distinction between KR and KP that has been widely adopted. _KR_ is used to refer to IF regarding the consequences in terms of goal attainment (e.g., the ball landed in the rough), and _KP_ is used to refer to IF regarding the movement itself (e.g., the path of the swing in a golf drive). Del Rey suggests that KR is more useful in open skills, and KP in closed skills. For example, supplementary KP in relatively closed gymnastic skills might include techniques such as videotaped replays and graph-check photographs. Appropriate supplementary IF for open skills, however, might be KR regarding the game conditions prior to or following a play. Football coaches use such methods routinely to restructure the conditions under which decisions were made and to point out relevant events that may have been overlooked by the players.

EVALUATIVE FEEDBACK

It has often been suggested that knowledge of the results of a movement (KR) is more appropriate to open skills, and knowledge of performance (KP) is more appropriate to closed skills. Thus in a closed skill, such as diving, feedback would be directed toward correcting the form of the movement, and in an open skill, such as passing a football, attention might be directed to whether the ball was thrown to the open receiver.

However, we need to be much more systematic in analyzing the performance

Was movement executed as planned?
(KP)

		Yes	No
Was goal accomplished? (KR)	Yes	"Got the idea of the movement"	"Surprise"
	No	"Something's wrong"	"Everything's wrong"

FIG. 4-9. Evaluative feedback. Performer reactions following comparison of *KR* and *KP*. (See text for further explanation.) (Modified from Gentile, A.M. A working model of skill acquisition with application to teaching. *Quest,* 1972, *17,* 3-23.)

situation to determine the most effective IF for the learner. As information processing tells us (Fig. 4-1), we need to determine which process in the chain is causing the problem: perceptual identification, decision making, or motor control.

Gentile (1972) presents a diagram highlighting the need for defining evaluative feedback more carefully (Fig. 4-9). Basically, Gentile is suggesting a comparison of KR (the outcome in terms of goal attainment) with KP (the movement plan that elicited it). The "surprise," "something's wrong," and so on, are obviously reactions, not decisions. But, as Gentile notes, these reactions are seen to lead to decisions on the part of the learner. Let's look at each of these boxes.

Yes-yes (got the idea of the movement)—The decision is that there is no problem. The Law of Effect (satisfaction) operates so that the likelihood of the same motor plan being used on the next attempt is high.

No-yes (something's wrong)—The goal was not attained, but the movement was executed as planned. What is the performer's decision? The obvious strategy would be to revise the movement plan. However, if the same result recurs, Gentile suggests that a different strategy would be required.

> Thus the "something's wrong" outcome would seem to require the learner to determine whether his environment/movement match or his initial identification of regulatory conditions was inadequate (p. 10).

Yes-no (surprise!)—According to Gentile, we don't really know what learners do in the case of the yes-no (surprise!) reaction. Marteniuk (1976) suggests that they might (1) modify their movement plan to try to bring the executed movement more in line with the planned movement or (2) tend to continue with the incorrect movement since it accomplished the goal (Law of Effect). In the latter case, he notes, the learners run the risk of learning an incorrect skill on a level that may limit their performance later. He suggests that the teacher would need to give supplementary KP regarding the proper movement (p. 197).

No-no (everything's wrong)—The no-no (everything's wrong) reaction could lead to several different decisions, including the decision to quit. Gentile can only express her hope that this would not be the case, since she believes that learners should come up with their own evaluations and action plans. As Marteniuk (1976) notes, however, if quitting appears to be the learner's decision, it would be hoped that the teacher or coach would step in and provide supplementary feedback (p. 197).

•   •   •

IF has too long been directed to the motor response without consideration of the fact that perceptual and decision-making problems can lead to performance problems. Rothstein (1979) has stated the need very well.

> By viewing information feedback as a means through which the performer is able to assess the success of each aspect of performance, and by realizing that feedback is a specialized form of input and thus subject to all the factors that govern input . . . , the teacher or coach should be able to provide information which is useful to performers and specifically related to the difficulties that may prevent them from achieving excellence (p. 225).

System development

If we are to design the performance-learning environment so that it is maximally adaptive, we need to take into consideration all of the factors operating. So far, the emphasis has been on how we might increase the individual performer's information-processing capacity. System development theory offers us the opportunity to consider how we might enhance performance by modifying other components of the performance-learning situation.

A basic assumption of a system development approach to optimizing performance is that the individual performer is considered only one component, albeit a major one, in a complex system composed of a variable number of mutually interacting components. Thus a system includes not only the dynamics of the individual performer or operator but also the dynamics of the machine, apparatus, or equipment being used, the dynamics of the environment (including other people) in which the performance is taking place, or a combination of these (Gagne, 1965, p. 35). Although the application of system development theory has been much more extensive (e.g., personnel management systems) than what is immediately relevant to our focus on individual skill development, the theory does offer some useful concepts for consideration by the practitioner.

The goal of system development is to optimize the performance of the system as a whole, whether that system be a relatively simple one, such as target archery, or a more complex one, such as driving a car. The concept of development is as important as the concept of system; that is, we want to develop not only the individual performer but also the environment and equipment. For example, performance in archery, springboard diving, golfing, skiing, riflery, and driving (the list is almost infinite) may be improved not only by individual training but also by the modification of equipment or machine design and other environmental factors, such as social interaction. In addition, the theory implies the possibility of modifying both equipment and the environment to accommodate individual differences and limitations (e.g., adjustable fulcrum on a diving board or automobile modifications for the handicapped).

Fitts (1962) presents a schematic diagram of a system approach to human performance (Fig. 4-10), which should help the practitioner appreciate the complexity of interactions (arrows) that influence system output.

SYSTEM COMPONENTS

In Fig. 4-10 the interacting components include man, environment, and machines. The nodes representing the performer (1, 2, 3) are comparable to the sensory input, central channel, and motor output boxes in the information-processing model used in this chapter. The environment (4) represents the performance-learning situation, including the instructor and other people. The machine components (6, 7, 8) can most easily by likened to an automobile in which there are both controls (steering wheel, brake) and display. However, for our purposes, the concept of machines would include such things as gymnastics apparatus and sports equipment.

FEEDBACK LOOPS

Note in Fig. 4-10 that the operator's performance is influenced by three primary feedback loops: (1) an internal loop (3-1) representing feedback from the movement itself, (2) an environmental loop (3-4-1), and (3) a man-machine loop (3-6-7-8-1). Thus the individual receives feedback information from both the environment and the machine and the interaction between them. The concern of the practitioner is to develop the environment and the machine in such a way that this feedback can enhance performance. Smith (1967) notes that the design of hand instruments is particularly significant to the type of precision control required in athletic or musical performance. The more fitted the instrument (as in shape and surface texture), the more precise is the sensory feedback resulting from its use (p. 67).

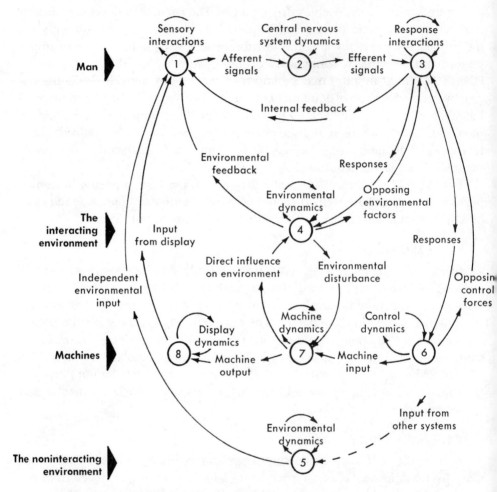

FIG. 4-10. A system development model of human performance. (See text for further explanation.) (From Fitts, P.M. Factors in complex skill training. In R. Glaser [Ed.], *Training research and education,* University of Pittsburgh Press, 1962.)

OPPOSING FORCES

On the right side of Fig. 4-10 are loops representing what Fitts terms *opposing forces,* which directly influence the performer's response without opportunity for central processing. For example, while driving we may hit a pothole in the road that pulls the steering wheel; while skiing we may contact ice unexpectedly. The desirability of maintaining a relatively flexible movement repertoire appears obvious. However, one of the best examples of machine development to decrease the influence of an opposing force in sports is the recent development of a fast running track at Harvard (McMahon & Greene, 1978). The design of the spring track was arrived at through a neuromuscular and mechanical analysis of running. In addition to decreasing the number of injuries, "the track substantially enhances a runner's performance, reducing the time of a well-run mile by several seconds" (p. 148). Such a system approach should help to emphasize that no one is ever performing in a vacuum, neither the learner nor the teacher or coach. This should be kept in mind as you proceed.

Sample thought sheet

1. Give an example (observed rather than hypothetical, if possible) of each of the following in operation in a teaching, learning, or performing situation.
   a. Overload of STS
   b. Chunking
   c. Rehearsal loop
   d. Overload of LCC
2. Differentiate between the two types of feedback in each set. Give an example of how you have used each type or could use it to best advantage in a teaching situation. Be specific regarding the skill or game.
   a. Intrinsic and supplementary
   b. Concurrent and terminal
   c. Immediate and delayed
   d. KR and KP
   e. Evaluative feedback
3. Observe a sports teaching situation.
   a. What were the inputs (regulatory cues, instruction, feedback)?
   b. Were any two of the inputs occurring at once?
   c. Where was student attention?
   d. How would you improve the situation?
4. Give an example of the development of a machine (equipment) to enhance performance in a specific motor skill.

References

Adams, J.A. A closed-loop theory of motor learning. *Journal of Motor Behavior,* 1971, 3, 111-151.
Adams, J.A. A closed-loop theory of motor learning. In G.E. Stelmach (Ed.), *Motor control: issues and trends.* New York: Academic Press, 1976.

Arend, S. Developing perceptual skills prior to motor performance. *Motor Skills: Theory into Practice,* 1980, *4*(1), 11-17.

Broadbent, D.E. *Perception and communication.* New York: Pergamon Press, 1958.

Del Rey, P. Appropriate feedback for open and closed skills acquisition. *Quest,* 1972, *11,* 42-45.

Eccles, J.C. *The understanding of the brain* (2nd ed.). New York: McGraw-Hill, 1977.

Evarts, E.V. Brain mechanisms of movement. *Scientific American,* 1979, *241*(3), 164-179.

Fitts, P.M. Factors in complex skill training. In R. Glaser (Ed.), *Training research and education.* Pittsburgh: University of Pittsburgh Press, 1962. (Republished New York: Wiley, 1965.)

Fitts, P.M. Perceptual-motor skill learning. In A.W. Melton (Ed.), *Categories of human learning.* New York: Academic Press, 1964.

Gagne, R.M. Introduction. In R.M. Gagne (Ed.), *Psychological principles in system development.* New York: Holt, Rinehart, and Winston, 1965.

Galambos, R., & Morgan, C.T. The neural basis of learning. In J. Field (Ed.), *Handbook of physiology: Section 1: neurophysiology, Vol. 3.* Washington, D.C.: American Physiological Society, 1960.

Gentile, A.M. A working model of skill acquisition with application to teaching. *Quest,* 1972, *17,* 3-23.

Gerard, R.W. Neurophysiology: an integration (molecules, neurons, and behavior). In J. Field (Ed.), *Handbook of physiology: Section 1: neurophysiology, Vol. 3.* Washington, D.C.: American Physiological Society, 1960.

Gervarter, W.B. *The nature of man and his programming.* Presented at Fall Conference of the American Society for Cybernetics, Washington, D.C., December 1971. (Mimeographed)

Harrison, B., & Reilly, R.E. *Visiondynamics: baseball method.* Visiondynamics: Success Through Perceptual Awareness, 23862 Wavespray Circle, Lacuna, Calif., 1975.

Henry, F.M. Increased response latency for complicated movements and a "memory drum" theory of neuromotor reaction. *Research Quarterly,* 1960, *31,* 448-458.

Kelso, J.A.S., & Wallace, S.A. Conscious mechanisms in movement. In G.E. Stelmach (Ed.), *Information processing in motor control and learning.* New York: Academic Press, 1978, pp. 79-111.

Loftus, G.R., & Loftus, E.F. *Human memory: the processing of information.* New York: Wiley, 1976.

Marteniuk, R.G. *Information processing in motor skills.* New York: Holt, Rinehart, and Winston, 1976.

McMahon, T.A., & Greene, P.R. Fast running tracks. *Scientific American,* 1978, *242,* 148-161.

Meade, M. Cybernetics of cybernetics. In H. von Foerster, J.D. White, L.J. Peterson, & J.K. Russell, *Purposive systems: proceedings of the First Annual Symposium of the American Society for Cybernetics.* New York: Spartan Books, 1968.

Miller, G.A. The magical number seven, plus or minus two: some limits on our capacity for processing information. *Psychological Review,* 1956, *63,* 81-97.

Pew, R. Toward a process-oriented theory of human skilled performance. *Journal of Motor Behavior,* 1970, *2,* 8-24.

Rothstein, J.A. Information feedback in coaching of highly skilled athletes. In P. Klavora & J.V. Daniel (Eds.), *Coach, athlete and the sport psychologist.* Toronto: University of Toronto School of Physical and Health Education, 1979.

Sage, G.H. *Introduction to motor behavior: a neuropsychological approach.* Reading, Mass.: Addison-Wesley, 1977.

Schmidt, R.A. Past and future issues in motor programming. *Research Quarterly for Exercise and Sport,* 1980, *51,* 122-140.

Simon, H.A. The information storage system called "human memory." In M.R. Rosenzweig & E.L. Bennett (Eds.), *Neural mechanisms of learning and memory.* Cambridge, Mass.: MIT Press, 1976.

Smith, K.U. Cybernetic foundations of physical behavioral science. *Quest,* 1967, *8,* 26-32.

Stallings, L.M. *Motor skills: development and learning.* Dubuque, Iowa: William C. Brown, 1973.

Stallings, L.M. Application of an information processing model to teaching motor skills. *Motor Skills: Theory Into Practice,* 1976, *1,* 12-22.

Stelmach, G.E. (Ed.). *Motor control: issues and trends,* New York: Academic Press, 1976.

Stelmach, G.E. (Ed.). *Information processing in motor control and learning.* New York: Academic Press, 1978.

Stratton, R.K. Information processing deficits in childrens' motor performance: implications for instruction. *Motor Skills: Theory into Practice,* 1978, *3*(1) 49-55.

Welford, A.T. The measurement of sensory-motor performance: survey and reappraisal of twelve years' progress. *Ergonomics,* 1960, *3*, 189-230.

Welford, A.T. *Fundamentals of skill.* London: Methuen, 1968.

Welford, A.T. *Skilled performance: perceptual and motor skills.* Glenview, Ill.: Scott, Foresman, 1976.

Whiting, H.T.A. *Acquiring ball skill: a psychological interpretation.* Philadelphia: Lea & Febiger, 1970.

Whiting, H.T.A. Theoretical frameworks for an understanding of the acquisition of perceptual-motor skills. *Quest,* 1972, *17*, 24-34.

5 CONCEPTS OF MOTOR CONTROL

In Chapter 3 we studied some of the major neuromuscular reflexes affecting movement, such as head righting and equilibrium, and in Chapter 4 we glanced briefly at the concept of motor control as one component of our information-processing model. Since the question as to how individuals control their movements is at the heart of our concern in teaching motor skills, it seems desirable to delve further into the concept of motor control.

It must be stated at the outset of this discussion that there is not yet sufficient knowledge of neurological functioning to explain motor control or motor learning; as practitioners, we still must base our instructional practice on theories. However, there are a number of theories of motor control with conflicting implications for teaching motor skills. A basic understanding of these theories and their differing implications would appear to be prerequisite to applying them in practice. Not all motor control theories are included here. Only those theories that have had, or are having, the greatest impact on instructional practice in physical education are considered.

In addition, it should be noted that much of movement control occurs automatically through intrinsic properties of the muscles themselves and by way of innate neuromuscular reflexes, such as the equilibrium reflex, some of which were described in Chapter 3. These mechanisms are not dealt with here where our interest is in how individuals learn to control their movements and to perform proficiently. The subtleties of touch and timing in the rendering of a piano concerto or the finesse demonstrated in a balance beam performance can hardly be accounted for by the operation of neuromuscular reflexes.

Let's first take another look at the information-processing model described in Chapter 4 (see Fig. 4-2) and especially at the box labeled motor control. Note that sensory information has been perceived, and an action plan to achieve a particular goal has been decided on. The motor control centers must now organize a set of commands to the muscles so that the movements to achieve the action plan can be carried out.

Notice that this description has involved the use of the following terms: *goal, action plan,* and *motor command.* We need to know what these terms mean before we can profit from a discussion of their possible role in motor control.

Goal, action plan, and motor command

As was emphasized in Chapter 1, authors use terms differently to achieve their purpose, but to avoid misinterpretation, and therefore misapplication, they are obligated to clarify the meaning they attach to the terms. The following definitions are constructed so as to be applicable by the practitioner.

Goal or objective of the skill—The phrase *goal of the skill* is used here interchangeably with the phrase *objective of the skill* to refer to the purpose of an act (e.g., to catch the ball, to stand on one's head, to put the arrow in the gold). The terms do not imply a specific movement, although in the case of some closed skills (standing on one's head), a particular movement may best achieve the objective.

Action plan—*Action plan* is used to refer to the directions given regarding the movement ("swing high," "follow through," "hit hard"). Although we as practitioners often specify a particular action plan for a learner, it should be emphasized that the action plan in operation is the one that different learners give themselves regarding the movement. For example, the practitioner may direct the learner to swing high while the learner is thinking hit hard. The point being made here is that the commands that go to the muscles are ultimately determined by the learner, not the practitioner.

Motor command—For an action plan to be carried out, neural impulses to the muscle (motor command) must be generated and organized so that the plan is carried out effectively (e.g., in a coordinated fashion). The fact is that we do not know how these neural commands are controlled. Basically, there are two theories that are discussed briefly in Chapter 4 and in more detail here: the closed-loop and open-loop concepts of motor control.

Closed- and open-loop concepts

Without doubt, the controversy between the closed- and open-loop theories of motor control has been one of the most heated and extensive battles in the field of motor learning for the past decade and beyond. This has resulted in a split similar to that which occurred between the connectionist and cognitive theories of learning; that is, researchers have been for one and against the other.

This split and bias have spread to practitioners as well, and since the two theories do imply important differences in instructional methods, the result has been to recommend skill practice based on one theory or the other rather than to recommend profiting from the contributions of both. For example, one of the major assumptions that practitioners have operated under over the years has been that the feedback from a movement (e.g., from the sensory organs in muscles, tendons, and joints) is a critical factor in both motor learning and performance. Thus we have encouraged attention to kinesthetic feedback (feel of movement), expecting that this would not only aid learning but also that it would allow the individual to perceive errors during performance and thus be able to make immediate corrections. Such an approach is based on a closed-loop concept of motor control, and, as we shall see, it has both advantages and disadvantages.

Recently, with the reemergence of open-loop theories of motor control, this emphasis on concentrating on the feeling of a movement during performance has been largely disavowed in the professional publications. In some ways this has been fortunate in that the limitations of this method of practice have been highlighted. However, any outright dismissal of the method as inappropriate in all cases would be unfortunate in that it would rob us of a technique that appears to be valuable in certain situations. There is no reason to believe that kinesthetic feedback does not contribute to motor control and learning; the question is how and when. Open-loop theories help us to answer these questions and at the same time offer us new possibilities for instructional practice.

Fig. 5-1 emphasizes that the primary theoretical difference between the closed-loop and open-loop concepts of motor control has to do with the importance assigned to the role of feedback from the movement itself (proprioceptive or kinesthetic feedback).

Thus the closed-loop concept basically assumes that peripheral feedback occurring during the performance of a skill acts as an error detection mechanism leading to error correction. For example, if I feel that I am too tense, I send messages to my muscles to correct the situation. Conversely, in the open-loop concept movement is generally seen as being controlled by centrally stored programs that are run off without recourse to peripheral feedback. For example, a batter anticipating a certain pitch preplans or preselects that action plan (swing) that is deemed appropriate for the anticipated pitch. This action plan is carried out without interference from the feedback from the movement. If the movement is executed properly and the pitch anticipated correctly, the ball is hit. If not, a strike results.

A broad analogy might be the difference between a traffic signal that changes when a car trips a plate set in the road (closed loop) and a fixed traffic signal that changes according to a preset time (open loop). Although it might seem that the

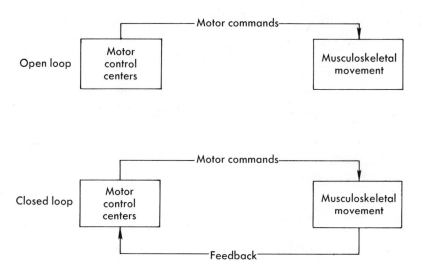

FIG. 5-1. Concepts of motor control: open loop and closed loop.

closed-loop mechanism is better, since it appears to be more flexible or adaptable to certain environmental traffic conditions, under other circumstances it may be more advantageous to have the signal operate under closed-loop control. For example, in very heavy traffic the trip mechanism cannot operate fast enough to be effective, and a traffic jam ensues.

As Schmidt (1980) notes, at their extremes, the closed-loop (peripheralist) and open-loop (centralist) views are absolutely incompatible. As we shall see later, however, they are not as incompatible as their proponents would have us believe. Nevertheless, since practitioners have tended to accept one or the other as a basis for instructional practice, it seems desirable to first look briefly at some of the practical implications of each. This is followed by a modified position to show how the two concepts might be integrated. Finally, some suggestions are made as to when the practitioner might want to use each to enhance learning or performance.

CLOSED-LOOP CONTROL

The closed-loop concept of motor control has traditionally dominated our thinking about motor learning and performance. For example, in target archery, as you draw the bow you may feel tension or trembling in the forearm. Because you have already learned that this forearm tension leads to ineffective shots, you immediately relax the forearm and switch to pulling with the back muscles. Thus the sensory feedback (tension) from the forearm muscles has acted as an error-detecting mechanism.

Note that the error detection depends on your previously having learned (and stored in memory) the proper feeling of the skill. This is the reason so much attention has been devoted in physical education to developing kinesthetic sense, even to the extent that we have had students practice skills with their eyes closed so that they could concentrate on the feeling of the skill.

This leaves us with the question as to how we learn to control movement in the early stages of learning before we have acquired the proper feeling of the movement. Fitts (1951) emphasizes that because the movement errors of beginners are relatively large, the sensory feedback or feel resulting from such movement cannot be error correcting.

Adams (1971, 1976) attempts to solve this problem within a closed-loop concept. He proposes that peripheral feedback from an ongoing movement is compared with a sensory image (perceptual trace) of past movements stored in memory. When there is a mismatch between the two, motor commands are generated to correct the movement.

However, since beginners have relatively poor movement images of a skill, they make use of feedback from other sources (e.g., vision, hearing, and supplementary feedback from the teacher) to help refine the movement. As the movement becomes more refined, the peripheral feedback from performance yields a more accurate image or perceptual trace in memory. Finally, this image or trace is sufficiently accurate to act as a "reference of correctness" for the skill, and the performer no longer needs supplementary information feedback (Adams, 1976).

OPEN-LOOP CONTROL

One of the predominate features of open-loop theories of motor control is the concept of motor programs. If, as recent evidence suggests, peripheral feedback from a movement is not essential in controlling the movement, then the central nervous system itself must be capable of organizing and carrying out an effective movement pattern without reference to the feedback produced by the movement. Thus the concept of motor programs, analogous to computer programs, has been postulated to be the basis for movement control. The individual preplans or preselects an action (stored in memory), which is then run off as planned (e.g., a bunt).

It should be noted that the concept of centrally stored motor programs is an assumption. We do not know whether such programs exist. Even if motor programs do exist, we do not know what characteristics of movement they control (e.g., sequencing, speed, force, or a combination of these). With these restrictions in mind, let's look at two of the open-loop concepts to see their implications for instruction.

Henry and Rogers (1960) postulate a neuromotor memory drum, analogous to an electronic computer in which the sensory-motor coordination pattern of each

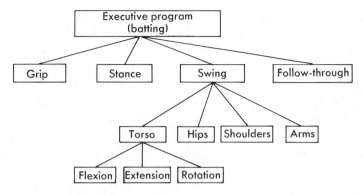

FIG. 5-2. A hierarchical motor program. (See text for further explanation.)

specific movement, whether innate or learned, is stored and the theory is used to support the contention that there can be little if any transfer between skills. Since the beginner has not developed a neuromotor program for a specific movement, the task is "carried out under conscious control in an awkward, step-by-step, poorly coordinated manner" (Henry, 1980, p. 164). Through extensive practice *on that specific movement,* the neuromotor memory drum is programmed (placed in permanent memory store), and thereafter the performer can execute the movement in a coordinated and automatic fashion.

Although it is clear from Henry's (1980) restatement of his theory that a complex motor skill or task may draw on several movement programs stored in memory, the concept of specificity remains. Thus a basketball player should have extensive practice in every shot possible until each shot is learned sufficiently for him to establish the particular motor programs required for each.

A major assumption of most motor program theories is that the motor control mechanisms are hierarchically organized; that is, there is seen to be an executive program with varying numbers of subroutines (e.g., Fitts & Posner, 1967). For example, in Fig. 5-2 such an executive program for batting is diagrammed. Thus batting would call on such subroutines as grip, stance, swing, and follow-through. Each of these in turn would call on a lower level of subroutines. For example, the swing may be seen to involve movement of the torso, hips, shoulders, and arms. Each of these would be seen as calling on other subroutines such as flexion and extension.

Such an arrangement, borrowed from computer technology, supposedly allows the skill to be run off in the proper sequence. However, the implications for learning and transfer should be noted. The executive program could be changed (e.g., to a golf drive) and could draw on some of the same subroutines. If the subroutines have not been learned, then the student would start at the next lower level. Fitts and Posner (1967) suggest that the lower level subroutines are basically learned in childhood. Later skill learning is then seen to be a matter of transferring subroutines to the new skill.

A motor program such as that diagrammed in Fig. 5-2 would seem to support our practice of breaking a skill down into parts (stance, swing, etc.) and our emphasis on teaching the details of movement. In addition, the concept appears to lend support to a movement fundamentals approach to physical education in which the child is taught basic movement patterns such as swinging and jumping. However, when such basic patterns are assumed to transfer automatically to skills requiring swings (golf and baseball) and jumping (rebounding and blocking), there are serious limitations to the concept that studies of skill specificity and transfer have emphasized. In addition, recent speculations (e.g., Kelso & Holt, 1980; Nichols, 1980; Schmidt, 1980) suggest that much of the coordination of muscular activity may be an automatic function of the muscles themselves and that motor programs, if they exist, may be much simpler than has previously been thought.

In any case, it is unlikely that the answer to the riddle of motor programs, when we get it, will look like the program outlined in Fig. 5-2, and practitioners should view with considerable caution applications to motor skill learning and performance based on this particular model. In addition, it should be noted that the concept of hierarchical programs as the controlling units of behavior (including motor control) is not sacred. Simon (1976), for example, speculates that other arrangements, such as production systems, may be more appropriate models for control systems—just a reminder that we're not locked into the concept of hierarchical motor programs.

Integrated concepts

Fortunately, many motor control theorists today (e.g., Evarts, 1979; Schmidt, 1980) agree that the control of movement probably involves both closed-loop (peripheral feedback) and open-loop (preprogramming) mechanisms, each operating under different conditions.

CONTROL OF BALLISTIC MOVEMENTS

There appears to be considerable evidence that very fast movements cannot be changed in a closed-loop fashion, since the movement is over before the feedback from the movement can be processed and a correction generated (Schmidt, 1980). Therefore it is assumed that rapid, ballistic-type movements, such as the downswing in a golf drive or the forward movement in a tennis serve, must be programmed in advance and carried out to their finish without opportunity for feedback correction during the stroke (Poulton, 1980). However, in slower movements there is time for the feedback processes to operate, and movement can then be controlled in a closed-loop fashion.

Presumably, then, in ballistic movements errors can only be corrected after the performance has taken place. This is usually assumed to be on the next trial. However, consider a basketball player making a one-handed shot for a goal. Experienced players often know as soon as the ball has left their hand whether it is going in the basket; that is, they have stored in memory what the wrist and finger movements should feel like. If, after releasing the ball, this feeling is not confirmed, they can follow up their shot for a possible rebound and second try. Thus, even though feedback cannot control a rapid movement (wrist snap), it may still provide information for follow-up action.

INTERMITTENT CONTROL

Another way the open-loop and closed-loop theories have been combined is by assuming that both mechanisms exist in a given motor task, but that they are important at different times in the action (Schmidt, 1980, p. 127). For example, in some tasks, such as moving to a target, the initial portion of the movement may be controlled by a preprogrammed process, while the end of the movement (nearing the target) may be controlled by a feedback process. As Schmidt (1980) notes, there has been some direct as well as indirect evidence showing that individuals tend to make feedback-based corrections in movement as they get closer to their target (p. 127).

In addition, some researchers (e.g., Poulton, 1975) have suggested that intermittent control can occur in continuous tracking movements.

> In these models, a small burst of activity is programmed centrally, the feedback resulting from the behavior is sampled, a decision is made about a correction and then another burst of activity is initiated, and so on (Schmidt, 1980, p. 127).

Poulton (1980) gives the following example of intermittent control in hurdling.

> The athlete touches the ground four times between one hurdle and the next. The first touch is landing after the last hurdle. Between them are two steps in which the athlete has to correct the position whether from being too far in front or behind (p. 358).

Presumably, as skills improve with practice, little or no correction during performance may be needed; prediction and preprogramming take the place of error correction.

Thus there is some evidence that at least two types of skills (discrete movements to a target and continuous tracking movements) may involve the shifting during performance from open-loop to closed-loop control and vice versa.

GOAL-DIRECTED (FLEXIBLE) CONTROL

Let's return for a moment to the analogy of open- and closed-loop control of traffic signals. Recall that in open-loop control the traffic signal may be preset to change on a fixed time basis; conversely, another signal may work in a closed-loop fashion by way of a trip that changes the signal according to traffic conditions. However, in very heavy traffic, the trip may not operate fast enough to be effective, and a traffic jam ensues.

By studying traffic patterns at different times of the day, engineers can anticipate changing needs, design a program to meet these demonstrated needs, and preset the signal accordingly. However, the signal can also be programmed to operate on a preset schedule (open loop) at heavy traffic times and by way of a trip mechanism (closed loop) at other times.

Such an analogy suggests that a major task of the practitioner may be to select the most appropriate method of control for a particular skill or a given task. However, although Schmidt (1980) suggests the possibility that under certain conditions individuals may choose or select the method of control, the notion of individual flexibility in the control of movement has received little research attention. In the absence of such evidence the practitioner is left the task of making some educated guesses.

Selecting the method of control

One of the most exciting speculations about movement behavior is that individuals may accomplish a particular action in a variety of ways. Hellebrandt (1958), for example, suggests that this is the result of a totally integrated neuromuscular endowment; when the neuromuscular components of one pattern become fatigued or disabled, the work load is spread to other motor units.

Schmidt (1980) implies that we may need to extend this concept of redundancy or flexibility in the neuromuscular system to our view of motor control mechanisms. Schmidt notes, "One can see a clear advantage for having a number of substitute mechanisms for accomplishing the same overall task" (p. 124).

If such choices are available, then the practitioner must ask when and under what conditions is feedback (closed loop) or program (open loop) control the more beneficial to performance or learning. Although directing his comments primarily to researchers, Schmidt (1980) suggests that we might look at (1) the attentional demands of the situation, (2) the accuracy requirements of the skill, and (3) the level of learning.

ATTENTIONAL REQUIREMENTS

Recall from the discussion of the limited concentration channel in the previous chapter (see Fig. 4-6) that we can only concentrate on one thing at a time. If, in performing a nonballistic skill, we are going to use concurrent feedback to change our action plan, attention or concentration space is required to initiate the correction (Schmidt, 1980). Thus the attention demand for the correction can be seen to interfere with the individual's overall capacity to attend to other aspects of the skill at the same time. Schmidt (1980) states the problem very well.

> If the demands of the situation are large (e.g., driving in traffic), then it is likely that the individual will abandon the relatively costly feedback-based mode of control in favor of a programmed mode since, once initiated, the program probably requires less attention. Such a shift in mode of control would enable more attention to be devoted to other aspects of the situation (p. 125).

For example, a skier on a crowded hill may find it advantageous to shift attention from feeling the snow and ice (through the skis) to watching the position and path of other skiers. Note, however, that to some extent this is a trade-off, since the skier's capacity to feel an ice patch and make immediate corrective movements is jeopardized. Thus we need to consider the accuracy requirements of a skill as well, and more will be said of this in the following section.

When a skill has few other attentional demands, the individual may choose to perform the skill by way of a feedback process, thus increasing accuracy. It is possible that a number of closed skills, such as individual events in synchronized swimming, fall into this latter category.

ACCURACY REQUIREMENTS

Schmidt (1980) notes that the selection of preprogrammed or feedback control of movement involves a trade-off between attention and accuracy.

> If the accuracy requirements of the response are not critical, or the costs of making an error are not very high, then the individual should be more likely to program responses to save effort. If, on the other hand, the accuracy requirements are critical and the costs of errors are high, then we would expect a shift in the control processes toward those involving feedback control (p. 126).

For example, in skills where the success of a performance is judged on the basis of form (e.g., balance beam), feedback control might be seen to lead to greater accuracy in the movement. However, this is a broad generalization, and evidence is limited.

In other situations we may wish to preprogram a movement and ignore concurrent feedback to achieve a particular goal. Of course, we do this whenever we inhibit neuromuscular reflexes (e.g., head-righting reflex in diving). But consider the downhill skier who can beat a competitor only by saving hundredths of seconds on the run. Rather than taking the run in the usual closed-loop fashion or under intermittent control, the racer goes all out by presetting his muscles. The cost may be high (a fall), but the end result (winning) is deemed worth it.

As Schmidt (1980) notes, there are times when it may be beneficial to apply intermittent control.

> Most of the responses we make (such as walking, throwing, pole-vaulting, etc.) involve more than one limb. It seems clear that we cannot attend to the feedback about the performance of all the limbs separately, and so we relegate much of the control to program processes (in those parts of the movement that have small accuracy requirements), while attending to only those parts of the movement that have critical costs for production of error (p. 126).

Let's return to our skier for an example. Making a turn (especially on top of a mogul) is a critical point, and the feeling is a signal for unweighting the skis. Following the turn, attention can be returned to other aspects of the skill (e.g., visually locating the next mogul).

LEVEL OF LEARNING

Notice that in the preceding discussion we were looking at how the experienced performer might control movement in various skills or situations. The ability to shift from feedback-controlled movement to a preprogrammed action plan assumes that the performer has an adequate program of action available. Obviously, the beginner, lacking the effective action plan produced by practice, cannot make the shift effectively.

The question remains as to how the learner controls movement *in the process of learning*. Schmidt (1980) suggests that at extremely low levels of proficiency there may be no motor program at all (p. 126). We have traditionally assumed that in this case (e.g., the absence of a program) the beginner carries out a new skill under conscious feedback control in, what appears to us, an awkward step-by-step manner. Unfortunately, we have tended to fit our instruction to this view of beginners by using part methods of instruction and by correcting details of their movement.

There are many reasons to question such an approach; some of these were discussed in Chapter 3 on neuromuscular mechanisms, and others are addressed later in this book. The point being made here is that there are alternatives, two of which (schema theory and cognitive organization strategies) are discussed in the remainder of this chapter.

A schema theory of motor learning

Dissatisfied with traditional open-loop and closed-loop theories of motor control, several motor-learning theorists have resurrected the notion of relational schemes or schema to account for motor performance and learning. That is, individuals are seen to store in memory not detailed copies of specific movements but rather ideas of relationships that can be used to produce variable movements.

Pew (1970), for example, notes that no individual performs two tennis drives in exactly the same way, although each may serve the same purpose. Thus what is stored as a result of a well-learned skill is not necessarily a fixed pattern of movement, but a set of relationships for the conduct of the skill. Effective learning is seen to lead to a memory of the skill in which an almost infinite variety of patterns of actions is possible. Which pattern is selected depends on the environmental conditions, as in steering a car or throwing a ball. Pew further suggests that maximal (adaptable) performance requires learning these schema (relationships) as in a problem-solving situation.

One of the schema theories that has had considerable attention recently is that of Schmidt (1975, 1976). Since this particular theory has found its way into school settings, it seems desirable to look at it briefly in terms of its assumptions, implications, and possible contributions and limitations. Readers who desire more theoretical detail would do well to begin with the references listed at the end of this chapter, especially Schmidt (1975, 1976).

ASSUMPTIONS

According to Schmidt (1977), schema theory has the advantage over both closed-loop theories and traditional open-loop theories in that, among other things, it can account for our ability to produce variations of movements (as in a tennis drive) to meet the particular environmental or game conditions. The movement is carried out by a program, but, in contrast to the other theories, this program is viewed as a generalized one.

> For example, any time I want to hurl something overhead, a dart, baseball, javelin, whatever, I use the same general program and in some way I modify it to meet the demands of the particular implement with which I am operating. . . . The program is the same, but I can ask the program to run slightly differently because of the particular situation I have before me (Schmidt, 1975, p. 3).

Schmidt (1977) likens such a program to a phonograph record. Although the motor program is seen to specify the sequence, force, and timing of muscle action, it could be run off rapidly or slowly, while maintaining its temporal patterning, much as a phonograph record can be run off at different speeds. Moreover, force of contraction could be varied just as we vary the volume at which a record is played.

Schmidt's schema theory proposes that every time a movement is performed, the individual stores the following four things in memory:

1. The initial conditions (the state of the muscles and the environmental conditions prior to movement)
2. The response specifications (the motor program, including its force, speed, and spatial characteristics)
3. The sensory consequences (the sensory feedback from the movement)

4. The response outcome (the success of the response in relation to the outcome intended)

Over the course of variable practice in the skill, the individual abstracts relationships (or schema) between these sources of information. Ultimately, although the specifics of the movement may be forgotten, the individual retains the general rule. The movement or a variation of it can be recalled based on a best guess estimate of what is appropriate in a particular circumstance. This best guess is based on the schema in memory between past movement specifications and outcomes.

Kerr (1978) gives an example of the operation of a schema for an overhand throw. There is a relationship between a particular distance to be thrown and the required muscular force, arm speed, and angle of release to reach the goal. As the learner continues to practice under variable conditions (e.g., at different distances), the distance to force-speed abstraction is strengthened until, as a result, the outfielder can throw accurately to second base from any position on the field.

IMPLICATIONS

There are several implications of this theory for instructional practice. It should be noted, however, that research evidence is inconclusive at this point, and the implications should be viewed as hypotheses to be tested.

Role of errors in learning—As Schmidt (1977) notes, with many learning theories, errors are regarded as evil. In schema theory, however, an error is just another movement that, like all movements, has the capacity to strengthen the schema. If the outfielder makes an unsuccessful throw to second base, for example, the error will be recognized (based on the schema in memory between past outcomes and past sensory consequences), the schema will be updated, and different responses will be produced on the next performance.

Role of feedback in learning—Schema theory is essentially an open-loop theory with strong emphasis on motor programming rather than on a closed-loop feedback control of movement. Schmidt (1977) views learning as "the generation of bigger and better motor programs that carry out movement without the need for feedback modification during movement" (p. 40). However, it is essential that the individual have information about movement outcome, as Schmidt (1977) notes, either from direct visual or kinesthetic confirmation (e.g., landing on one's back in a dive) or from supplementary KR or KP. This feedback is not used to control the movement in progress, but to strengthen the schema in memory for use in the next performance.

Role of variability in practice—One of the major predictions of Schmidt's schema theory of motor learning is that by increasing the variability of practice on a skill, we may increase the ability to perform similar skills. For example, Kerr and Booth (1977) found that children who practiced tossing an object to a target at both short and long distances were then better able to toss accurately to an intermediate target. Kerr (1978) suggests that perhaps we should have pitchers practice throwing wide to the left and right of the plate or have divers deliberately practice entering the water too long or too short. However, the schema theory implies that we might vary other aspects of performance as well, such as the weight of objects thrown and the speed of a movement.

Role of schema theory in movement education—Schmidt (1977) suggests that the schema concept has special significance for the structuring of movement education programs. However, he cautions that more research is needed and suggests that movement educators can help by doing some field testing. Specifically, he suggests that these practitioners consider working with the hypothesized components of motor programs, that is, vary a movement by changing its speed, force, or spatial characteristics. For example, have children slow down a particular movement pattern while holding its spatial dimensions and force characteristics constant. Then vary the force dimensions (e.g., change the weight thrown) while maintaining spatial dimensions and speed. In addition, by throwing an object overarm, sidearm, and so on, you could vary the spatial characteristics of a movement.

LIMITATIONS

Certainly, Schmidt's schema theory has exciting implications, particularly in its potential for giving some counterbalance to the extreme specificity theories now in vogue. However, Schmidt (1977) himself rightly cautions that there is some risk in applying the theory to practice. This is not to say that it should not be applied, but that, as with any theory, we need to be aware of the possible limitations, some of which are discussed here.

Specificity of skills—The concept of specificity of skills is emphasized throughout the remainder of this book. Suffice it to note here that research has convincingly demonstrated that our ability to perform one skill well does not predict the proficiency with which we will be able to perform another, even similar, skill. As Schmidt (1977) notes, the schema theory runs somewhat counter to this concept.

> One major difficulty seen in attempting to use these principles in movement education settings is that teachers will think that the motor programs subserve a far wider range of movements than might actually be the case. . . . This is important because if the schema for a given program is to be strengthened by such activity, we must be careful to choose movements that are governed by the same program. . . . We must consider the fact that movements that look very similar do not correlate very well, and they do not show much transfer, leading to the possibility that they are governed by different motor programs (p. 46).

The specificity-generality controversy is far from being satisfactorily resolved, and until such time as the limits of generality are more clearly established, continued experimentation with schema theories should be welcomed. Indeed, by considering the positive findings on transfer in children (e.g., Carson & Wiegand, 1979) that were sparked by the schema theories, you might speculate that the specificity of transfer of skills has a developmental dimension that needs to be accorded greater attention in our research.

Developmental aspects of memory schemes—Although some positive support for the schema theory has been forthcoming with children (primarily in terms of the efficacy of variable practice), results with adults have been less successful. Although several hypotheses have been advanced for this age difference (e.g., Moxley, 1979), it is possible that adults have already established a different and conflicting memory scheme for a particular task. Recall from our discussion of memory in the previous chapter (see Fig. 4-8) that memory appears to be flexible in terms of the forms in which it stores information. If this is true, then it is possible that individuals are capable of classifying information in a variety of ways (Simon, 1976). Certainly, observation of learners suggests that much of their efforts go into devising some kind of relational schemes. However, at this point there is little evidence to suggest that we all develop the same schemes. This is not to say that a particular scheme, such as that suggested by Schmidt, might not be more useful than others, only that the particular scheme adopted may be a function of the individual's experience.

Content of motor programs—The fact remains that we do not yet know what particular characteristics of movement might be controlled by motor programs. Schmidt (1977) suggests that they may specify the speed, force, and spatial patterning of a movement. More recently, however, there has been some evidence to suggest that motor programs may be more simple than previously conceived and that certain characteristics of movement may be functions of the muscles themselves (e.g., Kelso & Holt, 1980; Nichols, 1980; Schmidt, 1980). However, this lack of knowledge regarding the content of motor programs does not nullify a schema concept. The notion of helping children develop effective relational concepts for the learning and conduct of motor skills is one that should remain a primary consideration of the practitioner.

Perceptual motor organization and preselection

Recently, there has been some concern expressed over what would appear to be disproportionate attention to the motor processes in our so-called sports research publications (e.g., Salmela, 1979). It may be that we are becoming as obsessed with the motoric end as information-processing theorists have traditionally been with the input end. As Salmela (1980) notes, a great deal of motor skill learning and performance results from perceptual and cognitive processes.

One of the exciting recent developments may help bridge this gap. Diewart and Stelmach (1978) term this *perceptual-motor organization* (p. 251), that is, the perceptual or cognitive strategies by which individuals enhance their performance and learning.

Unfortunately, current research is developing its own jargon for these strategies, such as labeling or naming, depth of processing, coding, feedforward, and cueing. However, the results are starting to come in, and while there are apparently developmental differences (e.g., Thomas, 1980), evidence suggests that when individuals take an active part in organizing information (perceptually and cognitively as well as physically), this seems to enhance both performance and learning.

Although it is difficult to derive practical implications at this point, the concept has exciting potential. Consider the following conclusions from recent research cited by Diewart and Stelmach (1978).

1. Almost without exception, active movement is reproduced better than passive movement.
2. A movement whose relationship to another movement is known (e.g., longer, shorter) is reproduced better than when the relationship is not known.
3. Verbal labels or knowledge of movement relationships given to individuals result in improved performance (p. 252).
4. In addition, Kelso (1977a) has shown that preselected movements are retained more accurately than movements defined by the researcher.

With the possible exception of Kelso's (1977b) article dealing with the application of his preselection concept to anticipatory-timing skills and Thomas's (1980) article on developmental differences, little of this research has drawn direct implications for the practitioner. I hope that this gap will soon be bridged. As Diewart and Stelmach (1978) note,

> While findings are much too preliminary to begin theorizing about the mechanisms involved, they do stress the importance of cognitive activity in motor behavior and open the door for new and different types of experimenters. As theories and models of motor learning, specifically of perceptual-motor organization, are established, this knowledge should have direct application to the teaching and rehabilitation of motor skills (p. 263).

Sample thought sheet

1. Give an example of a motor skill that might best be executed under
   a. Closed-loop control
   b. Open-loop control
   c. Intermittent control
2. Describe a situation in which you have had to make a trade-off between the attentional and accuracy demands of a skill to achieve a goal.
3. a. Give an example of when attention to kinesthetic feedback might interfere with the performance of a skill (be specific with regard to the skill).
   b. Give an example of how kinesthetic feedback can be useful in performing a motor skill.
4. Describe how you might vary practice to generalize (form a schema for) a basic skill.

References

Adams, J.A. A closed-loop theory of motor learning. *Journal of Motor Behavior*, 1971, 3, 111-151.

Adams, J.A. Issues for a closed-loop theory of motor learning. In G.E. Stelmach (Ed.), *Motor control: issues and trends*. New York: Academic Press, 1976.

Carson, L.M., & Wiegand, R.L. Motor schema formation and retention in young children. *Journal of Motor Behavior*, 1979, 11, 247-252.

Diewart, G.L., & Stelmach, G.E. Perceptual organization in motor learning. In G.E. Stelmach (Ed.), *Information processing in motor control and learning*. New York: Academic Press, 1978.

Evarts, E.V. Brain mechanisms of movement. *Scientific American*, 1979, 241(3), 164-179.

Fitts, P.M. Engineering psychology and equipment design. In S.S. Stevens (Ed.), *Handbook of experimental psychology*. New York: Wiley, 1951.

Fitts, P.M., & Posner, J.I. *Human performance*. Monterey, Calif.: Brooks/Cole, 1967.

Hellebrandt, F.A. The physiology of motor learning. *Cerebral Palsy Review*, 1958, 28, 76-84.

Henry, F.M. Use of simple reaction time in motor programming studies: a reply to Klapp. *Journal of Motor Behavior*, 1980, 12, 163-168.

Henry, F.M., & Rogers, D.E. Increased response latency for complicated movements and a "memory drum" theory of neuromotor reaction. *Research Quarterly*, 1960, 31, 448-458.

Kelso, J.A.S. Planning and efferent components in the coding of movement. *Journal of Motor Behavior*, 1977a, 9, 33-47.

Kelso, J.A.S. Motor control mechanisms in timing behavior. In R.E. Stadulis (Ed.), *Research and practice in physical education: selected papers from the 1976 Research Symposium of the AAHPER National Convention*. Champaign, Ill.: Human Kinetics, 1977b.

Kelso, J.A.S., & Holt, K.G. Evidence for a mass-spring model of human neuromuscular control. In C.H. Nadeau, W.R. Halliwell, K.M. Newell, & G.C. Roberts (Eds.), *Psychology of motor behavior and sport—1979*. Champaign, Ill.: Human Kinetics, 1980.

Kerr, R. Schema theory applied to skill acquisition. *Motor Skills: Theory into Practice*, 1978, 3(1), 15-20.

Kerr, R., & Booth, B. Skill acquisition in elementary school children and schema theory. In D.M. Landers & R.W. Christina (Eds.), *Psychology of motor behavior and sport*, (Vol. 2). Champaign, Ill.: Human Kinetics, 1977.

Moxley, S.E. Schema: the variability hypothesis. *Journal of Motor Behavior*, 1979, 11, 65-70.

Nichols, T.R. What do spinal reflexes regulate and why? Paper presented at 27th Annual Meeting of American College of Sports Medicine, Las Vegas, Nevada, May 1980.

Pew, R. Toward a process-oriented theory of human skilled performance. *Journal of Motor Behavior*, 1970, 2, 8-24.

Poulton, E.C. *Tracking skill and manual control*. New York: Academic Press, 1975.

Poulton, E.C. Range effects and asymmetric transfer in studies of motor learning. In C.H. Nadeau, W.R. Halliwell, K.M. Newell, & G.C. Roberts (Eds.), *Psychology of motor behavior and sport—1979*. Champaign, Ill.: Human Kinetics, 1980.

Salmela, J.H. Psychology and sport: fear of applying. In P. Klavora & J.V. Daniel (Eds.), *Coach, athlete and the sport psychologist*. Toronto: University of Toronto School of Physical and Health Education, 1979.

Schmidt, R. The schema basis of motor control. In W.W. Spirduso & J.D. King (Eds.), *Proceedings of the motor control symposium*. Austin, Texas: University of Texas Printing Division, 1975.

Schmidt, R.A. A schema theory as a solution to some persistent problems in motor learning theory. In G.E. Stelmach (Ed.), *Motor control: issues and trends*. New York: Academic Press, 1976.

Schmidt, R.A. Schema theory: implications for movement education. *Motor Skills: Theory into Practice*, 1977, 2(1), 36-38.

Schmidt, R.A. Past and future issues in motor programming. *Research Quarterly for Exercise and Sport*, 1980, 51, 122-140.

Simon, H.A. The information storage system called "human memory." In M.R. Rosenzweig & E.L. Bennett (Eds.), *Neural mechanisms of learning and memory*. Cambridge, Mass.: MIT Press, 1976.

Thomas, J.R. Acquisition of motor skills: information-processing differences between children and adults. *Research Quarterly for Exercise and Sport*, 1980, 51, 158-170.

PART TWO

Factors influencing motor learning

6 AROUSAL LEVEL AND MOTIVATION

One of the most obvious conclusions to be derived from a study of behavior and learning theories is that motivation is seen to be of critical importance to both performance and learning; in reference to motor performance, one of the most frequently used motivational constructs is arousal. While the pervasiveness of this concept in the sports literature can be traced to problems of competitive anxiety, arousal should be seen as influencing all behavior: in children and adults, in the athletic and the nonathletic, in the classroom, and in the gymnasium.

As a number of sports psychologists have emphasized, we have too often assumed that the higher the level of arousal of individuals, the better their performance.

> The idea is, in other words, the more the players are "psyched up" or "high," the better will be the expected performance. This belief is the very reason why coaches consider their pre-game or mid-game motivational talks, also known as pep-talks, as the ultimate extension of their coaching ability (Klavora, 1979, p. 156).

Fisher and Motta (1977) state the problem very well: "Is this arousal necessary? If so, is high activation necessary for all team members irrespective of position? Are high levels of arousal equally effective for all sports?" (p. 98). To these questions might be added: How do I determine the best arousal level? How do I know what the arousal level of an individual is? What techniques can I use to control the level of arousal?

Since many of the traditional learning theories are implicitly, if not explicitly, theories of motivation, it might be assumed that the answers could be found in them. This is only partly true. You need only to consider the different concepts of motivation presented in these theories (Thorndike's Law of Effect, Hull's drive theory, Skinner's contingent reinforcement, and Lewins's concept of motivational learning as a change in needs and values) to realize the differing implications.

However, it is important to note that these motivational concepts have a common thread, namely, that motivation involves an emotional component whether this be called satisfaction, need, drive, or reward. While the incentive value of physiological or psychological needs and the efficacy of satisfaction and reward as motivational tools cannot and should not be denied, the fact remains that an understanding of the relationships (to the extent that we know them) between emotion, motivation, and physical performance may be seen as prerequisite to the design of specific motivational techniques to enhance motor performance and learning.

Intensity and direction of motivation

As Martens (1974, p. 156) notes, when so many different theories have used the concepts of arousal and motivation as explanatory concepts, the terms acquire a diversity of meanings. For the purposes of this book, the term *arousal* is used to refer to *the intensity of physiological excitation*. This may be viewed along a continuum extending from deep sleep at one end to high excitation at the other end.

However, performance motivation depends not only on arousal but also on the direction of that arousal toward the achievement of some goal. Unfortunately, the terms *motivation* and *arousal* are often used synonymously. Oxendine (1968, p. 195), for example, uses the term *demotivation* to refer to the process of decreasing arousal level. For the purposes of this book, however, it seems important to retain the traditional concept of motivation as being goal directed while at the same time emphasizing the influence of intensity of excitation (arousal) on goal achievement. Therefore *motivation* is defined here as *an internal factor that arouses and directs a person's behavior*. Martens (1974) distinguishes between the intensity and direction of behavior by drawing an analogy between human behavior and the behavior of an automobile.

> One dimension of an automobile's behavior is the speed with which the engine runs—it may idle very slowly or run very fast. The intensity of the engine's activity is described in terms of revolutions per minute; the intensity of the human engine is described in terms of a person's arousal level. . . . Not until it is known whether or not the car is in gear, and whether it is in forward or reverse gear can an automobile's behavior be adequately described (p. 157).

That the intensity (arousal) dimension of motivation is critical to motor performance appears evident from the research (Landers, 1980; Martens, 1971, 1974; Straub, 1975). The evidence for the effects of arousal on learning is less compelling if only because fewer studies have been conducted. However, when you consider that the effects of arousal have variously been attributed to interference with attentional and cognitive processes (Gerard, 1960; Landers, 1980), with neuromuscular patterning (Weinberg, 1978), and with cue utilization

(Easterbrook, 1959) or signal detection (Welford, 1976), then the difficulties that practitioners encounter when trying to teach or coach the overly aroused individual appear to be more than experiential phenomena.

It should be noted that research studies dealing with the performance-arousal relationship have used terms as varied as *drive, need, anxiety, stress, tension, level of aspiration, activation,* and *arousal.* This is not to imply that these terms are synonymous; rather, it suggests that these states have a factor in common, namely, the intensity dimension of behavior.

Unifying concepts of arousal

Despite the fact that arousal theories remain assumptive, the importance of arousal to performance and learning requires that some selection be made. The concepts presented here appear to be those most useful to the practitioner concerned with the effect of arousal on *motor* performance and learning. Those who desire a more comprehensive discussion of arousal theories in sport should refer to the references listed at the end of this chapter, especially Cofer (1976), Landers (1980), Martens (1971, 1974), Straub (1975), and Ulrich (1960).

It should be emphasized that any attempt to unify concepts of arousal runs the risk of oversimplifying what appears to be a very complex phenomenon with many variables. Therefore, while the focus of this chapter is on the implications of the concepts for instructional practice, an attempt is made to point out their limitations as well.

PHYSIOLOGICAL ADAPTATION

Historically, the efforts of physiologists to clarify the relationship between emotions and behavior relied on the concepts of homeostasis and adaptation. In its physiological sense, the term *homeostasis* should be familiar to you; it refers to the tendency of the body to maintain its internal environment within relatively constant, safe limits. *Adaptation,* physiologically, refers to the fact that the body attempts to adjust to any stimulus or situation that upsets this homeostatic balance.

One of the earliest theories of physiological adaptation to emotional stimulation was that proposed by Walter Cannon (1932). Although Cannon was concerned with specific sensations of emotion (hunger, pain, fear), he made a major contribution with his emergency theory. Briefly, Cannon's flight or fight theory speculated that intense emotional stimulation affects the visceral nervous system in such a way as to result in increased respiration; a shift in blood distribution from the viscera to the heart, brain, and skeletal muscles; and an increase in the secretion of epinephrine, which, among other things, mobilizes blood sugar, thereby providing the energy required to meet the emergency situation.

This emphasis on the peripheral physiological aspects of arousal would appear to be extremely useful when you consider the effect of arousal on physical performance. However, the fact remains that, in comparison with other animals, a human's behavior is seldom as simple as flight or fight. Primary survival needs have been supplanted to a large extent by so-called secondary needs or goals, and it is to the achievement of these goals that we direct our energies. It remains, therefore, for present-day investigators to explore the range of consequences of physiological adaptation in humans.

Hans Selye's concept of an adaptation syndrome emphasizes that the reactions of the body that occur as a result of its efforts to maintain homeostatic balance may be general as well as specific and, furthermore, that they may be detrimental as well as beneficial. When arousal is sufficiently intense to lead to general homeostatic upset (stress), the body mobilizes a system of defensive reactions involving the pituitary-adrenal hormones. Within limits, this defensive reaction resolves the stress. However, continued stress or intermittent periods of extreme stress gradually deplete this pool of adaptation energy, resulting in a breakdown of functioning (Selye, 1975).

In addition, Selye's concept emphasizes that the stress reaction can be elicited through different pathways. The physiological changes that characterize the general stress syndrome do not appear to differentiate between physical stressors (disease, temperature extremes, and heavy exercise) and psychological stressors (fear, anger, and the so-called social stressors such as noise and overcrowding). In addition, it appears that psychological stressors may more often be the eliciting agent for the stress reaction than are physical stressors (Levin, 1971; Ulrich, 1960). While the mechanisms by which the pituitary-adrenal hormones act to influence performance have yet to be fully explored, it seems certain that they affect not only muscular and visceral activity but also brain functioning (Landers, 1980; Levin, 1971; Martens, 1974).

Thus the concept of physiological adaptation emphasizes that while a certain intensity of arousal is beneficial, too much may be detrimental, and that this intensity may be brought about by psychological as well as physical stimuli. Since one of our traditional methods of motivation has been to increase arousal (in the form of competition, withholding approval, raising standards, or just admonitions to try harder), it would seem desirable to determine the extent to which techniques involving increased pressure may be beneficial or detrimental to the performance and learning of motor skills.

AROUSAL CONTINUUM

A continuum of emotional arousal has been proposed (Duffy, 1957; Hebb, 1955; Malmo, 1957) that helps break down the distinction between concepts

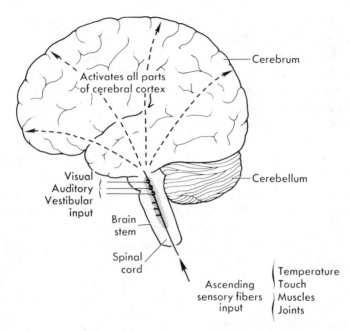

FIG. 6-1. Reticular-activating system (RAS). Shaded area indicates approximate location in the brain stem. Pathways *to* the RAS are depicted by solid lines; pathways *from* the RAS to the cerebral cortex are depicted by dotted lines.

previously considered separately (drive, tension, activation, stress, anxiety) and provides the practitioner a means of considering these states within a unitary framework.

Although the concept of physiological adaptation focused, for the most part, on the visceral effects of arousal (increased heart rate and blood pressure and various biochemical changes), arousal theorists generally emphasize the role of the brain stem reticular system, especially that part known as the reticular-activating system (RAS). As described by Martens (1974, p. 159), activity in the muscles and viscera of the body stimulates the RAS (Fig. 6-1), as does activity in the visual, auditory, and other sensory systems. Thus virtually any stimulation, internal or external, is manifested in a general activation of the RAS, which in turn has a generalized arousing effect on the cerebral cortex. In addition, the cortex itself has pathways to the RAS, and thus, as Hebb (1958, p. 170) emphasizes, the arousal system can be activated not only by sensory stimulation from peripheral sources (internal and external environment) but also by cortical activity itself. This might explain why in the initial stages of learning, when cortical activity may be high, further arousal may be detrimental to performance.

Martens (1974, p. 159) points out another important fact about the RAS; not only does it have diffuse pathways to the cerebral cortex but also pathways back to the muscular system itself. Some of the effects of arousal on the muscular and movement components of motor skills will be noted later.

The concept of an arousal continuum is based on the observation that the intensity of a response can vary independently from the direction (effectiveness) of the response, and for the practitioner this is one of the most important aspects of the concept. It emphasizes the fact that increase in arousal does not necessarily and inevitably lead to improvement in performance. Two basic theories based on the concept of an arousal continuum have been advanced to depict the relationships between arousal level and performance: the Hull-Spence drive theory and the inverted U hypothesis. The inverted U hypothesis has been selected here because it appears to be more widely applicable to the practitioner. Readers desiring more information on the differences between the two should refer to the references listed at the end of this chapter, especially Landers (1980) and Martens (1974).

Performance-arousal curves

The relationship between performance and arousal has been described as taking the form of an inverted U; that is, the level of performance increases with increase in arousal up to a certain optimal point (X in Fig. 6-2) beyond which further increases in arousal result in performance decrements. The important implication for the practitioner is that arousal is necessary for effective functioning and that there is an optimal (best) level essential for maximal performance. However, beyond this point, further arousal will be detrimental to performance.

For example, Klavora (1979), one of the few individuals to attempt to field-test the inverted U concept of arousal, presents data on the performance of high school basketball players at different arousal levels. The curve for one of these players is shown in Fig. 6-3 and, except for individual difference variations, is deemed by Klavora to be typical. Pregame arousal level as measured by the Spielberger State-Trait Anxiety Inventory (STAI scale) is shown on one coordinate, and level of performance (coaches' evaluation) is shown on the other. The dots represent performance level in each of 14 games. Klavora concludes the following:

> Various clusters of pregame arousal scores at both poor and average levels of performance indicate that indeed a basketball player may be performing poorly (or only at an average level) because of two quite different reasons: either he is psychologically not ready for the upcoming competition, or he is too excited about it (p. 160).

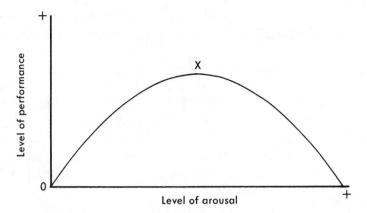

FIG. 6-2. Performance-arousal curve. Maximal performance is at point X, which in this case occurs at a moderate level of arousal.

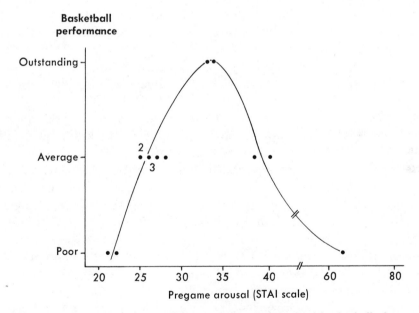

FIG. 6-3. Raw score profile (STAI scale) for a high school basketball player. Dots indicate pregame performance-arousal relationships in a 14-game season. (From Klavora, P. Customary arousal for peak athletic performances. In P. Klavora, & J.V. Daniel [Eds.], *Coach, athlete and the sport psychologist*. Toronto: University of Toronto School of Physical and Health Education, 1979.)

As Klavora notes, this player's arousal level has to climb about 12 points from a low level of approximately 20 on the STAI scale to reach the level that is conducive to outstanding performance.

The performance-arousal curves diagrammed in Figs. 6-2 and 6-3 appear to suggest that the best or optimal level of arousal is a moderate one. However, this is not necessarily the case. As Martens (1971) points out, "The nature of the task, the stage of practice, the inhibitory ability of the individual, and certain personality variables may separately or in combination alter the shape of the inverted-U" (p. 169). A consideration of these influences would seem prerequisite to the application of the inverted U concept to instructional and motivational techniques.

NATURE OF THE SKILL

Traditionally, studies relating performance to arousal level have been limited to the simple-to-complex dimension of tasks; that is, while the performance of simple skills might be expected to benefit from a high level of arousal, complex skills would be seen to require a low level. However, this approach appears to have limited applicability. For example, what constitutes a simple or a complex skill would appear to depend more on the individual's interpretation of the task than on the practitioner's. Thus it would seem desirable to suggest alternative approaches.

The approach that would appear to have the greatest applicability would be to examine the effects of arousal on each of the information-handling processes described in Chapter 4; we might then estimate the performance effects of different levels of arousal in accord with the information-processing demands of a particular skill. Unfortunately, although this approach is beginning to appear (e.g., Landers, 1980; Marteniuk, 1976; Welford, 1976), these explanations for the effects of arousal on performance are still limited primarily to a consideration of the perceptual demands of motor skills (signal detection, cue utilization, and attention). However, it is possible to approach the problem by examining the possible effects of arousal on the composite abilities required by a skill: motor, perceptual, and cognitive.

Motor abilities—Deese (1962) suggests that one of the most useful approaches to predicting the effect of discomfort arousal (stress) on physical performance is in terms of the motor requirements of the skill. Since the general physiological effects of stress include increased muscular tension and tremor, the effect of arousal on the performance of motor skills may be seen to depend on the movement requirements of the skill. For example, a motor skill that involves fast, ballistic movement should be facilitated by a high level of arousal, since increased muscular tension reduces the response latency of the movement, resulting in greater speed. Conversely, since a high level of arousal also results in increased muscular tremor and variability in corrective movement, motor skills involving tracking or aiming might be expected to show deterioration under stress. In addition, the quality (neuromuscular patterning) of movement appears to be adversely affected by high levels of arousal. For example, Weinberg and his colleagues (Weinberg, 1978; Weinberg & Hunt, 1976), using electromyography to measure neuromuscular patterning during a throwing skill, demonstrated that high-arousal subjects exhibited cocontraction of opposing muscles, resulting in inhibition of effective motion. Conversely, low-arousal subjects exhibited the sequential action of these muscles required for freedom of movement.

Perceptual abilities—A number of investigators have suggested that one of the primary effects of arousal on the performance of motor skills is on the perceptual abilities required by the skill. Easterbrook's (1959) cue utilization theory is an example.

> This model postulates that under low arousal an individual will have an overly broad perceptual range (so that) he/she accepts irrelevant and relevant task cues which affect performance. When arousal reaches an optimal level, only relevant task cues are attended to and perceptual selectivity increases. With further increases in arousal, it is argued that certain task relevant cues are eliminated as further perceptual narrowing occurs thus leading to performance deterioration (Hale, 1978, p. 51).

Hale (1978) cites the example of a guard in basketball who experiences difficulties in identifying teammates open for passes if too many or too few cues are attended to. Hale also refers to Nideffer's (1976) practical but untested suggestions for the teacher or coach. Since a broad focus (peripheral vision) is necessary in field hockey, fast-break basketball, and a double play in softball, a relatively low level of arousal could be seen as being beneficial to the performance of these skills. Skills requiring a narrow focus, such as hitting in softball, might be expected to improve with a higher level of arousal. However, inclusion of bowling, golf, and riflery as narrow-focus activities that might profit from high arousal is difficult to accept, since these activities would also subject the body to the muscular tremor effects of high arousal, thereby decreasing accuracy. It is important to note that perceptual narrowing is not limited to vision; presumably it occurs in auditory and other sensory modalities as well.

Cognitive abilities—One of the most obvious effects of high arousal is a decrease in the individual's ability to handle strategy problems. The pervasive general influence of the RAS (Fig. 6-1) throughout the cerebral cortex has been vividly demonstrated in the cerebral blood flow studies of Lassen, Ingvar, and Shinhoj (1978). Since level of blood flow to the cortex can be assumed to be indicative of the level of neuronal activity there, high arousal may be seen to engage these neurons to such an extent that they are unable to provide the cognitive integration necessary for high-level judgments and precisely graded

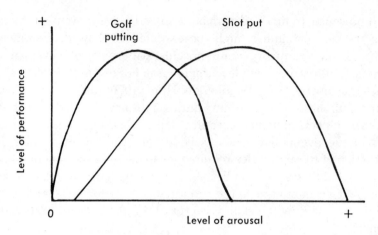

FIG. 6-4. Hypothesized performance-arousal curves for two motor skills.

responses. Conversely, moderate levels of arousal appear necessary, presumably to prime (sensitize) the cortical neurons so that they respond more readily. If this is true, then we need to determine the extent to which (and when) performance (or learning) of a skill requires a high level of cognitive activity (e.g., planning and analysis). Presumably, in these cases a relatively low level of arousal would be desirable.

Since the physiological effects of arousal influence perceptual and cognitive functioning as well as motor functioning, estimating the amount of arousal that will be beneficial to performance demands consideration of the extent to which a specific skill requires each of these components. Oxendine (1970) makes a noteworthy attempt to do just that. He suggests that a high level of arousal facilitates performance of skills that require strength and speed, but it interferes with the performance of skills requiring fine muscle coordination, steadiness, and high concentration or judgment. His table of suggestions for optimal arousal for various sports activities (Table 1), while admittedly speculative, serves to emphasize that the best arousal level for different skills may depend on the composite requirements of the activity.

As Oxendine points out, the job of determining optimal arousal level is not an easy one, because most activities require a combination of abilities. He gives the example of boxing in which the individual needs not only the strength and speed afforded by a high level of arousal but also the ability to analyze the moves of the opponent and make strategy judgments. Taking two of the skills listed in Table 1, a shot put and golf putting, and superimposing the estimated performance-arousal curves for each, we would come up with something similar to Fig. 6-4. Drawing

Table 1 □ *Optimal arousal level for some typical sports skills*

No. 1 Slight arousal	No. 2	No. 3	No. 4	No. 5 High excitement
Golf putting	Baseball pitching	Boxing	Running long jump	Football blocking and tackling
Field goal kicking	Batting	High jumping	Shot put	Sit-up, push-up
Basketball free throw	Diving	Most gymnastics skills	Swimming sprints	Weightlifting
Archery	Fencing	Soccer skills	Wrestling	
Bowling	Football quarterback	Basketball skills	Judo	
	Tennis			

Modified from Oxendine, J.B. Emotional arousal and motor performance. *Quest*, 1970, *13*, 23-32.

on your knowledge of these skills, can you give the rationale for the difference between the two curves, considering the motor, perceptual, and cognitive requirements of each? Two principles should emerge as you attempt this: (1) we must *know* a skill to estimate the best performance-arousal curve (and in fact you may want to modify these curves based on your expertise) and (2) such curves are still *estimates* or generalizations. For example, what is high-arousal? Low arousal? These are relative terms at best.

It should be noted that Oxendine's use of the term *skill* in Table 1 differs from the use of the term in this book. For example, the *activity* of tennis can be seen to consist of a number of *skills* (serve, lob, smash, dropshot), which because of their differing motor and perceptual requirements could be expected to be affected differentially by arousal level. The tennis teacher evidences knowledge of this fact by coaching a player to ease up on his lobs. It is possible, as we shall see later, to teach an individual to recognize the symptoms of arousal (particularly muscular tension) and to adjust this level quickly in terms of the demands of an activity at any given moment.

The desirability of analyzing the motor, perceptual, and cognitive requirements of a skill should be obvious. However, in determining the optimal arousal level, you must take into consideration not only the best arousal level for maximal performance on a well-learned skill, but also the best arousal level for maximal performance at earlier stages of learning the skill.

STAGES OF LEARNING

One of the basic assumptions of this book is that maximal performance at each stage of learning increases the likelihood of attaining higher levels of final proficiency within a given period of time. If this is true, then the practitioner needs to consider the variable effects that arousal level may have at different stages during the learning period.

Unfortunately, very little research is available, and, of those studies that have been done, most have been designed to test the Hull-Spence drive theory with conflicting results (Martens, 1971, 1974). Briefly, the Hull-Spence drive theory assumes that during the early stages of learning, incorrect responses are dominant; as learning proceeds, the habit strength of the correct response increases to the point that it equals and then exceeds that of the incorrect response. Since drive theory predicts that performance is a multiplicative function of drive and habit strength ($P = D \times H$), increases in arousal would be seen as impairing performance during early learning but facilitating it as the skill became well learned.

However, it is difficult to accept the drive theory as an explanation of performance during learning, predicting as it does that high arousal in the late stages of

Table 2 □ *Changes in motor and nonmotor ability requirements from
initial to final stages of learning*

	Initial stages	Final stages
Motor abilities	29.5%	74.5%
Nonmotor abilities	41.6%	10.5%

Based on data from Fleishman, E.A., & Hempel, W.E., Jr. Changes in factor structure of a complex
psychomotor task as a function of practice. *Psychometriks*, 1954, *19*, 239-252.

learning would necessarily facilitate performance. As Martens (1971, 1974)
notes, no consistent differences for either early or late stages of practice have
been found. It appears that Deese's (1962) conclusion is as true today as at the
time he wrote it: "No simple idea about the effect of stress (discomfort arousal)
during training is adequate" (p. 216). The fact remains that the practitioner, in
the absence of facts, must make some educated guesses. The following discussion assumes that the best arousal level at different stages of learning will depend, to some extent at least, on changes in the ability requirements of a skill
during learning, on the nature of the learning process itself, and on the instructional methods being used.

Changes in ability requirements—Fleishman (1962) and his colleagues
have demonstrated, rather convincingly, that the proportionate contribution of
motor and nonmotor (perceptual and cognitive) abilities to performance changes
as practice continues and proficiency increases. For example, if the abilities
contributing to a piloting skill (Fleishman & Hempel, 1954) are categorized as
motor (e.g., speed of movement) and nonmotor (e.g., spatial perception), the early
learning period is seen to require a predominance of perceptual and cognitive
abilities (Table 2). Since overarousal appears to lead first to a breakdown in
cognitive and perceptual functioning (Levin, 1971), high levels of arousal in the
initial stages of learning could be seen as being detrimental to performance.

Nature of the learning process—Many authors (e.g., Landers, 1978) have
focused on the attention demands of learning. In information-processing terms,
attention or concentration is seen as being of limited capacity, and when this
limited concentration channel or space is jammed by the neuronal effects of high
arousal, signal detection or cue utilization can be seen to be diminished. In
general we have assumed, as do Fisher and Motta (1977), that

> High levels of activation are more detrimental to the less experienced and less
> skilled athlete than to the experienced veteran competitor. This is not too surpris-
> ing since the less skillful must pay closer attention to such things as form, concen-
> tration and planned maneuvers. High levels of arousal are, therefore, more likely to
> disrupt their performances (p. 99).

The fact remains, however, that what little research there is on the effect of arousal at different stages of learning is equivocal. In addition, the practitioner, especially, should consider the possible effect of instructional methods on the learning process itself.

Instructional methods—It is unfortunate that so little effort has been given to determining or even hypothesizing the effects of instructional methods on the learning process (versus product). While this is understandable in view of the methodological problems involved and in view of our one-sided fascination with finding out how the nervous system functions (versus how it might be influenced to function), it has left us with practically no knowledge of how instruction itself might mediate nervous system activity and organization. For example, if the tennis serve is taught by a strict part method, then the individual may have to direct conscious attention to each part as it is introduced. The extent to which the beginner must pay closer attention to such things as form, concentration, and planned maneuvers, as noted in the quote by Fisher and Motta (1977), might be seen as being, at least in part, a result of the practitioner's organization of instruction. Thus the effect of arousal on performance, especially in the early stages of learning, could be seen to vary with differences in instructional methods.

INDIVIDUAL DIFFERENCES

Assuming that we can estimate the best arousal level for a specific skill at a particular stage of learning, we then need to consider the individual's current level of arousal and apply techniques designed to increase or decrease this level as needed. However, the problem is not as simple as might be thought. Individuals appear to differ both in their characteristic level of arousal and in the kinds of situations that arouse them. Thus some understanding of these individual differences seems prerequisite to the selection of motivational techniques.

Characteristic level of arousal—There seems to be considerable empirical support for the concept that, while individuals exhibit different emotional patterns in response to specific situations, they each have a characteristic level of arousal that influences their performance on a wide range of tasks. In Martens's (1974) parlance, some individuals tend to run their motors fast and others slowly, across all situations. This general arousal trait (often called trait anxiety or anxiety proneness) is held by Klavora (1979) to be "the most important factor affecting the arousal levels of athletes prior to competition and in training" (p. 162).

> The research reported here confirms what coaches have known from their experience; namely, that there are basically two kinds of athletes: the first kind are calm, low-strung, relaxed, composed players. The other kind are the nervous, high strung, excitable, anxious players (p. 162).

In general, research has shown that high arousal subjects perform less well under stress, and low arousal subjects perform better (e.g., Weinberg, 1978; Weinberg & Hunt, 1976). However, what is stressful to one individual is not necessarily so to another. We speak of this individual difference as situational arousal or state anxiety.

Situational arousal—There is no question that the arousal effect of any situation depends to a large extent on the individual's subjective interpretation of that situation. A common example is the learner who has a fear of the water. Less often recognized is the fact that almost any ingredient of the learning or performance environment may evoke situational arousal in the individual as, for example, the presence of an audience, the reaction of a teammate, opponent, or coach, or even a teacher's tone of voice or facial expression. This specificity of arousal has led some investigators (e.g., Landers, 1980; Martens, 1974; Sarason, Davidson, Lighthall, Waite, & Ruebush, 1960) to question the desirability of leaning too heavily on the concept of a general personality arousal trait. While accepting that such a trait may exist, some suggest that a situational approach may be more productive. While the suggestion has been directed primarily at researchers, the situational approach may have special merit for the practitioner. For example, an individual may exhibit arousal in a particular kind of situation, be it competitive, testing, or audience (Kroll, 1970). The practitioner who is aware of those situations that arouse an individual should be more effective in modifying the learning or performance environment (including instruction) so as to adjust the individual's arousal level toward the optimal. Note that this information might be used to either increase or decrease arousal. If a person is already at optimal arousal, we would want to avoid that situation if feasible; conversely, if the person is at a low level of arousal, we might use that arousal-inducing situation to increase it. However, before selecting a specific motivational technique, it would appear desirable to examine the alternatives available.

Direction of arousal

Assuming that optimal performance is the desired goal, then one of the critical roles of the practitioner in motivation is the adjustment of individual arousal level to a point consistent with this level of performance. However, before this is possible, we must estimate the player's current level of arousal to know whether to increase or decrease it. This is easier said than done. Kane (1970) points out one of the problems (Fig. 6-5). For any given level of performance (except the optimal) there are two possible levels of arousal: low (LA) and high (HA). Obviously, then, observation of level of performance cannot tell us whether an increase or decrease in arousal is needed to attain optimal performance.

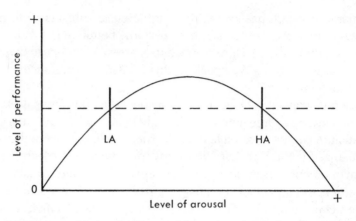

FIG. 6-5. Two possible levels of arousal for a given level of performance. Low arousal *(LA)* and high arousal *(HA)*.

ESTIMATING AROUSAL LEVEL

How, then, can we determine arousal level? One method used in research is to measure physiological indexes such as palmar skin conductance, blood chemistry changes, and circulatory responses to increased heart action. Obviously, such techniques are not readily available to the practitioner. While it may be possible, and at times advantageous, to observe the degree of skeletal muscle tension, this is a relatively crude index unless a baseline level for the individual has been established. In addition, there is some evidence (Shipman, Heath, & Oken, 1970) to suggest that the muscular and visceral manifestations of arousal may be or may become specific. Thus an individual might respond uniquely to a stressful situation with muscular tension in a specific group of muscles rather than with generalized muscular tension.

Sage (1977, p. 513) suggests that a rough measure of arousal might include observation of (1) hand tremor, (2) body perspiration, (3) eye dilation, and (4) restless and random fine and gross body movements. In addition, he notes that heart rate can be assessed without elaborate equipment.

Kane (1970) suggests that we might determine whether an individual's performance is indicative of too little arousal or too much (Fig. 6-5) by manipulating arousal level (e.g., applying stress) and noting the direction of the performance changes. Presumably, the performance of highly aroused individuals will decrease under applied stress, and the performance of those at low arousal levels will increase. The important concept for the practitioner is that observation of the directional changes in performance is very useful in determining if an individual is underaroused or overaroused. If, for example, an individual has been making relatively constant improvement and suddenly shows a significant decrease in proficiency, the possibility of overarousal should be considered.

In general, overarousal appears to lead first to a breakdown in cognitive and perceptual efficiency with a resultant decrease in the individual's ability to handle strategy problems and to attend to relevant sensory cues (Levin, 1971). Finally, there is often a breakdown in neuromuscular integration; the individual tends to revert to total body movement that appears clumsy. This suggests that we may be able to look to changes in the quality of performance to estimate arousal level.

Another method of estimating arousal level that may have possibilities, for the coach especially, is the use of anxiety or arousal inventories. Of the available anxiety scales, Martens (1971) recommends the Spielberger State-Trait Anxiety Inventory (STAI), which involves a self-report regarding feelings of tension, worry, and apprehension. However, this is a general inventory not specifically related to the sports situation. Martens (1977) has developed a Sport Competition Anxiety Test (SCAT), which he describes as being a "trait anxiety scale designed for measuring a predisposition to respond with varying levels of anxiety to competitive sports situations" (p. 18). SCAT items include statements such as the following:

1. Competing against others is fun.
2. Before I compete I feel uneasy.
3. I am a good sportsman when I compete.
4. I like rough games.
5. I get nervous waiting for the game to start.

As Kroll (1979) notes, both the STAI and the SCAT are directed toward estimating the level of arousal rather than its causes. He and his colleagues are working on a Competitive Athletic Stress Scale that "seeks to identify the causes of anxiety in athletic competition" (p. 215). The five major clusters of items identified include (1) somatic complaints, including such things as tightness, upset stomach, yawning, nervousness; (2) fear of failure; (3) feelings of inadequacy; (4) loss of control over events taking place; and (5) guilt feelings from such occurrences as hurting an opponent or losing one's temper. Kroll (1979) suggests that the scale may eventually serve as a diagnostic index of what athletes actually perceive as anxiety producers.

> On away games, for example, a different configuration of items may be causing anxiety as compared to home games. Different sports or different coaches may elicit identifiable item configurations. . . . In short, it may be possible to assess the causes of competitive anxiety in different athletes in different situations, and suggest training and coaching practices designed to reduce undesirable levels of anxiety by elimination of the stress stimulus elements which cause the emotional response (p. 219).

Meanwhile, however, both the STAI and the SCAT appear to be useful in the practical situation for giving an estimation of the level of a player's arousal. Recently, Martens, Burton, Rivkin, and Simon (1980) have reported on the reliability and validity of a Competitive State Anxiety Inventory (CSAI), which they feel supports its use in both its adult and child forms (p. 98).

Nevertheless, one of the most productive methods for a teacher or coach to get at the arousal problems of an individual remains that of systematic observation and dialogue, getting to know your players as individuals and observing their behavior in a variety of situations so as to determine not only the individual's situational arousal characteristics but also to observe changes in typical behavior that might signal arousal problems. In addition, talking with individuals can provide insights into personal problems that may be affecting performance.

REDUCING AROUSAL

Recently, the sports literature, both scientific and popular, has been rife with articles dealing with the management of stress or coping strategies, much of it directed to the problems of competitive anxiety. This is understandable on several counts. First, more people are engaging in competitive sport, whether it be running, racquetball, or little league soccer. Second, as the pressure to excel is increased, be it for the Olympics or at the local gymnastics camp, arousal tends to exceed the optimal. And third, but by no means the final count, as proficiency increases there is less room for error; that is, high-level competitors must perform at the very peak of the performance-arousal curve with the result, of course, that they are more apt to inch past that peak unless they have learned to finely tune arousal. When winning is measured in hundredths of a second, for example, there is little if any range for error.

As a result, new techniques for controlling arousal in sport have recently emerged: relaxation training, biofeedback, imagery, desensitization, autogenics, and even meditation and hypnosis. None of these are really new techniques; most have been borrowed from other disciplines, notably psychiatry and clinical psychology. The efficacy, the conditions, or the desirability of their application to sports situations remains to be determined. For this reason and because the use of some of the techniques would appear to require an expertise beyond that possessed by most teachers or coaches, they are mentioned only briefly here. Readers who wish to further explore the use of the techniques in sports would do well to begin with the readings edited by Klavora and Daniel (1979) and by Straub (1978).

Relaxation training—In 1938 Edmund Jacobson introduced a method of relaxation training that he called progressive relaxation (Jacobson, 1938). Since then, the technique has had wide acceptance and application. Unfortunately, little of this has been in schools, although the techniques are not difficult, as Jacobson notes in his most recent book, *Teaching and Learning: New Methods for Old Arts* (1973). Basically, the techniques are designed to develop awareness of tension in muscles and involve progression from maximal tension to complete relaxation; eventually individuals can learn to set muscles at the desired level of tension, one quarter of maximal, for example. There is also a progression from total body tension-relaxation to that of small body segments (hand, neck, forehead). Cratty (1971) has made modifications of these techniques for use with children, especially the hyperactive. However, since the techniques can provide a means of self-regulation, they can be used by the individual in arousal-inducing situations.

Biofeedback—Under normal conditions most of us have little awareness of our internal activity. With biofeedback, an individual is made aware of some aspect of this physiological activity by way of a visual or auditory display. As Zaichowsky (1980) notes, different methods of biofeedback have been used in training: (1) muscle feedback by way of electromyography, (2) skin temperature by way of thermal feedback, and (3) sweat activity by way of the Skin Potential Response. Brain wave activity, which can be demonstrated through electroencephalography, has been used for relaxation training but, according to Zaichowsky, is less effective than electromyography or thermal feedback. Recently, instrumentation to display heart rate and blood pressure during activity has become available, but experimentation in training is just beginning. Of course, the principle in operation is that we can learn to control physiological response through training even though we are unable to say specifically how we are controlling it. Biofeedback techniques, as currently used in the laboratory, depend on sophisticated electronic apparatus. However, as Harris (1978) notes, we can teach individuals to sense their own responses to stress (elevated heart rate, sweating, dry mouth, as well as degree of muscular tension); they can then respond to these responses with relaxation techniques. Frederick (1975) describes a method of biofeedback training without instrumentation for use by the teacher or coach.

Model training—Railo and Unestahl (1979) suggest that by gradually introducing stress elements into the training program, athletes are more effectively able to cope with stress as it occurs in the performance situation.

> First, working with athletes, we try to find out what factors or what situations they find difficult to control psychologically. Having defined these factors or situations, we try to introduce (copy or modulate) these factors into the training situation. . . . Depending on the sport, we use tapes from competitive situations, introduce stress elements in training, find training conditions that the athletes do not normally like, for example, windy weather, bad lanes, strange light, false judging, high expectations and so on (p. 256).

Such training would appear to be particularly useful where stressors are an inherent part of the performance situation.

Meditation—Techniques derived from Transcendental Meditation (TM), yoga, and Zen have been recommended by various sports figures to induce a relaxed state. Some have used meditation to overcome the destructive effect of brooding over past mistakes or trying too hard, claiming that it has a calming effect. Others have used it to improve concentration needed for body control, to force attention on relevant cues, to conserve energy, and to make it possible to put forth maximal effort without getting uptight (Alderman, 1978). Benson (1976) suggests that the word *one,* repeated over and over, can replace the traditional mantra used in TM. The principle assumed here is that by focusing on a single word or thought, the individual can successfully filter out arousal-inducing stimuli, including pain. Although there is little research on the effects of such techniques in sports, Layman (1978) suggests that physiological data and psychotherapeutic results indicate that meditation may be beneficial to athletic performance.

Desensitization—Systematic desensitization techniques involve conditioning an individual to be less sensitive to stress situations through the use of imagery. The method is basically one of classical conditioning. In general, the procedures involve pairing anxiety-producing situations with relaxation until the anxiety is alleviated. Ziegler (1978) describes a desensitization program consisting of five steps. First is an educational session including information regarding the effects of anxiety on performance, an interview involving pertinent medical information, the SCAT questionnaire, and the construction of a worry list of situations that the player finds anxiety producing. The second stage of the program is the development of the relaxation regimen. In the third stage the worry list is used to generate a hierarchical structure of anxiety-producing situations as shown on p. 135. The fourth stage, or desensitization session, begins with a period of relaxation, as described by Ziegler (1978).

> When relaxed the athlete is asked to imagine himself/herself in the first scene of the hierarchy for about 15 seconds. If any noticeable signs of tension or anxiety are felt, the athlete raises his/her hand and concentrates once again on the relaxation exercise. The pairing of the situation with relaxation continues until each situation, in order, has been successfully overcome (p. 261).

The final stage of the program involves the transfer to the competitive environment, which, as Ziegler notes, can be difficult to achieve. She suggests the use of biofeedback techniques and cognitive coping strategies such as thought stopping, autogenic phrases, imagery, and stimulus cueing, each of which is discussed briefly here.

Individualized hierarchy for a volleyball player who chokes during serve
(*only representative items included*)

1. During practice sessions
2. During pregame warm-up
3. During first play of game
4. When winning by wide margin; score 12-2
5. After I have made error
6. Serving for game point; score 14-13
7. Serving for game point; score 13-14

Modified from Ziegler, S.G. An overview of anxiety management strategies in sport. In W.F. Straub (Ed.), *Sport psychology: an analysis of athlete behavior* (2nd ed.). Ithaca, N.Y.: Mouvement Publications, 1978.

Thought stopping—The object of thought stopping is to replace negative thoughts with positive ones. For example, if a swimmer who is approaching a turn thinks, "I hope I don't miss this turn," his attention cannot be focused on the important cues for the turn. The swimmer must learn to recognize the negative thought, stop it ("No, my turns are good."), and replace it with a task-oriented thought ("Accelerate into the wall."). "The focus is changed from a negative to a positive performance-based suggestion" (Ziegler, 1978, p. 262).

Autogenics—There are several structured autogenic training programs (Hickman, 1979) that are designed to relieve stress through the use of either standardized or individualized verbalizations. Alexander (1969), for example, uses verbal commands that are specific to each individual.

> A teacher, working with his or her hands, provides the sensations and organization of the body while the student translates the sensations he is experiencing into verbal commands. For example, the teacher might place his hands on the student's neck and raise him from a sitting position, releasing and lengthening the neck while also positioning the head. The student articulates the accompanying sensations as "neck releasing and lengthening, head forward and up," or something of the sort (Hickman, 1979, p. 126).

Presumably, the student can in time elicit the head and neck relaxation by calling forth the verbal commands. However, autogenic phrases have also been used to elicit feelings of competency prior to performance (e.g., "I feel strong, relaxed, and capable."). Ziegler (1978) suggests that "words such as calm, warm, stretch, smooth, loose, lift, etc. can be useful in aiding the individual in retaining the appropriate focus for performance and beneficial in refining an individual's particular style" (p. 262).

Imagery—The use of imagery techniques in sport has been in vogue for some time and takes a variety of forms. Generally, it involves visualizing oneself performing a skill successfully prior to executing the skill. However, it has also been used as a method of rehearsal for game situations. Harrison and Reilly (1975), for example, list 10 visualization exercises that differ for pitchers, hitters, fielders, and base runners. One of the exercises for pitchers involves visualizing the execution of potential fielding plays: covering first base, backing up, fielding bunts, and so on (p. 59). The element most commonly emphasized in the use of visualization appears to be the vividness of the image. Ronan (1977), among others, cites evidence of muscular and brain wave activity during imagery to support his contention that the nervous system cannot tell the difference between an actual experience and an experience imagined vividly and in detail (p. 12). Thus vivid imagery ("Imagine the coldness of the water until you are shivering.") is seen as a kind of neuronal learning. Suinn (1978) suggests that mental imagery can be used for a variety of purposes: to practice technique, to practice strategy, to practice a general approach (e.g., being aggressive), to practice a difficult part of a course (e.g., ski run), to build confidence, or to become familiar with a specific performance situation by repeated mental rehearsal (p. 25).

Stimulus cueing—As Ziegler (1978) notes, inexperienced volleyball players often fail to respond to a ball until it comes speeding over the net. She suggests that they can be taught to cue in on the ball by saying "hit" as the ball is contacted on the serve. The object, of course, is to focus attention on the ball before it crosses the net, which in turn results in a readiness to respond.

Hypnosis—Pulos (1979) uses the terms *hypnosis, trance,* and *deep relaxation* interchangeably. He defines hypnosis as a process for making the subconscious conscious and suggests that it is a natural state that we slip into daily as in daydreaming, listening to music, or driving down a highway. He describes a program used to teach the athlete self-hypnosis.

> Athletes spend the remainder of the first session and subsequent sessions in "deep relaxation" or "trance" mentally rehearsing and visualizing themselves executing specific skills and general events or subconsciously reviewing problem areas in their sport. They are taught to suggest post-hypnotically that what they have executed ideally in their mind's eye they will be able to translate into action during practice or competition (p. 152).

Both Pulos (1979) and Pressman (1979) note the variety of situations amenable to hypnosis. "Self-hypnosis is also used to motivate the athlete to practice, to improve relaxation and sleep, to reduce the interfering aspects of stress upon concentration. . . ." (Pulos, 1979, p. 153). However, physical educators, in general, (e.g., Harris, 1978; Sage, 1977) have cautioned that the competence of the hypnotist and the ethical and legal considerations should be fully explored before hypnosis is employed.

INCREASING AROUSAL

That so much of the recent emphasis has been on methods of combating anxiety and reducing arousal tends to make us forget that it is often necessary to increase arousal. The fact that arousal is, to a large extent, qualitatively specific to the individual may appear to the practitioner to be an insurmountable barrier to the selection of arousal-producing techniques. However, since many of the methods discussed in the section on reducing arousal are designed to increase the individual's awareness of physiological states (e.g., degree of muscle tension), their possible use to teach an individual to increase arousal should be considered. There is no reason, for example, that relaxation training and biofeedback could not be used for this purpose. In addition, other techniques long used by teachers and coaches for increasing arousal are mentioned briefly here.

Intensity and variety of stimulus—Arousal can be attained and maintained by intensifying and varying a stimulus. An example would be raising your voice. However, this is effective only when it is not the usual procedure; yelling does not elicit high arousal if it is the habitual behavior of a teacher or coach. Kagan (1972) suggests that the discrepancy principle governs attention. Individuals pay more attention to events that are moderately different from those they are used to experiencing than they do to totally familiar or totally new events. Outwardly, this discrepancy elicits expressions of interest, surprise, and excitement. Carron (1978) notes that many coaches have a fixed, minimal repertoire of drills that are used over and over. He suggests that the coach consider using widely varied drills to provide the motivating effect of change (p. 46).

Exercise-induced activation—Since the sensory stimulation from muscles and joints feeds into the RAS (Fig. 6-1), movement itself can be used to increase arousal. Recently, the term *exercise-induced activation* has been used to refer to this phenomenon and may account for some of the positive effects of movement experiences in children with learning problems. However, care must be taken not to exceed the optimal level required for effective performance.

Arousal contagion—Arousal level may be catching. Teachers and coaches see this every day; a player or a team at a high pitch of excitement infects another player or team. While this can, and often does, have a negative effect by pushing an individual or team past the optimal arousal level, the principle can be used by the teacher or coach to either increase or reduce arousal. A soft tone of voice can do much to cool a player down, and a pep talk can indeed increase a player's arousal level.

Information feedback—Although the primary function of information feedback, as described earlier in this book, is to ensure an improvement in proficiency by giving information that will lead to error correction, it should be noted that information feedback tends to be motivating. Individuals receiving feedback approach their task with greater enthusiasm and diligence. It gives them a yardstick by which progress, or lack of it, can be seen. However, as Carron (1978) notes, care should be taken to avoid providing information that is readily available to the learner (p. 45). Redundant information does not have the same incentive value. In addition, progressive and realistic goal setting prior to participation can enhance the motivational value of information feedback.

Contingent reinforcement—Operant conditioning (behavior modification) was described in some detail in Chapter 2, and both positive and, at times, negative reinforcement can be effective not only for decreasing the incidence of a behavior (including arousal) but also for increasing it. However, as you recall, the techniques require adherence to specific criteria if they are to be effective. Siedentop (1978) summarizes these criteria: (1) target behaviors (e.g., "hustle," "work harder") must be specified clearly and be defined in observable terms, (2) behavior must be monitored to chart the effects of reinforcement, (3) the particular reinforcement must be clear to the individual and used only when the target behavior has occurred, (4) the least intrusive reward system should be used (the less motivated the individual, the greater is the need for strong external rewards such as T-shirts and patches) (p. 54). Although intrinsic rewards are often useful in initiating arousal, there is some indication (e.g., Gerson, 1978) that they may interfere with the development of intrinsic motivation. Suffice it to note here that a teacher or coach can reward (praise) manifestations of attention, excitement, and curiosity.

Incentive motivation—Before applying specific motivational techniques, it is desirable to determine why an individual is participating in the activity in the first place. As Halliwell (1979) notes, we can then begin to create an environment that will satisfy that need or expectation and thereby enhance motivation. Alderman (1978) reports rather consistent incentives, of young athletes (ages 11 to 18) at least: (1) the two strongest incentives are affiliation (e.g., making friends) and excellence (doing something very well), (2) stress (desire for excitement) is a consistent third, and (3) aggression (opportunity for intimidation) and independence (doing things without the help of others) are not strong incentives, either in individual or contact sports. He suggests that sports situations should be kept very social in nature and that each individual have the opportunity to become excellent (p. 140). Halliwell (1979) suggests that the incentive hierarchy noted by Alderman is not limited to young athletes. At any age we can achieve the desire to work harder by using techniques that provide opportunities for affiliation, excellence, excitement, and success. Specifically, he recommends that we (1) make sure that each individual feels that his contribution to the team is important, (2) base evaluation on performance rather than on performance outcome (e.g., playing well against a better team), (3) encourage players to accept personal responsibility for their own actions, (4) encourage players to develop team pride, (5) use innovative techniques to make practice exciting, and (6) encourage players to develop pride in performance through realistic goal setting and task analysis (pp. 190-195).

Goal setting—One of the most productive methods of directing arousal would appear to be that of setting and clarifying goals. As Halliwell (1979) notes, these goals should be specific, measureable, challenging, but attainable. In addition, participants who have a hand in setting their own goals are more highly motivated than those who do not (p. 191). However, the coach needs to assist in goal setting. Learners are prone to set a single long-term goal, whereas the provision for intermediate (short-term) goals (see Fig. 2-2) not only helps to maintain motivation and prevent frustration, but also allows for evaluation and revision as necessary. For example, a swimmer should set a seasonal time goal, but short-term (single meet) goals should also be set. In working with the coach, the individual can adjust these goals up or down as the season progresses. However, goals should not be thought of as being limited to skill proficiency. Individual training, practice, and commitment goals are important (McClements & Botterill, 1979), as are group goals established by the team as a whole (Zander, 1978).

SELF-ADJUSTMENT

The fact remains that any technique for adjusting arousal should eventually lead to self-regulation by the performer. The teacher or coach cannot always be on the spot nor can he expeditiously attend to each player's situational arousal during performance. However, most of the arousal-adjusting techniques can be learned by the individual. There are many techniques to assist individuals in controlling and directing their own behavior. However, as Harris (1978) notes, "These need to be incorporated into daily practice schedules as they must be practiced regularly for effective control. Coaches must learn that maximizing performance involves techniques beyond those of the game . . ." (p. 55).

It is unlikely that individuals will achieve such self-direction if they attribute their success or failure to unrealistic sources (e.g., poor officiating, bad luck). Therefore a brief glimpse at the attribution theory would appear desirable.

Attribution theory

Attribution theory and achievement motivation theory are derived from psychology but have relevance to teachers and coaches, as a review of recent literature attests to (e.g., Klavora & Daniel, 1979; Nadeau, Halliwell, Newell, & Rob-

Table 3 □ *Classification scheme for causal attribution*

Stability	Locus of control	
	Internal	**External**
Stable	Ability	Task difficulty
Unstable	Effort	Luck

Modified from Weiner, B., Freize, I.H., Kukla, A., Reed, L., Rest, L., and Rosenbaum, R.M. *Perceiving the causes for success and failure.* Chicago: General Learning Press, 1971.

erts, 1980; Straub, 1978). Basically, attribution theory states that we ascribe our performance (success or failure) to causes that may or may not be the actual cause. For example, Rejeski (1980) notes that there is a variety of causal explanations employed by athletes for failure such as the following:

(a) I just didn't run a very smart race.
(b) I've overtrained.
(c) My training regimen has been inefficient.
(d) The program was good; however, we just started too late.
(e) It seems I can never adapt to the changing environments (p. 34).

Table 3 shows four causal categories classified on the basis of locus of control (the extent to which individuals attribute their success or failure to external events or to their own actions) and stability. Effort and luck are seen to be factors that can fluctuate, while ability and task difficulty are seen as relatively stable for a participant or game situation at any specific point in time.

As Rejeski (1980) notes, many individuals either do not know the real cause of their success or failure or they do not want to know; they blame failure on external sources (task difficulty or bad luck) while attributing success to their own efforts or ability.

Rotella (1978) suggests that teachers and coaches should institute a planned program to bring attributions more into line with reality so that motivation can be productively directed. Among other things, he suggests the following:

1. Testing athletes on achievement motivation (self-scored) so that they can determine their own motivational levels
2. Providing information regarding attribution theory and its relationships to ascriptions of success and failure
3. Bringing in coaches or athletes who would be viewed as positive models and who can speak to the importance of realistic goal setting, confidence in one's ability, and feasibility of improvement through effort
4. Helping athletes set realistic goals, both terminal goals and intermediate sequential steps (see Fig. 2-2)
5. Assisting individuals in planning how to attain these goals

6. Drawing up a master list of all the competencies required for reaching goals (physical skills, conditioning strategies, etc.), beginning with each individual's weakest point

Finally, teachers and coaches must act on the understanding that they themselves probably have a significant impact on the attribution patterns of their players (Lefevbre, 1978).

Limitations and future directions

Both Martens (1974) and Landers (1980), among others, point out some of the limitations of the inverted U hypothesis of arousal. While some of the limitations are methodological and of primary interest to researchers, others have practical implications.

In the first place, the inverted U does not explain the relationship between arousal and performance; that is, we do not know why the performance-arousal relationship takes the form of the inverted U. While this chapter has drawn on some of the hypotheses that exist, there is very little research that tells us what aspects of performance are affected by specific levels of arousal. Martens (1974) notes the following:

> At least two broad research programs are needed to understand better the arousal-performance relationship. First, continued neurophysiological research to identify the arousal mechanisms in the brain and to explain how they interact with cognitive processes as well as the somatic system is fundamental to our understanding. Second, behavioral research to identify the yet unknown qualifications or mediating factors of the inverted-U relationship in terms of task, individual, and differences in arousal-eliciting stimuli is required (p. 183).

Many investigators (e.g., Landers, 1980; Martens, 1974; Shipman, et al., 1970) have noted that individuals respond or learn to respond in very specific ways to arousal; that is, an individual may respond to arousal in a specific mode (muscular, perceptual, cognitive, or behavioral) and even specifically within a modality (e.g., tension in a unique group of muscles). While this is an obvious limiting factor to a generalized view of arousal, it portends a trend that should have exciting possibilities for the practitioner. Landers (1980) notes, for example, that

> From an applied standpoint, the therapist must also understand which response component is primarily affected since the anxiety-coping techniques selected should be based on the type of anxiety response displayed by the individual athlete or student (p. 87).

For example, relaxation training would appear to be more appropriate for physiological reactions, whereas behavioral manifestations could be seen to be more amenable to contingent reinforcement and shaping.

The question remains as to how this specificity of response comes about. Is it learned? Do children respond in a more general fashion to arousal, and adults more specifically? Although we do not have the answers to these questions yet, learning has been hypothesized as a major factor in differences observed in arousal effects (Landers, 1980; Martens, 1974). It is hoped that the more we discover about this process or processes, the more we will be able to take it into consideration in our instruction and even, perhaps, to devise methods of directing arousal learning to the greatest benefit of the individual. For example, the application of various biofeedback techniques to the modification of some visceral responses (heart rate, blood pressure) led Jonas (1973) to title his book *Visceral Learning: Toward a Science of Self-Control.* Perhaps in the not too distant future we will include in our teaching of motor skills *visceral* motor skills.

The fact remains that the effects of arousal influence the motor, perceptual, and cognitive components of motor skills, either singly or in combination, and it is to a consideration of these abilities that the next chapter is directed.

Sample thought sheet

1. a. Select a specific motor skill. What is the optimal (best) arousal level for maximal proficiency for this skill?
   b. Draw a performance-arousal curve depicting this relationship.
   c. Justify your curve on the basis of the perceptual, motor, and cognitive requirements of the skill.
   d. Show how you might need to adjust this curve in the early stages of learning.
   e. Justify your early learning curve.
2. Give two different examples (actual rather than hypothetical, if possible) of each of the following in sports situations.
   a. Situational arousal
   b. Arousal contagion
3. Give a specific example of how you have used or could use each of the following techniques to maximize performance.
   a. Relaxation training
   b. Model training
   c. Desensitization
   d. Intensity and variety of stimulus
   e. Contingent reinforcement
   f. Goal setting
4. a. List the particular situations that you find are arousal inducing in your sports participation.
   b. List the symptoms of overarousal that you notice.
   c. Describe how you go about, or would go about, reducing your own arousal level as a performer, teacher, or coach.

References

Alderman, R.B. Strategies for motivating young athletes. In W.F. Straub (Ed.), *Sport psychology: an analysis of athlete behavior* (2nd ed.). Ithaca, N.Y.: Mouvement Publications, 1978.

Alexander, F.M. *The resurrection of the body.* New York: Delta Books, 1969.

Benson, H. *The relaxation response.* New York: Morrow, 1976.

Cannon, W.B. *The wisdom of the body.* New York: Norton, 1932.

Carron, A.V. Motivating the athlete. In W.F. Straub (Ed.), *Sport psychology: an analysis of athlete behavior* (2nd ed.). Ithaca, N.Y.: Mouvement Publications, 1978.

Cofer, C.N. *The structure of human memory.* San Francisco: W.H. Freeman and Co., 1976.

Cratty, B.J. *Active learning games to enhance academic abilities.* Englewood Cliffs, N.J.: Prentice-Hall, 1971.

Deese, J. Skilled performance and conditions of stress. In R. Glaser (Ed.), *Training research and education.* Pittsburgh: University of Pittsburgh Press, 1962. (Republished, New York: Wiley, 1965.)

Duffy, E. The psychological significance of the concept of "arousal" or "activation." *Psychological Review,* 1957, *64,* 265-275.

Easterbrook, J.A. The effect of emotion on cue utilization and the organization of behavior. *Psychological Review,* 1959, *66,* 183-201.

Fisher, A.C., & Motta, M.A. Activation and sports performance: some coaching guidelines. *Motor Skills: Theory into Practice,* 1977, *2,* 98-103.

Fleishman, E.A. The description and prediction of perceptual-motor skill learning. In R. Glaser (Ed.), *Training research and education.* Pittsburgh: University of Pittsburgh Press, 1962.

Fleishman, E.A., & Hempel, W.E., Jr. Changes in factor structure of a complex psychomotor task as a function of practice. *Psychometrika,* 1954, *19,* 239-252.

Frederick, A.B. Biofeedback and tension control. *Journal of Physical Education and Recreation,* October 1975, pp. 25-28.

Gerard, R.W. Neurophysiology: an integration (molecules, neurons, and behavior). In J. Field (Ed.), *Handbook of physiology: section 1, neurophysiology, vol. 3.* Washington, D.C.: American Physiological Society, 1960.

Gerson, R. Intrinsic motivation: implications for children's athletics. *Motor Skills: Theory into Practice,* 1978, 2(2), 111-119.

Hale, B.D. Anxiety and performance relationships. *Human movement potential.* Report of the Fall Conference of the Eastern Association of Physical Education for College Women, Hershey, Pa., October 1978, pp. 50-53. (Mimeographed)

Halliwell, W.R. Strategies for enhancing motivation in sport. In P. Klavora & J.V. Daniel (Eds.), *Coach, athlete and the sport psychologist.* Toronto: University of Toronto School of Physical and Health Education, 1979.

Harris, D.V. Coping strategies. *Human movement potential.* Report of the Fall Conference of the Eastern Association of Physical Education for College Women, Hershey, Pa., October 1978, pp. 39-44. (Mimeographed)

Harrison, B., & Reilly, R.E. *Visiondynamics: baseball method.* Laguna Niguel, Calif.: Visiondynamics, 1975.

Hebb, D.O. Drives and the CNS (Conceptual Nervous System). *Psychological Review,* 1955, *62,* 243-254.

Hebb, D.O. *A textbook of psychology.* Philadelphia: Saunders, 1958.

Hickman, J.L. How to elicit supernormal capabilities in athletes. In P. Klavora & J.V. Daniel (Eds.), *Coach, athlete and the sport psychologist.* Toronto: University of Toronto School of Physical and Health Education, 1979.

Jacobson, E. *Progressive relaxation.* Chicago: University of Chicago Press, 1938.

Jacobson, E. *Teaching and learning: new methods for old arts.* Chicago: National Foundation for Progressive Relaxation, 1973.

Jonas, G. *Visceral learning: toward a science of self-control.* New York: Cornerstone, 1973.

Kagan, J. Do infants think? *Scientific American,* 1972, 226, 74-82.

Kane, J.E. *Personality, arousal, and performance.* Paper presented at a symposium on psychological aspects of physical education and sports at Frostburg State College, Frostburg, Md., April 1970. (Mimeographed)

Klavora, P. Customary arousal for peak athletic performances. In P. Klavora & J.V. Daniel (Eds.), *Coach, athlete and the sport psychologist.* Toronto: University of Toronto School of Physical and Health Education, 1979.

Klavora, P., & Daniel, J.V. (Eds.). *Coach, athlete and the sport psychologist.* Toronto: University of Toronto School of Physical and Health Education, 1979.

Kroll, W. Theories and research on aggression in relation to motor learning and performance. In L.E. Smith (Ed.), *Psychology of motor learning.* Chicago: Athletic Institute, 1970.

Kroll, W. The stress of high performance athletics. In P. Klavora & J.V. Daniel (Eds.). *Coach, athlete and the sports psychologist.* Toronto: University of Toronto School of Physical and Health Education, 1979.

Landers, D.M. Motivation and performance: the role of arousal and attentional factors. In W.F. Straub (Ed.), *Sport psychology: an analysis of athlete behavior* (2nd ed.). Ithaca, N.Y.: Mouvement Publications, 1978.

Landers, D.M. The arousal-performance relationship revisited. *Research Quarterly for Exercise and Sport,* March 1980, *51*(1), 77-90.

Lassen, N.A., Ingvar, D.H., & Skinhoj, E. Brain function and blood flow. *Scientific American,* 1978, *239,* 62-71.

Layman, E. Mc. Meditation and sports performance. In W.F. Straub (Ed.), *Sport psychology: an analysis of athlete behavior* (2nd ed.). Ithaca, N.Y.: Mouvement Publications, 1978.

Lefevbre, L.M. Causal attributions for basketball performances by players and coaches. In F. Landry & W.A.R. Orban (Eds.), *Motor learning, sport psychology, pedagogy and didactics of physical activity.* Miami: Symposia Specialists, 1978.

Levin, S. Stress and behavior. *Scientific American,* 1971, 224, 26-31.

Malmo, R.B. Anxiety and behavioral arousal. *Psychological Review,* 1957, *64,* 276-287.

Marteniuk, R.G. *Information processing in motor skills.* New York: Holt, Rinehart and Winston, 1976.

Martens, R. Anxiety and motor behavior: a review. *Journal of Motor Behavior,* 1971, *3,* 151-180.

Martens, R. Arousal and motor performance. In J.H. Gilmore (Ed.), *Exercise and sport sciences review,* Vol. 2. New York: Academic Press, 1974, pp. 155-188.

Martens, R. *Sport competition anxiety test.* Champaign, Ill.: Human Kinetics, 1977.

Martens, R., Burton, D., Rivkin, F., & Simon J. Reliability and validity of the competitive state anxiety inventory (CSAI). In C.H. Nadeau, et al. (Eds.), *Psychology of motor behavior and sport—1979.* Champaign, Ill.: Human Kinetics, 1980.

McClements, J.D., & Botterill, C.B. Goal setting in shaping future performance of athletes. In P. Klavora & J.V. Daniel (Eds.), *Coach, athlete and the sport psychologist.* Toronto: University of Toronto School of Physical and Health Education, 1979.

Nadeau, C.H., Halliwell, W.R., Newell, K.M., & Roberts, G.C. (Eds.). *Psychology of motor behavior and sport—1969.* Champaign, Ill.: Human Kinetics, 1980.

Nideffer, R.M. *The inner athlete: mind plus muscle for winning.* New York: Thomas Crowell, 1976.

Oxendine, J.B. *Psychology of motor learning.* New York: Appleton-Century-Crofts, 1968.

Oxendine, J.B. Emotional arousal and motor performance. *Quest,* 1970, *13,* 23-32.

Pressman, M.D. Psychological techniques for the advancement of sport potential. In P. Klavora & J.V. Daniel (Eds.), *Coach, athlete and the sport psychologist.* Toronto: University of Toronto School of Physical and Health Education, 1979.

Pulos, L. Athletes and self-hypnosis. In P. Klavora & J.V. Daniel (Eds.), *Coach, athlete and the sport psychologist.* Toronto: University of Toronto School of Physical and Health Education, 1979.

Railo, W.S., & Unestahl, L. The Scandinavian practice of sport psychology. In P. Klavora & J.V. Daniel (Eds.), *Coach, athlete and the sport psychologist.* Toronto: University of Toronto School of Physical and Health Education, 1979.

Rejeski, W. Causal attribution: an aid to understanding and motivating athletes. *Motor Skills: Theory into Practice,* 1980, *4*(1), 32-36.

Ronan, D. *The swimmers' memorandum on mental training.* Fort Lauderdale, Fla.: 1977. (Mimeographed)

Rotella, R.J. Improving sports performance: implications of achievement motivation and attribution theory. *Motor Skills: Theory into Practice,* 1978, *2*(2), 120-127.

Sage, G.H. *Introduction to motor behavior: a neuropsychological approach* (2nd ed.). Reading, Mass.: Addison-Wesley, 1977.

Sarason, S.B., Davidson, K.S., Lighthall, F.F., Waite, R.R., & Ruebush, B.K. *Anxiety in elementary school children.* New York: Wiley, 1960.

Selye, H. *Stress without distress.* New York: Signet, 1975.

Shipman, W.G., Heath, H.A., & Oken, D. Response specificity among muscular and autonomic variables. *Archives of General Psychiatry,* 1970, *23,* 369-374.

Siedentop, P.D. The management of practice behavior. In W.F. Straub (Ed.), *Sport psychology: an analysis of athlete behavior* (2nd ed.). Ithaca, N.Y.: Mouvement Publications, 1978.

Straub, W.F. Classical theories of emotion: historical milestones. In C. Bard, M. Fleury, & J. Samela, (Eds.), *Mouvement: Actes du 7ᵉ Symposium Canadien en Apprentissage Psycho-Moteur et Psychologie du Sport.* Quebec: October 1975, 297-302.

Straub, W.F. (Ed.). *Sport psychology: an analysis of athlete behavior* (2nd ed.). Ithaca, N.Y.: Mouvement Publications, 1978.

Suinn, R.M. Psychology and sports performance: principles and applications. In W.F. Straub (Ed.), *Sport psychology: an analysis of athlete behavior* (2nd ed.). Ithaca, N.Y.: Mouvement Publications, 1978.

Ulrich, C. Stress and sport. In W.R. Johnson (Ed.), *Science and medicine of exercise and sports.* New York: Harper & Row, 1960.

Weinberg, R.S. The effects of success and failure on the patterning of neuromuscular energy. *Journal of Motor Behavior,* 1978, *10*, 53-61.

Weinberg, R.S., & Hunt, V.V. The interrelationships between anxiety, motor performance, and electromyography. *Journal of Motor Behavior,* 1976, *8*, 219-224.

Weiner, B., Freize, I.H., Kukla, A., Reed, L., Rest, L., & Rosenbaum, R.M. *Perceiving the causes for success and failure.* Chicago: General Learning Press, 1971.

Welford, A.T. *Skilled performance: perceptual and motor skills.* Glenview, Ill.: Scott, Foresman, 1976.

Zaichowsky, L.D. Tampering with performance—biofeedback and self-regulation. *Proceedings of the National Association for Physical Education in Higher Education: Annual Conference.* Champaign, Ill.: Human Kinetics, 1980, pp. 75-82.

Zander, A. Motivation and performance of sports groups. In W.F. Straub (Ed.), *Sport psychology: an analysis of athlete behavior* (2nd ed.). Ithaca, N.Y.: Mouvement Publications, 1978.

Ziegler, S.G. An overview of anxiety management strategies in sport. In W.F. Straub (Ed.), *Sport psychology: an analysis of athlete behavior* (2nd ed.). Ithaca, N.Y.: Mouvement Publications, 1978.

7 MOTOR SKILL ABILITIES

You will recall that the conceptual framework used in this book assumes that the learning of a skill is influenced by three major factors: (1) the state of the learner, (2) the nature of the skill, and (3) the methods of instruction. The state of the learner, in turn, is seen to be determined at least in part by the learner's arousal level and motivation and by the extent to which he possesses certain basic abilities.

While you are probably more familiar with motor abilities, such as strength and endurance, the information-processing model (see Fig. 4-2) suggests that we need to consider the input or perceptual side as well. In addition, certain central processing abilities, such as decision making, while more elusive, cannot be ignored. Assuming that we can identify such abilities, how can knowledge of them be used to enhance learning and performance?

Identifying the problem area—Obviously, if we are aware of the abilities required by a specific skill, this can help us determine whether an individual's problem is a perceptual one, a decision-making one, or a motor one. Too often we look only at the motor side of learning and performance problems.

Ability training—If we can identify where an individual's problem lies, presumably we can then proceed to develop the ability that is lacking through an appropriate training regimen. We have always been concerned with strength training or conditioning but have done very little with perceptual training. Unfortunately, we know little about the extent to which various perceptual abilities can be improved by training and about the extent to which such training might enhance performance of the skill (Rothstein, 1977b); this would appear to be a neglected area of research.

Advance information—There is some evidence (e.g., Parker & Fleishman, 1961) that if learners are given information regarding the major ability requirements of a skill prior to practice, they improve more rapidly than learners who are not given advance information. For example, if peripheral vision is critical to the performance of a skill, the individual who is aware of this would be seen as having the potential to progress more rapidly.

Developmental programs—It seems logical that if learners have already developed their perceptual and motor abilities, teachers and coaches would be able to move ahead with specific practice of the skill rather than having to spend so much time with general ability development. Obviously, we need to spend some time in physical education on developing and maintaining these abilities. A single sport does not have the potential for developing in an individual the array of abilities that can contribute to performance in a variety of activities.

However, it should be noted at the outset of this discussion that the notion there is a group of abilities, the development of which will contribute to the learning and performance of a wide range of motor skills, is not without its critics. Therefore some clarification of the specificity controversy and the position taken in this book in regard to it seems desirable.

Specificity of skills

Following in the wake of efforts by educational psychologists to identify a general intelligence factor were physical educators searching for a measure of general motor ability. As a result, a number of test batteries were developed, which were supposedly capable of predicting an individual's ability to learn or perform a variety of motor skills. However, Brace (1946), in a study to determine the validity of a number of such measures, concluded that none of the tests, including his own, were sufficiently predictive to justify their use. This, together with the evidence accumulated by Henry, Lotter, and Smith (1962), virtually erased the concept of a general motor ability or athletic index.

In its place there developed an ability-skill concept, that is, the idea that there are a number of abilities that contribute to the performance and learning of motor skills. McCraw (1949), for example, suggested that in learning a skill an individual might draw on a particular combination of abilities. Tentative concepts consistent with this idea were developed by Fleishman and his colleagues (Fleishman, 1962) and by Cratty (1966) and are summarized here briefly to clarify the position taken in this book in regard to the specificity of skills.

ABILITY-SKILL PARADIGM

Fleishman's (1962) concept assumes that an individual's ability to learn a particular motor skill is determined to a large extent by the level to which he has developed the perceptual and motor abilities required by that skill. One individual may be high on one ability and low on another, but presumably the individual who has a great many highly developed abilities can more readily become proficient in a variety of specific skills.

Although Fleishman (1962, p. 172) is explicit in his acknowledgment of the specificity of skills (the unique aspects of a skill that only practice on that particular skill will develop), his concept implies an ability-to-skill transfer; that is, learning a skill can be facilitated by the development of those perceptual and motor abilities basic to performance in a particular category of motor skills. For example, manipulative skills are seen to require different abilities than athletic skills. While athletic skills involve abilities such as strength, flexibility, and balance, manipulative and limb coordination skills involve abilities such as control precision and manual dexterity. The fact remains, however, that the specificity of skills is not as explicit in Fleishman's conceptual model as might be desired.

THREE-LEVEL THEORY

Cratty (1966) suggests that the factors that influence motor learning and performance may be grouped into three levels according to their degree of specificity. He conceptualizes these levels in the form of a triangle similar to that shown in Fig. 7-1. At the base level are those relatively consistent traits of an individual that influence almost all behavior whether it be verbal, cognitive, motor, or a combination of these. Included in these general supports of behavior is, for example, the individual's characteristic level of arousal. At the second or midsection level are the perceptual and motor abilities that are seen to contribute to the learning of motor skills. At the apex of the triangle are the skill specifics, such as the spatial-temporal patterning of the skill and its unique force and energy requirements. The learning of a motor skill is thus seen to involve (1) basic motivational and arousal traits, (2) the development of those perceptual and motor abilities required by motor skills, and (3) practice on the skill itself to develop its unique components.

SPECIFIC ADAPTATION

It should be noted that the content of each of the levels shown in Fig. 7-1 has been modified to reflect the particular abilities and specifics emphasized in this chapter. One of the most important inclusions in the task specifics is the adaptation of abilities to the specific skill. Henry et al. (1962), among others, have demonstrated rather convincingly that abilities are themselves (at least partially) specific to the skill; for example, a general training program for leg strength is not sufficient to develop the specific leg strength required of a person to rebound in basketball. Obviously, the force a muscle can exert in a particular skill is going to depend on the specific joint angles, among other things, used in that skill. The same is true of flexibility. Indeed, all of the abilities discussed in this chapter are assumed to require specific adaptation to a particular skill. More will be said of this in the section on training at the end of this chapter. Suffice it to emphasize here that there is a limit on the effectiveness of general training programs.

The position taken in this book is that, while every motor skill has its unique

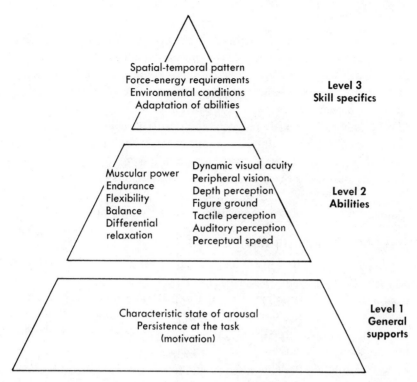

FIG. 7-1. Three-level theory of perceptual-motor learning. (Modified from Cratty, B.J. A three-level theory of perceptual-motor behavior. *Quest,* 1966, *6,* 2-10.)

characteristics, which only practice in that specific skill can develop, there are some basic abilities, the general development of which can contribute to learning motor skills. Such an assumption appears to be compatible, at present, both with the research and with common sense observation. When research findings appear to place limits on the generality of an ability, the limitations are noted in this book. However, the specificity controversy is far from being satisfactorily resolved, and until such time as its limits are more clearly established, the ability-skill concept appears to be both tenable and useful.

Any designation or list of the basic abilities contributing to motor skills is presently highly arbitrary and must be subject to change. The criteria for the selection of the abilities described in this chapter are (1) that they appear to be functional units, that is, amenable at some point both to development and to assessment, (2) that they have been identified in a number of studies, and (3) that they are relevant to physical educators. Unfortunately, the terms used to denote these abilities vary considerably. Therefore, wherever possible, alternative terms are noted, and examples of skills that require the ability are given.

Motor abilities

Motor abilities are discussed first, since you are probably more familiar with them than with perceptual abilities. Indeed, the professional literature is so replete with lists of motor abilities that any selection becomes somewhat arbitrary. In addition, recent investigations have demonstrated greater specificity of motor abilities than was conceived in earlier studies. Nevertheless, there appears to be a general consensus on at least four basic physical abilities that have emerged from studies of motor performance: muscular power, endurance, flexibility, and balance. Co-ordination, as a general ability, is questionable, but is included here for purposes of clarification. Differential relaxation is, unfortunately, seldom included in lists of motor abilities. It is hoped that this situation will change. Each of these abilities is mentioned only briefly here to clarify the nature of the ability.

MUSCULAR POWER AND ENDURANCE

Muscular strength refers to the contraction capacity of muscles. As such, it obviously underlies all motor performance. However, there is one thing that we are sure of and that is muscular strength, applied in performance, is not a single ability. Recently, the contraction capability of muscles has been differentiated on the basis of the energy source used to provide the contraction. Short-term, high-intensity contractions (characteristic of muscle action in sprinting) occur in the absence of oxygen and are called anaerobic power contractions. Long-term, low-intensity contractions (characteristic of muscle action in marathon running) require oxygen and are termed aerobic endurance contractions. Thus running the 100-meter dash and the marathon is called the "impossible double," because both call on different energy sources and require different kinds of training.

Some examples of activities requiring endurance (aerobic) ability are cross-country, in either skiing or track; 1500-meter events in swimming; and rowing. Examples of activities requiring muscular power (anaerobic) ability are basketball (in general), slalom in skiing and diving, and golf drives.

However, this is a relatively crude method of categorizing skills. For example, middle-distance running calls on a different anaerobic energy source than does sprinting. Therefore it seems desirable to classify skills according to their duration and intensity (Paup, 1980):

1. Anaerobic power skills, such as sprinting and golf drives, that last less than 30 seconds
2. Anaerobic power skills, such as middle-distance running, that last 1 or 2 minutes
3. Aerobic endurance skills, such as cycling and swimming, that last any-where from a few minutes to several hours

However, any specific skill usually calls on more than one of the energy systems. The practitioner needs to determine the predominate system and design training accordingly. Fox (1979, p. 198) presents a table noting the predominate energy system for various sports. More is said about specificity of training at the end of this chapter. Suffice it to note here that the strength of muscles is not only specific to the intensity and duration of the skill, but also to the particular muscle groups involved.

FLEXIBILITY

Corbin and Noble (1980) define flexibility as the "range of joint motion available in a joint or group of joints, mobility" (p. 23), and as they note, it is the "in thing" today among those who exercise regularly. It is seen to contribute not only to proficiency but also to the prevention of injury.

Flexibility is specific to each joint. Flexibility of the hip is not related to flexibility of the shoulder. This specificity of flexibility should be obvious when you consider that flexibility depends primarily on the elasticity and extensibility of connective tissue surrounding the muscle (deVries, 1980, p. 462).

In addition, static or extent flexibility is not the same as dynamic flexibility (deVries, 1980, p. 463; Fleishman, 1964). Static flexibility involves simple range of motion, such as slowly bending forward and touching the floor; dynamic flexibility is the ability to use the range of joint movement in the performance of a physical activity at the speed required in the performance (Corbin & Noble, 1980).

> For example, in gymnastics the "splits" may be done in the midst of a routine of several other important movements. To be able to perform the movement slowly or with an assist is irrelevant (p. 23).

Obviously, as with all abilities, flexibility must be adapted to the specific activity.

Although each skill has its own flexibility requirements, a general flexibility development program is desirable. This should include stretching each of the major muscle groups and joints. There are several techniques for developing flexibility; Corbin and Noble (1980) and deVries (1980, p. 467) suggest that passive procedures are probably best for most people. It is of interest that the changes brought about by stretching exercises last for 8 weeks or more after stretching is discontinued (deVries, 1980, p. 467).

Flexibility has been measured in a multitude of ways—from the use of simple tape measures to sophisticated electronic and photographic devices. According to Corbin and Noble (1980), the device used most often is the flexometer. This is a small instrument that can be strapped onto a body part and records range of motion in respect to a perpendicular established by gravity (deVries, 1980, p. 465). The important point is that no single joint action test nor even a limited battery of tests can adequately measure a person's flexibility (Harris, 1969).

Incidentally, one of the common misconceptions often associated with flexibility is that strength and flexibility are mutually exclusive; that is, an increase in one requires a decrease in the other. However, this is not the case. The main reason that individuals with strong muscles may lack flexibility is that they often fail to train for flexibility and vice versa.

BALANCE

Most studies of balance have given evidence of at least two types of balance: *static balance,* the ability to maintain body equilibrium in a relatively fixed position and *dynamic balance,* the ability to balance while in motion. Dynamic balance is essential in those sports requiring sudden changing movements. Singer (1975, p. 236) gives the example of a tennis player who has to move for the ball, regain balance, and then stroke the ball. A third type of balance, often referred to as *rotational balance,* is the ability to regain equilibrium after quickly turning the body on its axis and is related to the ability to recover from the stimulation produced in the vestibular apparatus of the ear by the spinning or turning movement.

Static balance is often measured by standing on one foot (often on a narrow balance beam) with the eyes either open or closed. The task is obviously harder with the eyes closed, since vision contributes significantly to balance. However, while most authorities seem to agree that both vision and vestibular functioning affect balance, less often emphasized is the fact that muscular capability is involved. For example, in a standing front scale on a balance beam, you will often see tremor in the individual's supporting leg; he is unable to hold the contraction of both flexors and extensors of the limb (cocontraction) to maintain a position.

Balance is obviously not a single ability. Sanborn and Wyrick (1969), in an attempt to find a predictor test for Olympic balance beam performance, concluded that "no one existing test of balance is sufficient to assess the motor performance component referred to as balance" (p. 181). However, tests are available for both static and dynamic balance that would appear to be acceptable gross screening devices. Static balance can be tested with the simple "stand on one foot" (preferably with eyes closed) as advocated by Fleishman (1964) or by the more sophisticated electronic ataxiameters that measure body sway (e.g., Kohen-Raz, 1976). Dynamic balance is more difficult to measure, if indeed it can be measured. Researchers have generally used the stabilometers (Singer, 1975, pp. 238 & 240) that require a person to balance on an unstable platform. In addition, practitioners have been observed using the bongo board as a screening and training device.

COORDINATION

Coordination is the most elusive of the so-called motor abilities, and in fact there is considerable question as to whether it should be considered a general motor ability, since both assessment and general development (training) potential are in doubt.

If we look at the multitude of performance tests used to identify coordination—shuttleruns, 30-yard dash, standing long jump, hopping, crossover steps, skipping, and cable jump—the problem should be obvious. In addition, while some authorities use the term *coordination,* others use the term *agility* (e.g., President's Council on Physical Fitness and Sport, 1971). Fleishman (1964) emphasizes the questionable status of coordination as a general ability, since agility and coordination tests seem to require other abilities such as dynamic flexibility.

The diversity of these tests and the lack of training techniques for coordination (short of practice on the specific skill) militate against the assumption of a general coordination ability at this time. Obviously, there is a specific coordination requirement for each skill. In addition, it appears that the learning of this skill-specific coordination is one of the major tasks in attaining proficiency in the skill (Fleishman & Hempel, 1955). Fleishman (1962) speculates that this "complex coordination, specific" factor might involve an "integration" ability. That is, while proficiency in the early stages of learning might depend primarily on the basic abilities required by the skill, higher proficiency might be the result of the individual's capacity to integrate or pattern these abilities.

Fitts (1962) notes the following on his survey of physical education instructors, coaches, and aviation instructors.

> Practically all instructors refer to the development of coordination. For the pilot this often means integration of hand and foot movements. For the swimmer, it means the integration of breathing, stroking, and kicking. For the golfer, it means integration of body, shoulder, arm, and wrist action. Timing of successive movement patterns, timing of body movements in relation to external objects, and the development of rhythm are also emphasized (p. 185).

Until there is evidence to the contrary, it would seem wise to dispense with the notion that coordination is a general ability, at least for the purposes of the practitioner, and to consider it instead a factor specific to each skill.

DIFFERENTIAL RELAXATION

Relaxation training as a method of modifying arousal level was mentioned in the previous chapter. The ability to selectively adjust (finely tune) muscle tension is important in developing proficiency in motor skills. In Fitts's (1962) survey of coaches and physical education teachers, Fitts found that one of the most frequent comments concerned the degree of tenseness-relaxation that could be observed in the movements of performers (pp. 185-186).

; (1964) defines relaxation as a "neuromuscular accomplishment
n reduction of tension in the skeletal musculature" (p. 3). He also
; between complete and differential relaxation.

> ete relaxation means relaxing all muscles of the body as completely as possi-
> . . Differential relaxation means differentiating between muscles that are
> necessary for an activity and those that are not. It also means differentiating be-
> tween strong and weak contractions of the active muscle and relaxing them as
> much as is consistent with doing the job at hand effectively. Thus differential
> relaxation should be practiced continually in connection with every activity (p. 3).

For example, modern dancers must learn to isolate movement for the body to
have the greatest freedom for expression, and large amounts of time are spent in
so-called technique training to achieve this capacity. Jacobson (1938, 1973) has
suggested some progressive relaxation training exercises that can be taught.
These were described in the section on reducing arousal in Chapter 6. Suffice it to
note here that for the most part this is a neglected area of training that should
begin early in physical education and continue into every skill-training program
so that it can be maximally effective.

Perceptual abilities

As was the case with motor abilities, any selection of the perceptual abilities most
important to motor skills is somewhat arbitrary. In addition, the predominance in
the physical education literature of the consideration of visual abilities, while
attesting to the importance of vision in the performance of so many of the sports
skills, has resulted in a neglect of auditory and tactile abilities. Therefore perceptual abilities have been categorized here according to the sensory modalities
(visual, kinesthetic, tactile, and auditory). While this method of classification
appears to be the most useful for the practitioner, it has limitations; these are
discussed in a separate section on intersensory integration.

Although the importance of perceptual abilities might be assumed to be more
critical in open skills, such as batting and catching, closed skills should not be
considered nonperceptual. For example, a modern dancer must take into account
not only the dimensions of the stage, or of different stages when performing with
a touring company, but also the movements in both space and time of the other
dancers.

VISUAL

The literature on visual perception is voluminous, and no attempt is made
here to be comprehensive in coverage. Rather, the purpose is to highlight those
abilities that appear in the physical education literature most consistently. Read-

ers who desire more information would do well to begin with Rothstein (1977a) and Whiting (1970).

Dynamic visual acuity (DVA)—Although static visual acuity (e.g., as measured by the Snellen chart) is the ability to see detail in a stationary object, DVA is the ability to see detail when either the object or the observer, or both, are moving. DVA thus requires proper functioning of the extrinsic eye muscles (oculomotor coordination) and of the internal accommodation (lens) system of the eyes. It is well known that we get a relatively accurate estimation of the speed of an object from our eye-head movement, but what of situations where the ball travels at speeds beyond the limits of oculomotor tracking? Whiting (1970, p. 42) notes that in baseball a fast ball takes a mere 0.43 to 0.58 seconds to travel the 60 feet from the pitcher to the plate and that batters must begin their swing when the ball is at least 20 feet from the plate. Although advanced performers obviously learn to predict the flight of the ball, Sharpe (1978) suggests that these performers must depend on the accommodation sytem of their eyes rather than on their eye-head movement. Although there is some controversy over whether advanced performers should continue to track the ball with their eyes past the point at which they need to make a prediction on the ball speed, Sharpe (1978) suggests that novices are more successful if they continue to track the ball; apparently this continued tracking helps build prediction capability. In any case, DVA is an important ability contributing to a large number of motor skills, and, according to Morris (1977, p. 17), there is a "simple, easily administered DVA test" that can also be used for testing static visual acuity (which he recommends) and for DVA training.

Peripheral vision—Field of vision refers to the entire area that can be seen without moving the eyes; peripheral vision is the lateral or outside part of this field. Peripheral vision has been reported to contribute to performance in basketball (Stroup, 1957), javelin and discus throwing, figure skating, and slalom (Rothstein, 1977b). In some cases it appears that its contribution lies in allowing the individual to better guide the throwing arm if the arm is seen; in most cases, however, the advantage lies in the detection of events occurring around the individual in a game (e.g., seeing a teammate open for a pass or an opponent moving in). As Rothstein (1977b) notes, peripheral vision contributes to anticipation so that a player is not taken by surprise. In addition, it is both easily measurable and trainable (Sage, 1977, pp. 264-265).

Depth perception—You need only to cover one eye to appreciate the role of binocular vision in depth perception. In binocular vision we are able to take the flat image from one eye and combine it with a flat image from the other eye to produce a three-dimensional view. However, there are also monocular cues for depth or distance perception, such as the changing size of objects as we or they move, shading, and the partial obscuring of a distant object by a nearer one (Sage, 1977, pp. 267-270). When you realize that the picture you view on television is flat or two-dimensional, you can appreciate how much of depth perception is learned. (An Olympic medal winner in the ski jump at Sapporo had vision in only one eye.) Thus it is not surprising that research on the contribution of depth perception to motor performance has been conflicting. Rothstein (1977b) suggests that dynamic depth perception (e.g., distance estimation of a moving object) may be more related to success in motor skills than static depth perception. Although there are a number of tests for static depth perception (Sage, 1977, p. 274), reliable tests for dynamic depth perception have not been developed (Rothstein, 1977b, p. 225). It appears, on empirical grounds, that depth perception can be improved through training (Sage, 1977, p. 275).

Figure-ground perception—Figure-ground perception refers to the ability to distinguish an object from its surrounding background. Smith (1970) cites the example of a ball getting lost against the background of a crowd as it rises into the air. Gallahue (1968) suggests that both lack of contrast (blending) between figure and ground and distracting complexity of figure-ground patterns can affect proficiency of a motor skill. For example, the blending of a white tennis ball with court lights or with the sky has led to the popularity of yellow tennis balls. In addition, Gallahue (1968) notes that children up to the age of 10 appear to be primarily ground dependent, and he suggests that cluttered walls and floor patterns, as well as lack of contrast between the object and its background, may lead to performance problems. Sage (1977, p. 284) notes that familiarity with the background in a given area seems to aid figure-ground selection at that site, and he suggests that one of the advantages to be gained from 1 or 2 days of practice at a strange sport area is improved figure-ground perception for that environment. Although figure-ground ability is enhanced with practice (Sage, 1977, p. 283), the specificity of the ability in sports would appear to call to question efforts at general training.

KINESTHETIC

We have long assumed that a major ability contributing to motor learning and performance is kinesthetic perception, or the feel of movement. Thus we have often gone to some lengths to heighten kinesthetic awareness as, for example, having learners practice movement patterns with their eyes closed. Teaching cues such as "Get the feel of the movement" and "Feel as though you're sweeping the ball" are still being used with the assumption that such cues will enhance learning. Recent investigations, however, have called into question the extent to which concentration on the feel of movement is effective or desirable. Pleasants (1971) states the problem well.

What is the feeling we're asking our students to experience? Does stressing the feel of a movement enhance learning? Is this an effective method of teaching? If so, how and when should we utilize this technique? (p. 224).

There are almost as many definitions of kinesthetic perception as there are authors. For our purposes, *kinesthesis* is defined as *the ability to perceive body movement exclusive of visual or auditory means*. In more popular terms it is the feeling of body movement.

It seems desirable to point out some of the limitations on the use of kinesthetic perception in learning and performance. In the first place, beginners can be seen as being limited in their use of kinesthetic perception to determine the correctness of their movement. Fitts (1951) notes that since the learner's movement errors are relatively large, perception of the erroneous movement cannot provide a correction function. Second, kinesthesis cannot be error correcting in fast movements, such as a kip, because the movement is over before the kinesthetic information can be processed. Third, even advanced performers can be seen as limiting their performance potential by concentrating on the feel of the act during performance. Borrowing on the concept of a limited concentration channel (LCC), described in Chapter 4, we can see that the high-level performer needs to concentrate on the regulatory cues (visual or auditory) essential to performance of that skill and on the strategy decisions that need to be made.

Why then should we be concerned about kinesthetic ability? In the first place, as learners improve in proficiency, the feel of the movement is stored in memory. This is why a golfer can say after a drive off the tee, "That didn't feel right." Notice, however, that this evaluation comes *after* the completion of the drive. As such, it can be useful knowledge of performance (KP), and along with knowledge of where the ball went (knowledge of results [KR]), it can provide information for correction on the next drive.

However, there is another way that emphasizing the feel of movement might be useful in teaching, and that is to "chunk" instructional information. For example, the cue, "Feel as though you're sweeping the ball," can give the learner an idea of the skill quickly, if the term *sweep* is familiar to him. However, caution must be used in such cases, since continued attention to feeling the movement detracts from attention to regulatory cues. In addition, as you recall, the spatial-temporal and force patterning of skills is specific. The feeling of a tennis serve is not the same as that of an overhand throw.

We don't have all the answers with regard to the role of kinesthetic perception in motor learning and performance. There is some reason to believe that it may play an important role in awareness of limb position prior to starting a movement pattern (e.g., the level of the racket arm just prior to a forehand drive in tennis) and that it may contribute to error correction during slow movements (Sage,

1977, p. 303), but the widespread practice of having learners concentrate on the feel of their movements during performance appears to have been largely discredited. Harrison and Reilly (1975) suggest that although going through a movement, such as a baseball swing or golf swing, prior to performance is a good training technique, once the individual steps to the plate or to the tee, concentration should be centered on the regulatory cues (e.g., the ball) not on the feel of the movement.

A major exception to this should be noted, however. When the feeling of movement is a performer's objective, whether in dancing, running, or fielding a ball, attention to kinesthetic perception is the key even though it may mean that the ball may not be fielded as successfully. It is hoped that the joy of movement will not become a neglected aspect of physical education.

TACTILE

Although the tactile sensors contribute to kinesthetic perception, as defined in the previous section, it seems desirable to consider it as a separate ability contributing to both motor learning and performance. Although kinesthetic perception is not very useful to beginners because of their large movement errors, tactile stimulation, especially through the feet, is an important source of information regarding shifts of weight. Thus youngsters learning to walk a beam can more readily make the change from visually guiding their movement (looking at their feet) by "listening to their feet." Smith (1970) suggests that we should allow children to do more activities barefoot rather than allow their foot sensation to be masked by sneakers. In addition, she suggests providing play areas with different surfaces (sand, grass) and terrain (flat, sloping). However, continued concentration on tactile sensation has the same limitations as attention to kinesthetic perception; concentration needs to be focused on the purpose of the act.

AUDITORY

Despite the fact that audition is one of the most common means by which both children and adults receive information, we have given little attention to its abilities in physical education. These abilities have implications for motor learning and performance, and they are discussed briefly here.

Sound localization—Our ability to localize the source or direction of sound contributes to our perception of space. For example, information about what goes on behind us in a game (movement of players or of the ball) is dependent to a large extent on sound localization. In addition, individuals tend to initiate movement toward the source of sound. Smith (1970) suggests that we should give sound cues from the direction in which the movement is to be made.

Rhythm discrimination—Rhythm is the temporal patterning of sequential stimuli. According to Smith (1970), children learn to discriminate rhythm through auditory means before they do so visually. She suggests that training to move to auditory rhythmic patterns should begin in the preschool years. Presumably, such training may help the child learn to discriminate the temporal patterning of movement skills in later years (p. 32).

Figure-ground selection—Similar to visual figure-ground differentiation, auditory figure-ground selection involves selecting relevant stimuli from among an array of sounds. A common example is the problem that football linemen may have in distinguishing the quarterback's signals over the noise of the crowd. Less obvious is the problem of attending to verbal instruction when it blends with the noise in the pool or gymnasium. The practitioner has the dual responsibility of controlling background noise to facilitate attention to instruction and of training in figure-ground selection when noise is an inherent part of the performance situation. For example, the football lineman needs to learn to filter out extraneous noise so that he hears the quarterback's signals.

INTERSENSORY INTEGRATION

The classification of perceptual abilities into separate modalities (visual, kinesthetic, tactile, and auditory) gives an oversimplified view of perception, since the functioning of any one system is affected or modified by the other systems (Williams, 1977). When proficiency in a particular motor skill depends on the independent functioning of a specific modality, efforts must be made to decrease interference from other systems. However, the cooperation of systems is usually facilitating. For example, orienting ourselves in space can be accomplished visually or by tactile or auditory means; however, it is usually the result of the integration of sensory systems (e.g., visual-auditory or visual-tactile). Fig. 7-2 may help you to appreciate the complexity of perception.

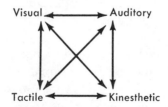

FIG. 7-2. Intersensory integration.

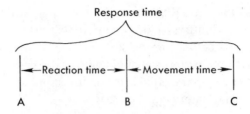

FIG. 7-3. Components of response time. *A*, Presentation of stimulus; *B*, initiation of response; *C*, completion of response.

Components of response time

Probably no other single measurement has been used as much in the study of motor skill learning as has response time. However, response time is most profitably thought of, not as a single ability, but as consisting of a number of components, each of which may have important implications for the practitioner. In addition, different investigators use somewhat differing terminology. Therefore it seems desirable to clarify the terms used in this book before discussing the practical implications.

In Fig. 7-3 *response time* is used to refer to the time from the presentation of a stimulus until the completion of the response to that stimulus. In research this often involves a relatively simple act, such as depressing a lever in response to a visual, auditory, or tactile stimulus. In practical terms, it could be the time from the moment the ball leaves your opponent's racket until you hit it with yours.

This response time can be divided into two phases: (1) *reaction time* (RT), the time from the presentation of the stimulus until the initiation of a movement response, and (2) *movement time* (MT), the time from the initiation of movement until contact with the ball. This distinction between RT and MT is an important one for the practitioner. RT and MT show very little correlation; that is, an individual may react very quickly to a particular stimulus (e.g., a fastball pitch) but have slow MT (e.g., due to poor biomechanics or lack of sufficient muscular power to bring the bat around quickly). In addition, RT itself may be of two types: (1) simple or reflex RT and (2) choice reaction time (CRT), involving a decision among two or more responses.

There is a component of RT that would appear to have important implications for the practitioner, and that is *perceptual speed*. As defined above, RT involves not only perception of the stimulus but also the decision to respond to the stimulus with a particular movement. Thus measurement of RT has usually included the time necessary not only to identify a stimulus, but also to generate a motor program to the muscles. From the practical standpoint, there are times when a teacher or coach may want to work on perceptual speed independently from RT. For example, a batter may be seen as having, at the minimum, two tasks: (1) to correctly *identify* a pitch and (2) to *choose* a motor response that will meet the objective of the game at that point in time (e.g., bunt). Since the ability to quickly identify a stimulus (perceptual speed) may be a trainable component of RT, it is included in the following discussions of the components of response time.

PERCEPTUAL SPEED

If a batter's problem lies in the inability to quickly identify a pitch, the practitioner may want to consider Marteniuk's (1976) suggestion. He recommends that the player view videotapes of pitches taken from behind the plate to learn to decrease the time he needs to identify a pitch (p. 7).

However, the practitioner needs to determine the specific task that is to be presented. For example, if the problem only occurs with a certain kind of pitch (e.g., a fastball), practice should be with that pitch. If the problem lies in an inability to discriminate quickly between two or more kinds of pitches (e.g., fastball and curve), pitches should be varied.

Needless to say, the player's task (e.g., "Indicate all the fastballs in a given variable sequence" versus "Indicate the kind of pitch: fastball, curve to the outside . . .") should be kept constant; only as the individual is ready to proceed to a higher level of identification (overload) should the task be changed. Overload is discussed further in the section at the end of this chapter on training. Suffice it to note here that the goal is to increase perceptual speed in the easier task before moving to the harder task.

There are other visual abilities, mentioned earlier, that would appear to profit from specific training in perceptual speed. For example, peripheral vision is an ability that may be seen as having important contributions to make to proficiency in basketball. Not only can we work to widen a player's field of vision, but we also might want to increase the speed with which peripheral vision operates. We should consider all perceptual abilities, auditory and tactile as well as visual, as possible candidates for training in perceptual speed. This is a very neglected area of research, and there is much to be learned.

SIMPLE REACTION TIME (RT)

There are a number of skills where RT training rather than training in perceptual speed would appear to be the more productive. When a specific movement response is to follow a specific stimulus, then practice should involve the initiation of the movement. The swimmer needs to react motorically as fast as possible to the sound of the starting gun. Timing devices for starting blocks in both track and swimming are available. In addition, there is considerable information on RT that should be useful to the practitioner in such cases (Sage, 1977). In summary, (1) RT to an auditory stimulus is fastest; a close second is RT to tactile stimuli, while RT to a visual stimulus (e.g., light) is about 20% slower than to auditory and tactile stimuli; (2) RT to tactile stimulation decreases as the site of stimulation occurs closer to the brain; (3) up to a point, the greater the intensity of the stimulus, the faster the RT; (4) RT is faster when a stimulus is preceded by a warning signal, such as "take your mark" in racing; and (5) attention to the stimulus (sensory set) rather than to the movement to be made (motor set) apparently results in a faster RT in racing starts (pp. 237-244).

CHOICE REACTION TIME (CRT)

RT in most motor skills is seldom as simple as that represented in a racing start. Usually, performers must make a choice or choices, and this increases RT. We speak of this as CRT. The choice may be a perceptual one, a motor one, or both. Whiting (1970) notes, for example, that in any ball game the particular response made will depend not only on the flight of the ball but also on the position of other players and the game strategy being used (p. 44).

Beginners are usually faced with a bewildering array of stimuli and need the practitioner's advice on where attention should be directed as well as on appropriate movement responses. At high-skill levels, players appear to have learned what cues are worth attending to, and therefore their CRT diminishes. Whiting (1970) suggests that this is usually brought about by a combination of experience in different game situations and good coaching. Although not speaking to coaches, Miller (1965, p. 213) suggests that we need to *train* for decision making at a cognitive level. According to Miller, the following kinds of information should be available to the decision maker: (1) the stimulus event that signals the need for a decision, (2) the goal priorities, (3) the response options and their implications, (4) the time allowable for a decision, and (5) the general strategy rules for selecting response alternatives. He emphasizes that when such information is lacking, training degenerates into an attempt to teach "all about the situation" after which the performer is thrown into the task where he either sinks or swims.

One of the most useful things the practitioner can do, it would seem, is to train players as to *when* each of the kinds of information noted in Miller's list should be attended to. For example, when a batter steps to the plate, most of the information should have already been considered. In addition, the information should not be given all at once; as you recall, short-term store (STS) is limited both by the amount of information it can handle and by time.

Obviously, the task of decision making in game strategy is often delegated to the coaches or to the team captain. Sometimes the quarterback calls the plays; at other times the plays are sent in from the bench. At times a coach will use a set play as in basketball; the game situation is anticipated (predecided), and an established and well-practiced play is run off without recourse to further decision making. In any case, both the practitioner and the performer need to know *who* is responsible for making *what* decisions and *when*. One method of training team members in systematic decision making is to have them serve in a coaching capacity (e.g., first- or third-base coach in baseball).

Miller (1965) makes a useful distinction between decision making and problem solving. He defines decision making as "the cognitive processes that lead to the selection of one from among a 'known' set of response alternatives—where these are known by the decisionmaker" (p. 222). On the other hand, he defines problem solving as "the activity of *inventing* or *improvising* resources and response alternatives beyond those already known to the operator" (p. 223). He suggests that we need to educate as well as train for inventive acts and implies that it is not sufficient to provide opportunities for problem solving; we need to provide, in addition, the criteria and time needed for contemplative analysis of the problem.

MOVEMENT TIME (MT)

As shown in Fig. 7-3, MT is the time taken from the start of a movement to its completion. Recall that RT and MT are relatively independent of each other; that is, an individual may react slowly to a specific stimulus (either because of perceptual problems or decision making demands) but evidence rapid speed of movement. Of course, the reverse is also possible, or the individual may be fast or slow in both.

However, the fact that RT and MT measures do not correlate does not mean that there are not important relationships between the two. Consider the following example in baseball batting (Hay, 1973).

> From the instant the ball is released by the pitcher, the batter has roughly half a second in which to hit it before it passes behind him into the catcher's mitt. During this time his first task is to evaluate the pitch and make his decision as to whether or not he will swing at the ball. In this part of the process, the longer the batter can study the flight of the ball before making his decision . . . the more likely it is that he will make the correct choice. . . . Having made the decision to swing, the batter's second task is to bring his bat around to meet the ball. . . . the shorter a batter's swing time, the longer his [viewing and] decision time and thus the higher the level of performance that he can produce (p. 211).

Breen (1967) reports the swing times of a number of major league players. He compares those players with high batting averages to a major league hitter whose batting average was less than .300. Using Breen's data, Hay (1973) depicts the

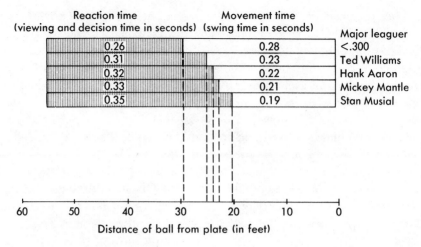

FIG. 7-4. Reaction time (RT) and movement time (MT) in batting. (Modified from Hay, J.G. *Biomechanics of sports techniques,* Englewood Cliffs, N.J.: Prentice-Hall, 1973; Based on data from Breen, J.L. What makes a good hitter. *Journal of Health, Physical Education, and Recreation,* 1967, 38, 36-39.)

relationship of swing time to the time allowable for perceptual and decision processes (p. 212). Fig. 7-4 indicates the respective lengths of each for a fastball pitch traveling at 104 feet per second. It should be noted that other interpretations of the time factors in batting exist (e.g., Newell, 1978). However, the important point being made here is that the batters with the shorter swing time (MT) can delay the commitment to swing until the ball is closer to the plate, thus allowing themselves more viewing and decision time (RT).

While we do not know the extent to which perceptual speed can be improved with practice, MT is primarily a result of practice. This involves not only the adaptation of motor abilities, such as muscular power and flexibility, to the specific skill, but also practice of the specific coordination requirements of the skill.

ANTICIPATORY TIMING

One of the most obvious talents of high-level performers is to make decisions on the basis of anticipation. For example, in the description of the skill of batting in the previous section, a batter was seen as having to anticipate from the initial flight characteristics of the pitch where and when the ball will cross the plate and to select and time a motor response so that it would be effective. Rothstein (1977a) describes anticipatory timing tasks.

These types of tasks require the performer to *predict* the future position of an object or target on the basis of current information and then organize and initiate a motor response so that its completion *coincides* with the arrival of the target at a predetermined point (interception point) (p. 205).

Various terms have been used to label this ability: *coincidence anticipation, prediction,* and *interval timing.* The term *anticipatory timing* is chosen here to emphasize that we are concerned both with perceptually anticipating the arrival of the object and with the timing of the motor response so as to intercept the object.

Although the difficulty of this task appears more obvious in open skills, such as intercepting a football, there is no reason to believe that the answers to anticipatory timing, when we get them, would not be useful in closed skills. Meanwhile, the question for the practitioner is how to assist the learner so that anticipatory timing might be developed more readily. There are three basic research approaches to the problem. Each of these has different implications for the practitioner.

Ability approach—Traditionally, research has attempted to determine the sensory and perceptual abilities, such as visual acuity and peripheral vision, contributing to proficiency. However, as Rothstein (1977b) notes, even assuming that we identify the perceptual abilities involved, we do not really know the extent to which such abilities might be increased by training, nor do we know whether improvements achieved through perceptual training will transfer to a specific anticipatory task such as throwing to a moving target. Recently, visual and perceptual ability training has become big business (e.g., Harrison & Reilly, 1975). To what extent is such training a viable technique for developing anticipatory timing? What little research has been done is equivocal (Rothstein, 1977b). However, we need to continue to seek answers, including field-based research.

Integration of input and output—Rothstein (1977a) notes that we need to study anticipatory timing in terms of all the information-processing components, rather than just the input or perceptual side. Motor control theorists (e.g., Kelso, 1977) are hypothesizing input-output interactions that have exciting possibilities for expanding our understanding of anticipatory timing. Kelso (1977), for example, speculates that when we preselect a movement, this "primes" the sensory systems so that they can process information more readily (called feedforward). Since the sensory systems can then handle information more easily, this frees the LCC to give attention to other details of the environment.

> For example, consider the highly skilled baseball outfielder reacting to a line drive. . . . The orientation of the player relative to the ball can be handled by feedforward, with central sensory systems ready to process incoming information. At the same time, however, sensory feedback systems can be directed toward other cues, such as the positional status of opposing players relative to the base (p. 250).

While admittedly speculative, this concept suggests that by preselecting a movement (influenced by past experience, of course), the individual can more readily process the information needed to effectively time the response. However, Kelso (1977) notes the developmental aspects of feedforward control: "That is, the beginner cannot adequately predict what the effects of his movement will be and hence must rely on continually monitoring peripheral feedback" (p. 250).

Developmental aspects—Stadulis (1972) emphasizes the developmental aspects of anticipatory timing and draws some implications for the practitioner.

> The physical educator, in preparing a program of instruction for coincidence-anticipation skill, should emphasize the nature and goal of the task first. Then he should stress the importance of visually focusing on the source of the object. After these preliminary phases, the learners should practice the interception movement response required for the particular skill. When the movement response seems reasonably learned, monitoring the object flight should be emphasized (p. 72).

Cratty (1980) also suggests that anticipatory timing tasks need to be simplified for children.

> Thus, even normal youngsters in their first experiences with moving objects should not have to deal with more than one stimulus at a time (not people and balls together); should be standing relatively still themselves when asked to judge where a moving object will arrive; and should be asked to judge the movement of things that are within a close distance to their bodies—from five to ten feet away (p. 137).

Ridenour (1977), however, reports highly developed object interception during the first 6 months of life. Wade (1980), studying anticipatory timing in children from 8½ to 14 years of age, notes differences that suggest that the younger and older children may apply different strategies. He and his colleagues are continuing to attempt to evaluate the relative contributions of perception and movement in anticipatory timing (p. 109).

It is hoped that research will soon answer the question as to whether anticipatory timing can be more readily developed by part practice (e.g., perceptual practice and motor practice) or by variable whole practice in which the individual is seen to build up input-output relational schemes between perception and action (e.g., Schmidt, 1977) or both at different ages. Meanwhile, it would seem that all avenues of investigation should continue, and practitioners should not lock themselves into practices implied by a single theory. As Stadulis (1972) notes,

> Too few task component and development analyses have been attempted for the many motor skills physical educators teach. It seems imperative that motor skills be studied and analyzed, from many different emphases, if we are to arrive at optimal teaching strategies in physical education (p. 73).

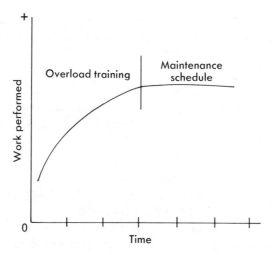

FIG. 7-5. Work performed during overload training and maintenance schedule.

Principles of training

It is not within the purview of this book to deal with particular training or conditioning regimens. However, a major assumption of the ability-skill concept is that ability development can contribute to motor skill learning. Therefore it seems desirable to emphasize two major principles of training—overload and specificity—together with a brief example of each.

OVERLOAD

As was noted above, the ability-skill concept presupposes that abilities can be improved with practice. The question is, What kind of practice? The overload principle used so successfully in the development of muscular strength and endurance is assumed to be applicable to other abilities as well. Briefly, the overload principle requires that a person subject whatever is to be developed to a progressively increasing work load. Once a desired level is reached, the ability can be maintained by continuing at approximately that level. Fig. 7-5 depicts this relationship.

In motor ability training this overload may be achieved by progressively increasing (1) the speed of the performance, (2) the weight load, (3) the number of repetitions, or (4) a combination of these.

> For example, suppose an athlete, at the beginning of a program, can curl 80 pounds eight times before fatigue sets in. That amount of overload may be used until the athlete can make perhaps twelve lifts before becoming fatigued. At that

time, the load should be increased to such a degree that the number of repetitions to the point of fatigue is once again reduced to eight. This pattern should be repeated as often as required throughout the duration of the program (Fox, 1979, p. 122).

Overload training presumably applies to the development of all abilities. For example, flexibility training requires that the muscle be stretched beyond its normal length. In passive stretch, stretching until it hurts may be effective.

SPECIFICITY*

The evidence for specificity in training in muscular power and endurance is overwhelming (e.g., McCafferty & Horvath, 1979). Not only does training have to be designed in terms of the type of muscular strength required but also in terms of the specific muscles involved in the activity. Thus training for high-intensity, short-term (anaerobic) activities, such as sprinting, requires a different training regimen than for low-intensity, long-term (aerobic) endurance events, such as marathon running. Paup (1980) has summarized some of the considerations in regard to *metabolic specificity* and their implications for the practitioner:

1. For training purposes, the practitioner-trainer must determine the predominate energy system used for muscle contraction in the specific skill: anaerobic power activities, such as sprinting, that last up to about 30 seconds; anaerobic activities, such as middle-distance running, that last between 1 and 2 minutes; or aerobic endurance events, such as running, cycling, and swimming, that last from a few minutes to several hours. For improvement to occur through training, the specific intensity and duration of the training activity must simulate the intensity and duration of the activity. Thus sprinting activities are not improved by distance running and vice versa.

2. Training using upper body musculature does not improve performance in activities, such as cycling and running, that involve lower extremity musculature. In a like manner, a high level of fitness for swimming does not transfer to running even though the intensity and duration of the workouts are similar. Obviously, then, training must involve the specific muscles that are to be used.

A training program, even when designed for the particular muscle groups involved in an activity and for the intensity and duration of that activity, does not suffice to bring about the specific muscular strength or endurance required for high proficiency on that skill. As was noted at the beginning of this chapter, abilities must be adapted to the specific skill. Fox (1979) notes that this type of specificity is most apparent in athletes who participate in back-to-back seasonal

---

*I am grateful to Dr. Donald C. Paup, Professor of Exercise Physiology at The George Washington University, for his contributions to this section.

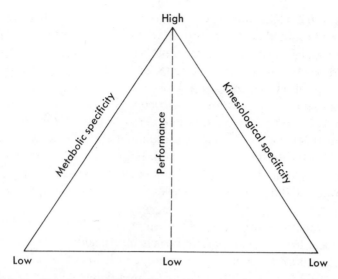

FIG. 7-6. Predicted performance relationship to levels of specificity in training: metabolic specificity and kinesiological specificity. (From Paup, D.C. Personal communication, August 1980.)

sports. "Thus the football player who is in excellent condition to play football is in poor condition to play basketball," despite the fact that both activities involve the same general muscle groups (p. 124). Logan and McKinney (1977) recommend specific resistive exercise through the plane of motion, range of motion, and joint angles "used by the athlete while performing skills in the athletic contest" (p. 253). Paup (1980) terms this *kinesiological specificity,* and in Fig. 7-6 he depicts the mutual contribution of metabolic specificity, mentioned earlier, and kinesiological specificity to peak performance. As can be seen, only as training becomes specific in either or both components, can performance on a specific skill be expected to improve through training.

GENERAL DEVELOPMENT PROGRAMS

If abilities are so specific, what then can be said in favor of the ability-skill concept and ability development? It seems important here to make a distinction between training and education. In training we are most often concerned with conditioning the individual for peak performance in a specific skill (e.g., marathon running); in education we are charged with developing in individuals the capacity for engaging in whatever activities they may select—now or later. Thus a general ability development program always has been and should remain a major focus of physical education.

However, the evidence on specificity of abilities suggests that such developmental programs should be different from what they have been in the past. If you are going to develop flexibility, for example, all of the major muscle groups and joints should be stretched. Fox (1979, pp. 346-352), for example, recommends consideration of all of the following areas: Achilles tendon, neck, back, hamstrings, groin, spine and waistline, quadriceps, shoulder and chest, ankle, abdominals, and hip. In the general development of strength, isokinetic exercise, in which maximal tension is developed throughout the full range of joint movement, would appear to be the most useful, since this could be seen as having greater transfer to a variety of skills. In addition, interval training can be regulated so as to develop either the anaerobic or aerobic energy systems (Fox, 1979, p. 199).

The fact remains, however, that few such systematic general development programs appear to be in operation in the schools. In addition, while considerable information exists for the design of motor development programs (e.g., Fox, 1979; Lamb, 1978), there is little systematic attention to perceptual development programs in physical education. While such programs have been advocated (e.g., Cratty, 1979), most have been designed for children with learning disabilities (e.g., Ayres, 1972; Kephart, 1971). Harrison and Reilly (1975), among others, have devised some general training techniques for eye control and concentration that might hold some interest for the practitioner, and optometric training programs have been advocated. However, research is lacking on the effectiveness of such programs (Rothstein, 1977b). This would seem to be a very neglected area and one that physical educators should pursue.

Sample thought sheet

1. For each of the perceptual and motor abilities listed below, give a specific example (not used in the text) of a motor skill requiring a high level of the ability.
   - a. Muscular power
   - b. Endurance
   - c. Flexibility
   - d. Static balance
   - e. Dynamic visual acuity
   - f. Peripheral vision
   - g. Figure-ground differentiation
   - h. Sound localization
2. Select a specific game situation. List the factors that you as a teacher, coach, or performer must consider to determine the strategy (decision choices) you will take.
3. Give an example (not used in the text) of each of the following in terms of a specific motor or perceptual ability.
   - a. Overload training
   - b. Specificity of training
4. Describe how you would expect overarousal (discussed in Chapter 6) to affect each of the skills you listed in No. 1 above.

References

Ayres, A.J. *Sensory integration and learning disorders.* Los Angeles: Western Psychological Services, 1972.

Brace, D.K. Studies in motor learning of gross bodily skills. *Research Quarterly,* 1946, *17,* 242-253.

Breen, J.L. What makes a good hitter. *Journal of Health, Physical Education, and Recreation,* 1967, *38,* 36-39.

Corbin, C.B., & Noble, L. Flexibility: a major component of fitness. *Journal of Physical Education and Recreation,* June 1980, *23,* 57-60.

Cratty, B.J. A three-level theory of perceptual-motor behavior. *Quest,* 1966, *6,* 2-10.

Cratty, B.J. *Perceptual and motor development in infants and children* (2nd ed.). Englewood Cliffs, N.J.: Prentice-Hall, 1979.

Cratty, B.J. *Adapted physical education for handicapped children and youth.* Denver: Love, 1980.

deVries, H.A. *Physiology of exercise.* Dubuque, Iowa: William C. Brown, 1980.

Fitts, P.M. Engineering psychology and equipment design. In S.S. Stevens (Ed.), *Handbook of experimental psychology.* New York: Wiley, 1951.

Fitts, P.M. Factors in complex skill training. In R. Glaser (Ed.), *Training research and education.* Pittsburgh: University of Pittsburgh Press, 1962. (Republished, New York: Wiley, 1965.)

Fleishman, E.A. The description and prediction of perceptual-motor skill learning. In R. Glaser (Ed.), *Training research and education.* Pittsburgh: University of Pittsburgh Press, 1962. (Republished, New York: Wiley, 1965.)

Fleishman, E.A. *The structure and measurement of physical fitness.* Englewood Cliffs, N.J.: Prentice-Hall, 1964.

Fleishman, E.A., & Hempel, W.E., Jr. The relation between abilities and improvement with practice in a visual discrimination reaction task. *Journal of Experimental Psychology,* 1955, *49,* 301-310.

Fox, E.L. *Sports physiology.* Philadelphia: Saunders, 1979.

Gallahue, D.L. The relationship between perceptual and motor abilities. *Research Quarterly,* 1968, *39,* 948-952.

Harris, M.L. A factor analytic study of flexibility. *Research Quarterly,* 1969, *40,* 62-70.

Harrison, B., & Reilly, R.E. *Visiondynamics: baseball method.* 23862 Wavespray Circle, Laguna Niguel, Calif.: Visiondynamics: Success Through Perceptual Awareness, 1975.

Hay, J.G. *Biomechanics of sports techniques.* Englewood Cliffs, N.J.: Prentice-Hall, 1973.

Henry, F.M., Lotter, W.S., & Smith, L.E. Factorial structure of individual differences in limb speed, reaction, and strength. *Research Quarterly,* 1962, *33,* 70-84.

Jacobson, E. *Progressive relaxation.* Chicago: University of Chicago Press, 1938.

Jacobson, E. *Teaching and learning: new methods for old arts.* Chicago: National Foundation for Progressive Relaxation, 1973.

Kelso, J.A.S. Motor control mechanisms in timing behavior. In R.E. Stadulis (Ed.), *Research and practice in physical education: selected papers from the 1976 Research Symposia of the AAHPER National Convention.* Champaign, Ill.: Human Kinetics, 1977.

Kephart, N.C. *The slow learner in the classroom* (2nd ed.). Columbus, Ohio: Merrill, 1971.

Kohen-Raz, R. The role of static balance in cognitive development. In U. Simei (Ed.), *Motor learning in physical education and sport: proceedings of an international seminar.* Israel: Wingate Institute for Physical Education and Sport, 1976, pp. 281-289.

Lamb, D.R. *Physiology of exercise.* New York: MacMillan, 1978.

Logan, G.A., & McKinney, W.C. *Anatomic kinesiology* (2nd ed.). Dubuque, Iowa: William C. Brown, 1977.

Marteniuk, R.G. *Information processing in motor skills.* New York: Holt, Rinehart and Winston, 1976.

McCafferty, W.B., & Horvath, S.M. Specificity of exercise and specificity of training: a subcellular review. *Research Quarterly,* 1979, *48,* 358-371.

McCraw, L.W. A factory analysis of motor learning. *Research Quarterly*, 1949, 20, 316-335.

Miller, R.B. Task description and analysis. In R.M. Gagne (Ed.), *Psychological principles of system development*. New York: Holt, Rinehart and Winston, 1965.

Morris, G.S.D. Dynamic visual acuity: implications for the physical educator and coach. *Motor Skills: Theory into Practice*, 1977, 2, 15-30.

Newell, K.M. Decision processes of baseball batters. In W.F. Straub (Ed.), *Sport psychology: an analysis of athlete behavior* (2nd ed.). Ithaca, N.Y.: Mouvement Publications, 1978.

Parker, J.F., & Fleishman, E.A. Use of analytical information concerning task requirements to increase the effectiveness of skill training. *Journal of Applied Psychology*, 1961, 45, 295-302.

Paup, D.C. Personal communication, August, 1980.

Pleasants, F. Kinesthesis: that uncertain feeling. *The Physical Educator*, March 1971, pp. 36-38.

President's Council on Physical Fitness and Sport. Basic understanding of physical fitness. *Physical Fitness Research Digest*, 1971, 1, 1-12.

Ridenour, M.V. The development of static and dynamic spatial relationships influencing object interception in infancy. In R.E. Stadulis (Ed.), *Research and practice in physical education: selected papers from the 1976 Research Symposia of the AAHPER National Convention*. Champaign, Ill.: Human Kinetics, 1977.

Rothstein, A.L. Prediction in sport: an information processing approach. In R.E. Stadulis (Ed.), *Research and practice in physical education: selected papers from the 1976 Symposia of the AAHPER National Convention*. Champaign, Ill.: Human Kinetics, 1977a.

Rothstein, A.L. Prediction in sport: visual factors. In R.E. Stadulis (Ed.), *Research and practice in physical education: selected papers from the 1976 Symposia of the AAHPER National Convention*. Champaign, Ill.: Human Kinetics, 1977b.

Sage, G.H. *Introduction to motor behavior: a neuropsychological approach* (2nd ed.). Reading, Mass.: Addison-Wesley, 1977.

Sanborn, C., & Wyrick, W. Prediction of Olympic balance beam performance from standardized and modified tests of balance. *Research Quarterly*, 1969, 40, 174-184.

Schmidt, R.A. Schema theory: implications for movement education. *Motor Skills: Theory into Practice*, 1977, 2, 36-38.

Sharpe, R.H. Visual information-processing in ball games: some input considerations. In F. Landry & W.A.R. Orban (Eds.), *Motor learning, sport psychology, and the didactics of physical activity*. Miami: Symposia Specialists, 1978.

Singer, R.N. *Motor learning and human performance* (2nd ed.). New York: Macmillan, 1975.

Singer, R.N. *Motor learning and human performance* (3rd ed.). New York: Macmillan, 1980.

Smith, H.M. Implications for movement education experiences drawn from perceptual-motor research. *Journal of Health, Physical Education, and Recreation*, April 1970, pp. 30-33.

Stadulis, R.E. Motor skill analysis: coincidence-anticipation. *Quest*, 1972, 17, 70-73.

Steinhaus, A.H. Facts and theories of neuromuscular relaxation. *Quest*, 1964, 3, 3-14.

Stroupe, F. Relationship between measurements of field of motion perception and basketball ability in college men. *Research Quarterly*, 1957, 28, 72-76.

Wade, M.G. Coincidence anticipation of young normal and handicapped children. *Journal of Motor Behavior*, 1980, 12, 103-112.

Whiting, H.T.A. *Acquiring ball skill: a psychological interpretation*. Philadelphia: Lea & Febiger, 1970.

Williams, H.G. Sensory-motor integration: an overview. In R.E. Stadulis (Ed.), *Research and practice in physical education: selected papers from the 1976 Research Symposia of the AAHPER National Convention*. Champaign, Ill.: Human Kinetics, 1977.

8 SKILL ANALYSIS

Because the nature of a skill is an important factor in learning that skill, we need to ask ourselves how skills differ. For example, you are already familiar with the categorization of motor skills as open or closed. However, there are a number of classification schemes for motor skills, each of which may serve a particular purpose. It is not my intention to present each of these in this chapter. Readers who desire more information on classifications of motor skills would do well to begin with the article by Merrill (1972).

The more important question for the practitioner is What kinds of skill analysis will contribute to the design of more effective instruction? For example, motor skills are often classified as either fine or gross, depending on the size of muscle groups involved or the spatial dimensions of the movement, but this differentiation is not very useful to the practitioner. Since the main purpose of this book is to present concepts applicable to the practical situation, discussion is purposely limited to methods of skill analysis that can be seen to have application to instruction and training. Obviously, not all applicable methods of skill analysis can be included. For example, kinesiological or biomechanical analysis of a skill is a critical prerequisite to teaching a skill effectively. However, the concepts presented here, if used together with biomechanical analysis, should provide the practitioner with a more complete basis for designing instruction.

Expert opinion

One approach to analyzing the nature of a specific skill is to "tap" the experiences of those people who devote their energies to teaching or coaching that skill. A common method of gaining this information is by attending workshops and clinics. Most practitioners are sincerely interested in skill analysis, and the experiences of those who have expertise in the development of specific skills are valuable sources of information. However, as practitioners we need to be cognizant of the fact that experience does not replace research; we must always be aware that new information may be forthcoming that may call into question a popular view of the essential elements of a skill. Consider the following example in golf putting.

One of the traditional admonitions of golf instructors when teaching a putt has been "Keep your eye on the ball." Cockerill (1980), however, has found that low-handicap golfers perform equally well when looking at the hole. In addition, nongolfers in the study tended to putt to the right of the hole when looking at the ball rather than at the hole. Cockerill suggests that the "eyes on the hole" method, used from the beginning, might lead to greater accuracy in the long run.

This would appear to be a logical conclusion if you take into consideration some of the information-processing demands of the golf putt and compare them with those of other target skills, such as throwing a ball. As Cockerill (1980) notes,

> When individuals are able to hold an object to be projected at a target, they invariably attend to the target when taking aim, thereby affording themselves continuous monitoring of the perceived distance between the projectile and the target. However, when putting a golf ball, perhaps in order to ensure that the clubhead makes good contact, vision is focused upon the ball with the associated need to remember the precise distance from ball to hole. Since concentration upon making a sound stroke is likely to be greater than upon retaining an image of target distance, it is likely that there will be rapid decay in maintaining the latter (p. 379).

Cockerill suggests that by emphasizing a square club face at impact, practitioners can teach beginners a mechanically sound, smooth putting stroke that is consistent over a range of distances while using the "eyes on the hole" approach (pp. 383-384).

What does this say about the efficacy of expert opinion in skill analysis? Only that the opinion needs to be considered together with other methods of skill analysis. Certainly, it is difficult to argue with the successful coach or performer. However, in the long run the question for the practitioner is How much more successful or effective can I be? It becomes a matter not of good or bad teaching, but of good teaching and better teaching.

In addition, definitive methods of skill analysis could contribute much to the value of workshops and clinics. With such methods it is possible that communication between individuals with expertise in a specific activity could result in models of the structure of the skills that would lead to more effective instructional and training programs. In the remainder of this chapter several such methods are presented for consideration. However, they will be most useful if the practitioner views them as cumulative steps to skill analysis.

Factor structure

One approach to analyzing the nature of a skill has been by means of factor analyses. A description of these techniques is beyond the scope of this book.

Suffice it to note here that the results depend, to a large extent, on the subjective interpretation of the researcher using the techniques. Generally, the elements (e.g., abilities) supposedly required by a skill are hypothesized from the literature, a battery of tests, including performance tests on the skill, is used to measure each of the abilities administered, and the resulting correlations are subjected to factor analyses. The researcher comes up with a set of skill requirements, which, through the factor analyses, are shown to be relatively independent of each other (e.g., have low correlations).

The most extensive work on the ability composition of motor skills has been that of Fleishman and his colleagues (Fleishman, 1964, 1972). Fleishman's (1964) ability-skill concept was described briefly in the previous chapter. It assumes that the extent to which individuals possess the particular abilities required by a skill will influence, in part, both their rate of learning that skill and the proficiency they attain.

Despite the fact that there has been some criticism of Fleishman's use of factor analysis (e.g., Bechtoldt, 1970; Henry, 1970), the ability-skill concept and its usefulness to the practitioner, at least, has gained wide recognition. Therefore it seems desirable to go into the findings of Fleishman and his colleagues in more depth. These can best be analyzed by referring to Fig. 8-1.

The skill involved in Fleishman and Hempel's study (1954) was a piloting task that required coordinated manipulation of stick and rudder in response to visual patterns. Scores obtained at eight different stages of practice were correlated with performance on a battery of printed and apparatus tests. The findings noted here, however, are not limited to this particular skill; over 20 years' work by Fleishman and his colleagues, studying a wide range of psychomotor skills, led to the conclusions (Fleishman, 1972, p. 99) that are summarized here:

1. A particular combination of factors contributes to performance on a specific skill.
2. There is a change in the nature of the factors that contribute to performance as proficiency increases from beginning to terminal stages of learning.
3. A factor specific to performance on the skill increases with practice and, indeed, comprises the major component of the skill in the later stages of learning.

To appreciate the implications of these findings for skill analysis, and therefore instruction, each is discussed here in more depth.

ABILITY COMPOSITION OF A SKILL

In the piloting skill analyzed by Fleishman and Hempel (1954) the particular abilities contributing to proficiency can be seen in Fig. 8-1 (e.g., psychomotor coordination and speed of movement). Obviously, not all motor skills require the

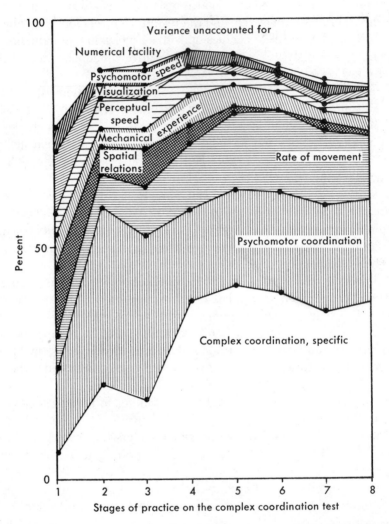

FIG. 8-1. Changes in factor structure of a psychomotor skill. (From Fleishman, E.A., & Hempel, W.E., Jr. Changes in factor structure of a complex psychomotor test as a function of practice. *Psychometrika,* 1954, *19,* 239-252.)

same combination of abilities. Fleishman (1962, 1964) differentiates between psychomotor abilities (derived primarily from studies of manipulative skills and limb coordination tasks) and abilities in the physical proficiency area (athletic skills). While the athletic skills are seen to involve abilities such as strength, flexibility, and balance, manipulative skills have been shown to involve abilities such as those shown in Fig. 8-1.

In addition, even when different skills require some of the same abilities, the extent to which each ability contributes to proficiency of the skill will probably differ. For example, ankle, shoulder, and trunk flexibility seem to contribute to more effective performance in swimmers; research with joggers, however, shows no better performance among the more flexible than the less flexible (Corbin & Noble, 1980, p. 58). This is not to say, however, that flexibility is not desirable in joggers, only that it is not a limiting factor. The exact minimum necessary is probably specific to each skill; levels of the ability greater than the minimum may not result in greater levels of proficiency (Corbin & Noble, 1980, p. 58). This suggests that an important criterion for the practitioner hypothesizing the abilities contributing to proficiency on a skill might be the extent to which lack of the ability would be a limiting factor.

The unfortunate fact is that few factor analyses of specific sports skills have been carried out, and also unfortunate is the fact that the prospects for this situation changing in the near future do not appear promising. Nevertheless, as Singer (1975) notes, "The recognition of those abilities required for task proficiency assists in understanding task requirements more fully" (p. 227).

In the absence of studies of the ability composition of specific skills, the practitioner is left the task of hypothesizing the contributing abilities by subjectively analyzing the skill. There are obvious dangers in this, but the advantages appear to outweigh the disadvantages as long as the practitioner keeps in mind that the results of such subjective analyses are hypotheses, not facts. Obviously, the practitioner cannot be expected to arrive at a percent contribution for each of the abilities as shown in Fig. 8-1; however, a gross estimate of the major abilities contributing to the skill, in the order of their importance, is possible. Such an estimate for the skill of baseball batting is shown on p. 178.

There is little doubt that this type of skill analysis could be useful to the practitioner. Some of these uses were discussed in the previous chapter and included (1) aiding in identification of an individual's particular performance problem (e.g., dynamic visual acuity or flexibility), (2) structuring an individualized training program to meet the performer's deficiencies (e.g., power), and (3) giving advance information to help ensure that performers will make use of the ability in the game situation (e.g., peripheral vision). As Parker and Fleishman (1961) have demonstrated, when instruction stresses the particular ability re-

---

Hypothesized ability composition of baseball batting

Abilities are listed in order of their importance to high proficiency

1. Anticipatory timing, including
    perceptual speed
    reaction time
    movement time
2. Dynamic balance
3. Muscular power of forearm and triceps
4. Flexibility of upper extremities and neck
5. Visual figure-ground
6. Depth perception

From Breen, J.L. Personal communication, December 1980.

quirements of a skill, learners show more rapid progress. This suggests that although performers may possess the abilities required, they are more apt to make use of them when given knowledge regarding their contribution to proficiency. In addition, if we as practitioners are cognizant of the ability composition of a skill, we can design preseason training so as to help fulfill the individual's potential in these abilities. Thus an analysis of the ability composition of a skill would appear to be helpful as long as we keep in mind its subjectivity and continually work to revise and refine it.

CHANGES DURING PRACTICE

A common assumption is that an individual's level of performance in the early stages of learning is somehow indicative of the final proficiency that he can attain. Such as assumption is implicit in the practice of selecting team personnel on the basis of their performance in initial practice sessions (and may also account, at least in part, for the designation of some individuals as slow learners). However, Fleishman (1972) and his colleagues have demonstrated, rather convincingly, that the ability composition of a skill may change as practice continues and proficiency increases. For example, in Fig. 8-1 the rate of movement contributes more to proficiency in the later stages of practice than in the earlier stages. Moreover, the ability composition of the skill becomes relatively stabilized in the later stages of practice (Fleishman, 1972, p. 99). In Fig. 8-1 the ability composition of the piloting task is essentially the same from a midlearning point (stage 5) through the terminal session (stage 8). This suggests that although the practitioner might best proceed by analyzing the ability composition of a skill in terms

Table 4 □ *Percent contribution of motor and nonmotor factors during initial and final stages of learning a psychomotor skill*

	Initial stages	Final stages
Motor factors	29.5%	74.5%
Nonmotor factors	41.6%	10.5%

Modified from Fleishman, E.A., and Hempel, W.E., Jr. Changes in factor structure of a complex psychomotor test as a function of practice. *Psychometrika*, 1954, *19*, 239-252.

of its requirements at high levels of proficiency, the fact that the beginner may require somewhat different abilities cannot be ignored. Therefore we need to examine this change in ability requirements in more depth.

If the factors contributing to performance on the piloting skill, as shown in Fig. 8-1, are classified as *nonmotor* (spatial relations, perceptual speed, visualization, etc.) or *motor* (coordination, rate of movement, etc.), there will be a shift from initial to final stages of practice, as shown in Table 4, in terms of the percent contribution of each of these categories of abilities. Although the ratio of nonmotor to motor abilities could be expected to vary with the nature of the skill (the contribution of motor abilities could be expected to be greater in athletic skills), the question of interest to the practitioner is What is the nature of these nonmotor factors that contribute to proficiency in the early stages of learning?

Fleishman and Hempel (1955) suggest that perceptual learning of the spatial characteristics of a skill is a minimal but necessary requirement for early progress; however, once the spatial characteristics are learned, other abilities assume increasing importance. There are other conditions that may be operating as well. The most obvious of these are the methods of instruction used by the practitioner. If early instruction is primarily visual, you would expect that visual abilities would appear as early learning requirements. In like manner, verbal abilities would be seen to be required if instruction is predominantly verbal. It is important to note that studies of the ability requirements of specific skills have often failed to differentiate between those ability requirements intrinsic to the skill itself and those that may be a function of the learning process or the methods of instruction (e.g., Stallings, 1968). Thus the practitioner needs to differentiate between the requirements of the *skill* and the requirements of the *task* imposed on the learner by the methods of instruction.

Analyzing a skill in terms of its information-processing demands is discussed later in this chapter. Suffice it to note here that this method of analysis suffers the same problem. We need to take into consideration the fact that much of early learning is perceptual and cognitive in nature, not just because of specific perceptual requirements of the skill, but also because of the need to perceptually "get the idea of the skill" and to interpret instruction.

INCREASE IN SPECIFICITY

Fleishman (1972) and his colleagues, among others, have demonstrated that a factor specific to performance on a particular skill increases in importance during learning and, indeed, comprises the major factor contributing to proficiency in the final stages of practice. In the piloting task, represented in Fig. 8-1, Fleishman and Hempel (1954) term this a "complex coordination specific" factor, and Fleishman (1962) suggests that it might include an "integration" factor, that is, the capacity to integrate or pattern the basic abilities required by that particular skill. Cratty (1966) suggests that the specifics of a skill might include such factors as its unique energy, force, and velocity requirements, as well as the specific spatial-temporal dimensions of the movement.

Although the nature of this skill-specific factor remains speculative, its importance to skill analysis and to the design of effective instruction requires that some assumptions be made. Fig. 8-2 is an attempt to dissect the skill specifics by bringing together information on the specificity of skills presented earlier in this book. Basically, the information provided by Paup (1980) in Fig. 7-6 has been superimposed on a modification of Cratty's (1966) three-level theory (see also Fig. 7-1) with some additions. Let's look at the top level of the triangle in Fig. 8-2 labeled skill specifics. While highly speculative, this conceptualization assumes that there are at least three skill-specific factors: (1) kinesiological specificity, (2) metabolic specificity, and (3) environmental specificity.

Kinesiological specificity—Kinesiological specificity would include the unique spatial-temporal and force patterning of the skill. Even though a tennis smash may appear (especially to the beginner) to look like an overhand throw pattern or a badminton smash, they are not the same. Anderson (1979), in an electromyographic and cinematographic study of the overhand throw and tennis serve, found important differences in the patterning of the two skills. Although she suggests that because of these differences reference to one to facilitate transfer to the other may not be advisable, such use in the initial stage of learning to "get an idea of the movement" may not be detrimental if the practitioner is aware of the specificity of each and emphasizes differences as practice proceeds.

Metabolic specificity—Metabolic specificity was described in some detail in the previous chapter. The energy source needed for muscular power events was seen as being different from that required for endurance events. In addition, strength is specific not only to the intensity and duration of the skill, but also to the specific muscles involved. Obviously, both the kinesiological and the metabolic specificity of skills demand not only that the practitioner analyze the skill in terms of these requirements, but also provide for practice on the skill as a whole. Fleishman (1972) notes that retention of proficiency on a skill is a function not

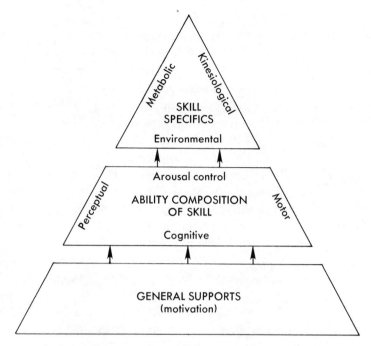

FIG. 8-2. Ability composition of a skill and skill specifics.

only of the individual's initial prepractice abilities, but also of the specific habits acquired in practicing the skill itself (p. 103).

Environmental specificity—An unfortunate fact is that we often think of a skill as a movement pattern executed in isolation of the performance situation. Although at this point it is hoped that you will have been convinced that the practice of hitting a ball off a batting tee ignores some of the basic requirements of batting (e.g., perceptual identification and anticipatory timing), less often recognized is the fact that *all* the ingredients of the performance environment (e.g., batter's box, catcher, umpire, baserunners) should be present in the learning environment if maximal proficiency is to be ensured in the actual performance situation. In addition, uncontrollable distractions, such as altitude, sun, and audience, must be made a part of the learning situation. It is problematical when each of these can be introduced, depending on the particular learner; the best advice would appear to be "the sooner, the better" (Arnold, 1978). In any case, it should be obvious that skills need to be analyzed in terms of what is required for proficiency in the actual performance situation, not as movements carried out in isolation.

OPTIMAL AROUSAL LEVEL

Chapter 6 on arousal level and motivation emphasized that skills differ in the optimal arousal level conducive to proficiency on the skill; arousal control was viewed as the process of increasing or decreasing arousal level consistent with the perceptual, motor, and cognitive abilities required by the skill. Although Fleishman and Hempel (1954) did not test for arousal level in their study, Fleishman (1962) did suggest that part of the "variance unaccounted for" in Fig. 8-1 might be motivational in nature. Therefore arousal control is included as part of the ability composition of a skill shown in Fig. 8-2.

When considering the evidence for a change in the ability requirements of a skill during learning, you would also expect that the optimal arousal level for early learning would be different than for later stages of learning. The early learning period, characterized by heavy perceptual and cognitive demands, could be expected to require a relatively low level of arousal.

In summary, the practitioner needs to analyze a skill in terms of its perceptual, motor, and cognitive requirements (and associated optimal arousal level) as these change during learning. In addition, the increasing specificity (metabolic, kinesiological, and environmental) of the skill must be considered. Although metabolic and kinesiological specificity are not a focus of this book, they are critical aspects of skill analysis. The need for considering environmental specifics is emphasized throughout this book.

Scales for skill analysis

It has already been noted that skills can be dichotomized on the basis of any one of several criteria, as, for example, open or closed, fine or gross. However, motor skills are seldom a matter of either-or. Thus the concept of continuums or scales to differentiate skills appears to be more useful to the practitioner. A particular skill can then be described as falling on different portions of several scales. However, not all such scales are particularly useful to the practitioner (e.g., fine to gross and simple to complex). The scales discussed in this section are those that appear to have the most relevance to the practitioner in the design of instruction.

CONTINUITY AND COHERENCE

According to Fitts (1962), movements (or stimuli), regardless of their particular form, can be specified by several characteristics, including their degrees of continuity and coherence. These are mentioned briefly here to give you an idea of the concept of a continuum or scale.

Continuity—The continuity of a skill is determined by the duration of its movement sequences and the occurrence of pauses between sequences (Fitts,

1962, p. 181). Several motor skills have been placed on a continuum from continuous to discrete in the scale below.

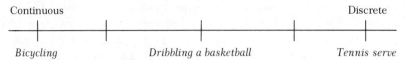

In this scale, bicycling falls toward the continuous end of the scale and a tennis serve toward the discrete end. When discrete movements follow each other rapidly, the skill is often called a serial skill (e.g., typing). Continuous skills can generally be learned more rapidly than discrete skills and are usually retained longer because repetitions of the movement (practice to overlearning) are an inherent part of the skill.

Coherence—A skill is coherent to the extent that there is dependence between successive movements (Fitts, 1962, p. 181). Thus walking, skating, and diving are relatively coherent skills. As shown in the scale below, swimming and handwriting are skills that might be placed nearer the middle of this scale.

The assumption in the scale is that few motor skills, as defined in this book, can be classified as noncoherent. (You are encouraged to construct your own scales on the basis of your experience.) The more coherent a skill, the more difficult it is to break it down into parts for the purposes of instruction and practice and, at the same time, maintain its integrity as a specific skill. For example, a cartwheel depends on the momentum from the initial parts of the movement to achieve the maximally effective inverted position.

SELF-PACED–EXTERNALLY PACED

Fitts (1962) suggests that the analysis of skills might begin with a determination of the nature of the stimulus and movement conditions prior to the execution of the skill. In certain skills the body is at rest prior to the beginning of the movement, and the object involved (e.g., basketball goal, golf ball) is relatively fixed or stable. Other skills are initiated while both the individual and object are moving. Specific skills illustrating these and intermediate conditions are shown on the scale below, ranging from self-paced skills to externally paced skills.

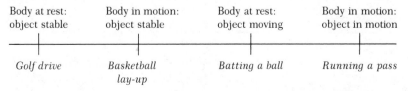

The interest here is in the extent to which the nature of the skill allows the individual to "get set" for the action, that is, the extent to which the action is self-paced or externally paced. It should be noted that the skill must be viewed as including the situation in which the skill is performed. For example, in a basketball foul shot the performer is at rest prior to the shot, whereas in shooting from the floor the performer is usually in motion or at the least constrained by the movements of opponents in the time allowable to "get set" for the shot.

Fitts (1962) notes that as an individual moves from left to right on the scale shown above, skills become more difficult to analyze in terms of their constancies, that is, the essentials of the movement that increase the likelihood of success. "Only the end result appears to be constant and only by considering means-end relationships is the nature of the constancies revealed" (p. 179). For example, the basketball player, in making a field shot for the goal, will use whatever type of shot (hook, lay-up, jump) is needed to score. More will be said of this later; however, the need for realistic (scrimmage) practice in such a situation is obvious.

OPEN-CLOSED

Closely related to Fitts's (1962) analysis of skills in terms of their pacing is the more recent designation of skills as open or closed. As you recall, open skills are skills in which the particular action plan or movement is regulated by variable or changing events in the performance environment. The field shot for the goal, mentioned in the previous paragraph, is an example of an open skill. Conversely, the performance of closed skills is regulated by a single set of environmental conditions (Arnold, 1978). Thus the swimmer in performing a racing start reacts to the sound of the starting gun with a consistent movement. Note that a particular motor skill (e.g., a racing start) can be both closed and externally paced. Therefore the pacing of a skill and its categorization as open or closed should probably be considered independently. Later the desirability of profiling a skill on the basis of several criteria will be emphasized.

On the scale below are certain skills ranging from closed to open in terms of the extent to which effective execution of the skill requires adapting movement to the particular performance conditions. It should be obvious that skills lying on the right of the scale require a flexibility of movement response, while those on the left require a relatively stereotyped movement.

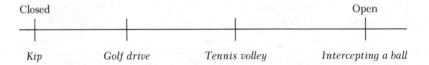

Closed   Open

Kip   Golf drive   Tennis volley   Intercepting a ball

Arnold (1978) cites target archery as an example of a closed skill (performed in a relatively fixed environment and requiring the development of a highly consistent movement pattern).

> Indeed, the learner is instructed to position his/her body in a consistent location on the shooting line, draw to a consistent anchor point, employ a consistent point of aim . . . (p. 84).

Conversely, successful performance in tennis stroking, characterized by variable game conditions (ball position, speed, spin, and opponent's position), requires a diversification of movement.

> Not only must the learner develop, for example, both baseline and net shots, forehand as well as backhand, but the learner must also acquire the ability to make subtle alterations in each general type of shot in accord with the specific requirements of each situation which occurs during game play (p. 84).

This suggests that while the practitioner's emphasis in closed skills may be on developing consistency of movement, in more open skills the emphasis would be on providing variable practice opportunities. Arnold (1978) lists four implications for teaching, each of which is discussed briefly here.

1. MAKE THE GOAL OF THE ACTIVITY CLEAR TO THE LEARNER. Too often the goal is perceived by the learner as moving in a particular stereotyped way. This is only useful in skills such as diving and gymnastics where the form of the movement is the basis for judging the success of the performance. In all other skills the particular movement employed is only a means to an end. This should be considered applicable to closed as well as open skills. For example, in a racing start for individual swimming events, the selection of the particular type of start (conventional or grab) and even the particular form within each type should be determined by their effectiveness (speed) for a particular individual (Brey, 1980). The most effective form is whatever best achieves the goal.

2. PROVIDE REALISTIC PRACTICE CONDITIONS. One of the most essential of the practitioner's tasks is to provide realistic practice conditions without overloading the LCC. This is more difficult in open skills such as those involved in basketball, volleyball, and football. Provision must be made for moving players and opponents while at the same time providing gamelike variations. For example, the traditional squad-type relay drills (e.g., lay-ups in basketball) would appear to be of little value as far as learning to use the skill in a game is concerned. Arnold (1978) suggests that minigame situations involving two or more players may provide a means of simplifying the complex environment of an open skill while maintaining the requisite openness of performance conditions (p. 85).

3. DIRECT ATTENTION TO THE ESSENTIAL ASPECTS OF THE SKILL. The essential aspects of a closed skill are by definition its movement characteristics, such as its spatial-

temporal patterning. In an open skill attention must be directed to the regulatory cues, to the external changing events to which the individual's movements must conform if they are to be successful. As Arnold (1978) notes, the learner cannot develop anticipatory skills by batting a stationary ball from a batting tee or by practicing tennis strokes without reference to court position or opponents (p. 85). As we shall see, the problem lies in how to simplify practice for the beginner while maintaining the essential aspects of the skill.

4. PROVIDE FOR VARIABLE PRACTICE IN OPEN SKILLS. Diversification of movement patterns that are necessary to meet the changing demands in open skills will not occur if the learner repeatedly practices one shot or one stroke for long periods of time. As Arnold (1978) notes, the practitioner must provide for systematic variation in the practice situation. She suggests putting students into the actual game situation very quickly. "Game-related practice on specific skills can then follow as the need for the skill arises from game play" (p. 86). Arnold (1978) concludes the following.

> If the requirements of skills differ critically, and if the demands on the learner differ critically, then clearly we should *teach* open and closed skills differently. Don't plan lessons for open skills around movement. . . . Rather, plan in terms of environmental situations: for example, baseline strokes, net play, midcourt techniques, etc. Don't impose form unless it is *truly* the goal of the task. Do analyze tasks, relative to both perceptual and motor requirements (p. 86).

INTRINSIC FEEDBACK

Fitts (1962, p. 182) suggests the desirability of determining the amount and type of information feedback available in a task. Some skills have a great deal of intrinsic feedback; that is, execution of the skill provides the performer with information about the movement (knowledge of performance [KP]) or about the results of the movement (knowledge of results [KR]). For example, in target archery learners can see immediately the extent to which they have missed the goal. Other activities (e.g., ballet, gymnastics) involve skills that have little intrinsic feedback, at least in the early stages of learning. Obviously, in the latter a primary task of the practitioner is to provide supplementary feedback.

In addition, devising a method for automatic supplementary feedback would appear desirable for those skills that have little intrinsic feedback. For example, mirrors in ballet, a line strung above the tennis net, or a simple tape measure in broad jumping provides means for the performer to measure success or progress immediately. The teacher's time may then be spent in working with students who are not progressing by suggesting new ways to approach the performance of the skill.

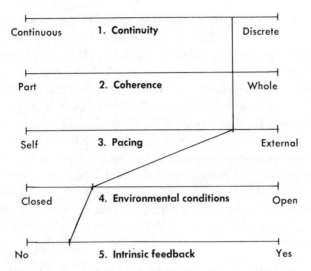

FIG. 8-3. Scaled profile for a racing start in swimming.

A SCALED PROFILE

By placing all of the scales just discussed in relationship to one another, it is possible to construct profiles for specific skills that may be useful to the practitioner. Such a profile for a racing start in swimming is shown in Fig. 8-3. Let's look at some of the instructional implications the practitioner might derive from such a profile.*

1. Since the start is discrete (performed once at the beginning of a race), it requires practice time in addition to that involved in swimming the event if the individual is to achieve a high level of proficiency.

2. The racing start is highly coherent; that is, each part is dependent on the previous one. Therefore the start needs to be practiced as a whole. The whole in this case involves not only the preparatory phrase, "Take your mark," and the takeoff from the platform but also the transition from hitting the water to the beginning of the actual stroking.

3. The racing start is externally paced by the sound of the gun or beeper. Therefore, to learn the proper timing, practice should be with the sound of the gun or beeper. (Incidentally, the word *go* is not a sufficient substitute if the greatest transfer to the actual performance situation is to occur.)

*I am grateful to Betty Brey, Women's Swimming Coach at The George Washington University, for her review of this section.

4. Despite the fact that the racing start is externally paced, it is a relatively closed skill, since the sound of the gun is the only regulatory cue and the movement for any one individual needs to be consistent. However, because variability exists in the time between the starter's signal ("Take your mark") and the sound of the gun, this variability should be built into the practice sessions.

5. There is little intrinsic feedback available in this skill. Although the swimmer gets kinesthetic feedback from the performance of the skill (KP), it is KR (speed) that provides the most useful information. KR can be provided through various timing devices. An electronic circuit can be rigged, which will record the time between the sound of the gun and the takeoff from the platform or, preferably, between the sound of the gun and a specified distance down the lane. In the latter case, coaches have been able to make use of a stopwatch, although this is obviously less accurate.

Concentration (attention) demands

In Chapter 4 on information processing emphasis was given to the fact that an individual can concentrate on only one thing at a time. Therefore it would seem desirable that we analyze, for any specific skill, where concentration (attention) should be directed to perform the skill at the highest level of proficiency. In a tennis drive, for example, should players concentrate on the ball, on the movements of opponents in the court, or on the selection, initiation, and control of their own movements?

It is unfortunate that we have little research to guide us in such analyses. However, Cockerill's (1980) contention, described earlier in this chapter, that in golf putting the player may be better off looking at the hole rather than the ball suggests that our traditional assumptions about where attention should be directed during the performance of particular skills need to be tested. Meanwhile, the practitioner would do well to make some educated guesses based on this concept of the LCC.

Recall that attention in the LCC may be directed to the perceptual (regulatory) cues, to the selection of a particular response or action plan, or to movement control (Fig. 8-4). We cannot expect an individual to concentrate on all of these at the same time. Anyone who has watched an infant learning to walk will appreciate this fact. At first the infant concentrates on the motor aspects of the skill and if, during this phase, attention is diverted (e.g., by a loud noise), loss of motor control ensues. Very soon, however, the infant is able to give attention to directional commands ("Come here") and to manage stairs and different terrain. In the case of walking, all aspects of performance are finally relegated to an automatic level, and attention can be directed to thought processes unassociated with walking.

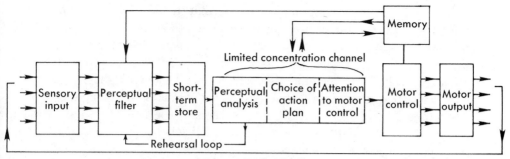

FIG. 8-4. Limited concentration (attention) channel (LCC) shown within the context of an information-processing model.

Similar, but not necessarily parallel, changes occur in the learning of most new motor skills, and the simplification or sequencing of skill learning is one of the practitioner's major tasks. Therefore it seems desirable to approach this discussion of the attention demands of skills first in terms of what is required for high proficiency and then in terms of early learning problems.

HIGH PROFICIENCY DEMANDS

We need to start any analysis of the attention demands of a skill in terms of what is needed in the actual performance situation; that is, we need to ask ourselves Where should the performer's attention be directed to achieve the highest proficiency? Only by starting with attention requirements at this level can we later determine what aspects of a skill (perception, decision making, or motor control) we need to make automatic during the instruction-learning phase.

Obviously, skills will differ in their attention demands. For example, it seems probable that in batting the attention should be on the pitch; in a racing start attention needs to be on the sound of the gun. While recognizing that limited examples run the risk of fostering rigid thinking, let's look at a specific skill— baseball batting—to see how an analysis of attention demands might proceed.*

Although the most effective focus of attention in baseball batting remains somewhat controversial, we will assume here that it should be directed to the most essential regulatory cues; that is, the batter needs to concentrate on the pitcher's release and the initial flight of the ball to predict the most effective action plan (e.g., not to swing, to swing high, or to swing low).

---

*I am grateful to Dr. James L. Breen, Professor and Chairman of Human Kinetics at The George Washington University and former batting consultant to the Baltimore Orioles, for his review of this section.

Although you might be prone to assume that the decision not to swing or to swing high or low requires attention or concentration space, there is some argument that this is not necessarily the case. Because the ball is traveling at such high speed, the batter must initiate the swing almost as soon as the ball has left the pitcher's hand and, therefore, can sample only the initial flight characteristics of the ball. There is no question but that the batter makes a decision; the question is whether this must be a conscious decision. If the batter, through variable practice during learning, has built up relational schemes in memory, an action plan can automatically be elicited.

This does not mean that for each type of pitch there is one automatic action plan. As was emphasized in Chapter 5, relational schemes in memory can be versatile. For example, the batter will have gathered much information prior to the pitch that will influence the action plan. The coach, for example, may signal for a bunt or sacrifice fly, or the batter may have noted a weakness in the opposing team's infield positioning. Each of these situations places contingencies on the batter's action plan that will be elicited by a particular pitch.

Does the experienced batter need to give attention to motor control? We have all seen a batter check or stop a swing. However, the stimulus for the check is most likely to come from attention to regulatory cues rather than from attention to movement control. The batter, for example, may have determined that the estimate of the pitch was in error. Whether such a determination is achieved by continuing to view the ball after the initiation of the swing is a matter of current research, and we do not yet have the verdict (Sharpe, 1978). However, the point being made here is that the decision to check the swing is based on perceptual analysis rather than on attention to movement control.

Assuming that this analysis of baseball batting is correct, we would then say that concentration in this particular skill *during performance* should be directed to the pitch rather than to decision making or motor control. Having made this determination, we can now proceed to a consideration of some of the attention problems during early learning.

EARLY LEARNING DEMANDS

It is hard for us as adults to recall the difficulties encountered by the beginner, since we have already relegated much of our performance to an automatic level. Not only is the individual who is learning a new motor skill faced with a bewildering array of sensory input that may or may not be relevant to the performance of the skill, but he also has yet to achieve the motor sequencing of the skill.

The process of shaping a skill by way of successive approximations is at the heart of skill learning. However, there is little research available that can guide

Perception ⟶	Decision ⟶	Movement ⟶	Intrinsic feedback
Number of relevant cues?	Number of decisions?	Consistency? Coherence?	Quantity?
Duration?	Sequence?	Precision of results?	Quality?
Intensity?	Time allowable?	Continuity?	Timing?
Confusing stimuli?	Other?	Conflicting reflexes?	Other?
Other?		Other?	

FIG. 8-5. Items that contribute to the components of motor performance. No attempt is made to list the items by priority, since this will differ with the nature of the skill. (Modified from Billing, J. An overview of task complexity. *Motor skills: theory into practice,* 1980, 4 [1], 18-23.)

the practitioner in determining the most effective way to proceed. Unfortunately, an all-too-common procedure for simplifying a skill has been to break the skill down into its movement parts without consideration of the coherence of the skill or of its perceptual or cognitive demands.

Billing (1980) takes a different approach that appears to have special merit for the practitioner. He suggests that we need to look at skill complexity, not only in terms of the movement components, but also in terms of the perceptual and decision-making requirements of the skill. Fig. 8-5 is a tentative list of some of the factors that need to be considered when analyzing skill complexity and determining effective methods for simplifying the attention demands of a skill during learning. The instructor's task is to identify from the list the most important items to manipulate to simplify a particular skill. Obviously, the attention demands for high proficiency in the actual performance situation need to be kept in mind.

Perceptual complexity—As Billing (1980) notes, if a large number of regulatory cues must be attended to, as in a basketball game, this complicates early learning. If regulatory cues are available for only a short duration, as in baseball batting, task difficulty increases. If intensity of regulatory cues is limited (e.g., white ball against a white background), the skill becomes more difficult. If conflicting stimuli such as the faking movements of an opponent are present, the difficulty of the performance increases. Each item can be manipulated by the practitioner to decrease or increase the complexity of the skill.

Decision making—The learner must translate perceptual information, compare it with past experience in memory, and select an appropriate action plan. Billing (1980) gives the example of a three-on-two fast break in basketball. The performer has to make several decisions: Dribble or pass? If dribble, what path? If pass, to whom? Where to go after the pass? Obviously, the practitioner must simplify the decision-making complexity of this task for the beginner, and Billing (1980, p. 21) makes some specific suggestions for doing so. However, the actual game requirements need to be kept in mind. A major task of the practitioner is not just to simplify the skill for the beginner but also to build up to the high proficiency demands.

Motor act complexity—Reduction of task difficulty by breaking a skill down into parts or by slowing down the speed of a movement has been a standard practice in physical education. However, as was noted earlier in this chapter, if one part of a skill is dependent on a previous part (coherent), part practice should be considered questionable. In addition, when a movement is slowed down, essential aspects are often lost. For example, observe an individual execute a tennis drive in slow motion; the hip rotation essential to the power phase of the stroke is lost. (This is not to say that slow motion is not a useful way to demonstrate certain aspects of the skill; however, extended slow motion practice of a skill should not be a standard procedure.) Obviously, some skills are not coherent and can be broken down (e.g., ball toss for the tennis serve).

Billing (1980) analyzes a tennis forehand to show how each of the components (perceptual, decision making, and movement) might be manipulated by the practitioner to reduce the attention demands of the skill during learning: (1) Hitting an effective forehand requires perception of the court, net, trajectory and speed of the ball, opponent's position, and so on. Reduction of perceptual load could include stroking from a specific court position, delivering the ball with a consistent trajectory and speed and from a standard position, reducing ball speed and spin, and using colored balls. (2) The decisions as to what stroke, where placed, where and when to hit, and what to do afterward can be predetermined and specified to reduce the decision-making demands on the learner. (3) The difficulty of the motor actions could be reduced by beginning with a side-to-the-net position, starting with the racket back, and so on (p. 23).

As has been noted, the practitioner must keep in mind the specificity of skills and plan on gradually increasing the complexity of the skill until it meets the requirements for performance at high levels of proficiency. In addition, as Billing (1980) notes, a skill could be complex in both perceptual and decision-making demands but require only a simple motor response (e.g., a move in chess). Conversely, a skill may involve movement that is complex (twisting somersault) but has minimal perceptual and decision-making requirements (p. 22).

Table 5 □ *Representative psychomotor behavior classified by traditional subject matter categories*

Physical education and recreational skills	Communication skills	Language skills	Vocational skills	Fine art skills
Sports	Typing	Speech	Crafts	Instrument playing
Dance	Handwriting	Facial expression	Tool use	Painting & drawing
Exercise	Shorthand	Gestures	Equipment operation	Singing
WILL WE EVER CROSS THE WALLS OF TRADITION?				

Modified from Merrill, M.D. Taxonomies, Classifications and theory. In R.N. Singer (Ed.). *The psychomotor domain: movement behavior.* Philadelphia: Lea & Febiger, 1972.

Future directions

Obviously, skill analysis is a critical task for the practitioner and is addressed again in Chapter 10 on instructional tasks. However, we do not have, as yet, a single viable classification system for motor skill analysis that meets all instructional needs. At the present time, it appears that we must rely on an approach, such as that described in this chapter, in which several methods of skill analysis are used.

It is hoped that this situation will change in the not too distant future. Indeed it must. Already physical educators are beginning to take on new instructional tasks dealing with a broad range of psychomotor skills, developmental as well as rehabilitative. We need a method of skill analysis that will cut across a number of areas concerned with motor learning.

The traditional classification scheme is shown in Table 5. As Merrill (1972) notes, this traditional method of classification is based on the fact that instruction is generally centered on individuals who seldom overlap the categories. Our educational system trains musicians to teach instrument playing and coaches to teach sports. However, Merrill (1972) asks some very cogent questions that need to be answered.

> Do task characteristics exist which are common across these lines? Do similarities exist which are more useful than the differences in content? If a satisfactory taxonomy of psychomotor behavior, with accompanying instructional and evaluational strategies, were developed, would a specialist trained in its use have something to contribute across subject matter lines? Would we let him?

One of the most promising candidates for helping us bridge the gap across different categories of motor skills is information processing. If we continue to (1) *refine* our theoretical models, (2) *validate* them in the practical situation, and (3) *translate* them into instructional procedures applicable to the practitioner, we will enormously increase our potential for improving performance and learning, not only in sports skills but in all types of skills, rehabilitative as well as developmental.

Sample thought sheet

1. Select a specific motor skill.
   a. List the major perceptual, motor, and cognitive abilities required for high proficiency (see Chapter 7).
   b. List these in order of their importance to high proficiency.
   c. In the case of muscular power, endurance, and flexibility, be specific with regard to the part of the body involved (e.g., neck flexibility).
2. Select one open and one closed motor skill.
   a. Describe how you would approach teaching each.
   b. Come prepared to demonstrate, if possible.
3. Select a specific motor skill.
   a. Construct a scaled profile for that skill, using the format shown in Fig. 8-3.
   b. Draw implications for teaching the skill.
4. Select a specific motor skill.
   a. Where should attention be concentrated to perform at peak proficiency?
   b. How can you simplify the skill in the early stages of learning?

References

Anderson, M.B. Comparison of muscle patterning in the overhand throw and tennis serve. *Research Quarterly,* 1979, *50,* 541-553.

Arnold, R.K. Optimizing skill learning: moving to match the environment. *Journal of Physical Education and Recreation,* November-December 1978, pp. 84-86.

Bechtoldt, H. Motor abilities in studies of motor learning. In L.E. Smith (Ed.), *Psychology of motor learning.* Chicago: Athletic Institute, 1970.

Billing, J. An overview of task complexity. *Motor Skills: Theory into Practice,* 1980, 4(1), 18-23.

Breen, J.L. Personal communication, December 1980.

Brey, B. Personal communication, November 1980.

Cockerill, I.M. Visual control in golf putting. In C.H. Nadeau, et al. (Eds.), *Psychology of motor behavior and sport—1979.* Champaign, Ill.: Human Kinetics, 1980.

Corbin, C.B., & Noble, L. Flexibility: a major component of fitness. *Journal of Physical Education and Recreation,* June 1980, *23,* 57-60.

Cratty, B.J. A three-level theory of perceptual-motor behavior. *Quest,* 1966, *6,* 3-10.

Fitts, P.M. Factors in complex skill training. In R. Glaser (Ed.), *Training research and education.* Pittsburgh: University of Pittsburgh Press, 1962.

Fleishman, E.A. The description and prediction of perceptual-motor skill learning. In R. Glaser (Ed.), *Training research and education.* Pittsburgh: University of Pittsburgh Press, 1962.

Fleishman, E.A. *The structure and measurement of physical fitness.* Englewood Cliffs, N.J.: Prentice-Hall, 1964.

Fleishman, E.A. Structure and measurement of psychomotor abilities. In R.N. Singer (Ed.), *The psychomotor domain: movement behavior*. Philadelphia: Lea & Febiger, 1972.

Fleishman, E.A., & Hempel, W.E., Jr. Changes in factor structure of a complex psychomotor test as a function of practice. *Psychometrika*, 1954, *19*, 239-252.

Fleishman, E.A., & Hempel, W.E., Jr. The relation between abilities and improvement with practice in a visual discrimination reaction task. *Journal of Experimental Psychology*, 1955, *49*, 301-310.

Henry, F.M. Individual differences in motor learning and performance. In L. Smith (Ed.), *Psychology of motor learning*. Chicago: Athletic Institute, 1970.

Merrill, M.D. Taxonomies, classifications and theory. In R.N. Singer (Ed.), *The psychomotor domain: movement behavior*. Philadelphia: Lea & Febiger, 1972.

Parker, J.F., & Fleishman, E.A. Use of analytical information concerning task requirements to increase the effectiveness of skill training. *Journal of Applied Psychology*, 1961, *45*, 295-302.

Paup, D.C. Personal communication, August 1980.

Sharpe, R.H. Visual information-processing in ball games: some input considerations. In F. Landry & W.A.R. Orban (Eds.), *Motor learning, sport psychology, pedagogy and didactics of physical activity*. Miami: Symposia Specialists, 1978.

Singer, R.N. *Motor learning and human performance* (2nd ed.). New York: MacMillan, 1975.

Singer, R.N. *Motor learning and human performance* (3rd ed.). New York: MacMillan, 1980.

Stallings, L.M. The Role of visual-spatial abilities in the performance of certain motor skills. *Research Quarterly*, 1968, *39*, 708-713.

9 RETENTION AND TRANSFER

Implicit in the whole concept of education and teaching is the assumption that what we teach will be relatively well retained. Equally as implicit is the idea that learning is cumulative; that is, what we learn today is built on past learning and will in turn enhance our capacity for future learning (transfer). However, these assumptions tend to be highly oversimplified both in popular sports literature and in the minds of many practitioners.

The extent to which motor skills are well retained depends primarily on the conditions of practice, and transfer, as we shall see, may interfere with rather than enhance the learning of new skills. Because the conditions of instruction, including practice, largely determine whether positive rather than negative results will be achieved, these conditions need to be clarified before Chapter 10, Instructional Tasks, is discussed.

Retention and overlearning

In popular terms retention refers to our capacity to remember, whether this be an event in history, a telephone number, or a motor skill. As such, it obviously involves long-term store or memory. In some ways it is unfortunate that most of our research on retention has been with verbal material, because this has given the impression that memory is somehow limited to verbal or cognitive skills. This is not acceptable when the task of enhancing the retention of motor skills is addressed. Although part of the learning of any motor skill is obviously cognitive, much of it is also neuromuscular, and practitioners must widen their view of remembering to include neuromuscular conditioning or, in information-processing terms, the degree of automation of motor control.

Fortunately, experimental definitions of retention more closely meet our needs than does the popular concept of retention as remembering. Experimentally, the term *retention* is used to refer to *the extent of proficiency on a skill remaining after a period without practice*. The usual procedures for determining amount of retention are shown in Figs. 9-1 and 9-2.

196

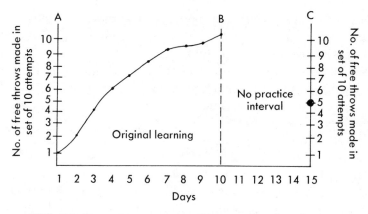

FIG. 9-1. Retention as measured by percent of proficiency.

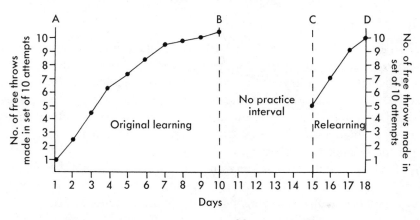

FIG. 9-2. Retention as measured by rate of relearning.

In Fig. 9-1 retention is measured by comparing proficiency (point C) following a no-practice interval with proficiency at the end of practice (point B). If the individual made 10 out of 10 free throws at point B and 5 out of 10 free throws at point C, this would indicate a 50% retention level.

In Fig. 9-2 retention is measured by comparing the rate of relearning with the rate of original learning. If the individual originally took 10 days of practice to make 10 out of 10 free throws and then, following a no-practice interval, took 4 days to regain the original proficiency, this indicates a savings of 6 days or 60% retention. This type of comparison would seem to give a better estimate of retention of motor skills than would a single score (as shown in Fig. 9-1), since rapid relearning often occurs in motor skills.

The purpose of this discussion is not to suggest that the practitioner embark on the measurement of retention but rather to point out the practical implications of the concept of retention for the physical educator or coach. Obviously, the teacher is concerned not only with students' developing current proficiency but also with ensuring students' sufficient retention so that they can continue to participate long after formal instruction has been completed. In addition, the coach is obviously concerned about the degree of loss in proficiency during the off season or layoffs. Thus we must be concerned with understanding retention and the factors that influence it. Only then can we plan instruction and practice in such a way as to enhance proficiency.

The amount of retention that can be expected is determined primarily by the level of proficiency originally attained (point B in Figs. 9-1 and 9-2). Other factors, such as the nature of the skill and the type of activity engaged in during the no-practice interval, play a secondary role. Each is discussed briefly here.

ORIGINAL LEARNING

There is little doubt that the most important factor in retention is the level of proficiency attained during original learning; that is, the higher the proficiency at point B in Figs. 9-1 and 9-2, the greater the retention at point C. Fleishman and Parker (1962), in studying the retention of a piloting skill involving coordinated arm and foot movements, found a near linear relationship between the degree of proficiency attained during initial training and the level of retention following varying intervals of no practice (9 to 25 months). Purdy and Lockhart's (1962) study of the retention of several gross motor skills produced similar results. The greater the proficiency attained in original learning, the greater the retention.

You might be tempted to conclude that the more practice, the better. However, this is only partially true if we recognize that there is only so much time available to the teacher or coach or, indeed, to the learner. A player may well be able to achieve a goal of making 100 consecutive free throws, but the question is, To what extent is the time necessary to achieve this high level of proficiency justifiable? At what point in practice do we get diminishing returns for the time spent? The answers to these questions require a consideration of the concept of overlearning.

OVERLEARNING

A recent analysis of coaching practices in mainland China (Salmela, 1979) demonstrated that much of the gymnastic skill that the Chinese have recently developed is due not to new procedures or innovative techniques but to the application of learning principles that have been known for many years, namely, specificity of practice and overlearning (p. 18). The fact remains, however, that

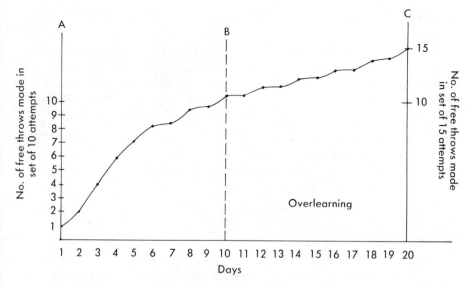

FIG. 9-3. Overlearning. (See text for further explanation.)

these principles, as important as they are to teachers and coaches, are seldom properly applied in practice. Therefore the focus of this section is on the *practitioner's role* in overlearning.

Do not confuse the term *overlearning* with the term *overload* used in Chapter 7 on motor skill abilities. Overload training for muscular power, for example, refers to the schedule for gradually increasing the work load a muscle can handle. *Overlearning*, in contrast, refers to *the continuation of practice on a skill after attaining a criterion level of performance.*

In Fig. 9-3 the criterion for learning is 10 successful free throws out of 10 attempts. If the individual continues practice until 15 out of 15 free throws are made, we would say that 50% overlearning has occurred. However, there are other ways that overlearning might be scheduled. For example, in more qualitative skills, such as in gymnastics, we might specify the learning criterion as a score of 9 in each of two successive trials. Overlearning might then be achieved by increasing the required score, or if this is not an attainable goal for the individual, we might specify the overlearning goal as three successive trials of 9.

It should be noted here that there are other viewpoints on what constitutes overlearning. The term is sometimes used to refer to continued practice on a skill irrespective of whether an improvement in proficiency occurs (Melnick, 1971; Oxendine, 1968). For example, an individual having reached the criterion proficiency of 10 out of 10 successful free throws would continue practice while maintaining this proficiency level. The assumption in this view of overlearning is that the extra practice allows the learning that has taken place to "set" or "consolidate."

However, although increments in improvement obviously decrease as individuals approach their physiological or psychological limits, Fitts (1962) maintains that they never reach a true plateau. The viewpoint taken in this book is that overlearning is most profitably thought of as an extension of practice past the criterion level of learning to achieve the relatively small increments of improvement characteristic of the later stages of learning, although these small improvements may not be measurable. This view of overlearning is explicit in Krueger's (1929) classic study; the learning criterion was six trials without error, and 50% overlearning was nine trials without error.

Obviously, overlearning requires proportionately more time than early learning. In Fig. 9-3, for example, the time taken to achieve 50% overlearning (point C) was 10 days, the same amount of time that was taken to achieve the learning criterion (point B). This is true because the learning rate begins to decrease as proficiency reaches higher levels; this is indicated by the relative flattening out or plateauing of the learning curve in Fig. 9-3. As we become more proficient in a skill, the less room there is for improvement, and these smaller increments of improvement take longer to achieve as we approach the limits of performance.

Therefore we have to ask ourselves, as practitioners or performers, how much extra time we want to devote to achieving higher levels of proficiency. Is it worthwhile to practice until we can make 100 consecutive free throws? In laboratory studies 50% overlearning has generally been shown to be advantageous, but practice beyond this has diminishing returns for the time spent (Singer, 1975, p. 366). Thus, in the example shown in Fig. 9-3, extending practice to achieve a proficiency level of 20 out of 20 free throws (100% overlearning) would not result in a sufficiently greater increase in retention to warrant the extra practice time required.

However, there are other factors that need to be taken into consideration before establishing the most desirable amount of overlearning for a particular skill. Each of these is discussed briefly here.

Overlearning as habit formation—When we realize that overlearning results in establishing a habit, we must ask ourselves whether the habit formed will be advantageous or detrimental in the actual performance or game situation. Habits are very difficult to break—try writing a sentence without dotting your i's or crossing your t's. Thus practicing single skills for long periods of time in isolation from the performance situation is particularly suspect. This is especially true of open skills, such as tennis strokes, which require variable practice. Conversely, closed skills, as in gymnastics, may profit from extended drill.

Drill versus variable practice—It is misleading to equate *drill*, in its popular

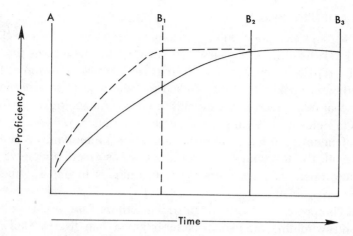

FIG. 9-4. Relationship of rate of learning to overlearning as a function of time. At faster learning rate *(dotted line)*, overlearning occurs during B_1 to B_2; at slower learning rate *(solid line)*, overlearning requires extension of time from B_2 to B_3.

sense, with overlearning. Open skills, such as batting, can also profit from the application of the overlearning principle. In this case, however, the extra practice associated with overlearning is devoted to practice with the varying pitches and other changing situations that occur in a game situation. The learning criterion in batting might be a certain batting average and the overlearning criterion, a specified increase in batting average. However, there are obviously closed skills in which practice of a particular stereotyped movement is the best method to achieve overlearning (e.g., discus). In such cases, however, the practitioner must recognize that extended drill has problems of its own. Often it becomes boring to the learner, and techniques for enhancing motivation become critical. Often, setting short, intermediate goals during the overlearning period helps to maintain motivation.

The unfortunate fact is that we seldom bring our students to the point of overlearning, that is, to the point where their learning curves begin to plateau (point B in Fig. 9-3). One of our excuses has been that we just do not have the time to bring students to a higher level of achievement. However, since retention is dependent on the level of proficiency attained, the question becomes one of how to attain higher proficiency in a given amount of time. The thesis of this book is that we can increase the learning rate by applying certain learning concepts. As shown in Fig. 9-4, by increasing the learning rate (dotted line), we have time (B_1 to B_2) that can be devoted to overlearning that was not available at the slower learning rate (solid line). The faster one learns, the more time left for overlearning.

NATURE OF THE SKILL

Almost without exception, motor skills have been shown to be well retained even after intervals of up to 2 years. The small proficiency losses that do occur appear to be rapidly recovered in early relearning trials (Fleishman & Parker, 1962). Purdy and Lockhart (1962) studied the retention of several motor skills, including a foot volley, lacrosse throw and catch, and balancing on a bongo board. The subjects, retested following a year without practice, retained 94% of their original proficiency, and relearning was rapid. Since retention was so high after this long layoff, the investigators suggested that, as practitioners, we might be spending too much time reviewing basic techniques in our intermediate and advanced classes.

Some skills appear to be better retained than others. Continuous skills, such as bicycling and swimming, are usually better retained than discrete skills, such as a golf drive or tennis serve. This should not be surprising, since repetitions of movement are typical of continuous skills. You need only to consider how little proficiency is lost in bicycling even after years without practice.

Another factor that needs to be considered in predicting the retention of motor skills is the ability structure of the skill. For example, retention of proficiency in gymnastics or any skill requiring a high level of muscular power, endurance, or flexibility can be expected to show considerable loss unless a high level of fitness has been maintained. However, it is probable that the loss would be regained fairly quickly following a retraining program.

INTERIM ACTIVITIES

The type of activity engaged in during the no-practice interval (e.g., between seasons) also influences the retention of proficiency of a skill. Thus a swimming coach may caution a long-distance swimmer not to engage in diving; a tennis coach may encourage or prohibit a player from participating in racketball or squash, depending on that coach's understanding, or lack of it, regarding the effect of interim activities on skill retention.

In general, traditional studies have suggested that very different activities (e.g., swimming and ballet) or very similar activities (e.g., bowling and duck pin) cause the least interference, while those that are moderately similar (e.g., tennis and badminton) appear to cause the most. However, this is a broad generalization that requires a consideration of the concept of transfer before it can be used wisely by the practitioner.

Transfer

Education assumes transfer. Whether it is the English teacher who expects that writing compositions will have a favorable effect on all communication skills or the physical education teacher who claims that lead-up games are a desirable prerequisite to more complex sports, both are assuming transfer. Land drills in swimming are assumed to transfer to performance in the water, and physical conditioning is expected to contribute to a proficiency in a variety of motor skills. Obviously, not all of these assumptions are equally valid. Writing may have little effect on oral communication, and certain kinds of physical conditioning may in fact be detrimental to performance on a specific motor skill. Thus transfer may be positive, negative, or nonexistent. Therefore before the principle of transfer can be used by practitioners to enhance an individual's proficiency, an understanding of both its potential contributions and its limitations is imperative.

One typical experimental pattern for transfer is shown below. Group A learns

Group A	Group B
Learn task x	
Learn task y	Learn task y

task x, then task y; Group B learns only task y. Assuming that the groups are matched, if Group A learns task y faster than Group B, there is said to be positive transfer from task x to task y. For example, if Group A requires only 20 trials to learn task y, while Group B requires 25 trials, task x is said to have contributed 25% to the learning of y. Conversely, if Group A takes more trials to reach the criterion level of proficiency than Group B, task x is said to have interfered with the learning of y (negative transfer). Thus the degree of transfer may be placed on a continuum, as shown on the scale below.

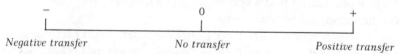

task x, then task y; Group B learns only task y. Assuming that the groups are

Most of the studies of transfer have been in terms of skill-to-skill transfer. However, this is a relatively limited notion of the concept of transfer. *Transfer* is defined here as *the effect that previous practice has on subsequent learning or performance.* This allows us to consider not only transfer from one motor skill to another, but also transfer from practice to performance, from abilities to skills, from limb to limb (bilateral or cross transfer), from principles to skills, and from one developmental stage to another throughout life.

Almost all of our instructional practices make some kind of assumption regarding transfer. For example, we expect that what is learned in practice drills will transfer to the game situation or that the individual who knows tennis well will be able to learn racketball or badminton more readily.

What creates these assumptions, in general, is that there is seen to exist between the two tasks some similarities, either between the stimulus situations (ball or bird and net in badminton and tennis) or between the movement responses of the two skills (overhand throw and tennis serve) or between both stimulus and response (badminton smash and tennis smash). However, some of the perceived similarities between skills may be illusions; that is, the skills appear similar, especially to the novice, while in fact they may be sufficiently dissimilar so that negative rather than positive transfer is likely to occur.

Efforts to predict the transfer effects between tasks on the basis of their stimulus and response similarities have resulted in a number of hypotheses, the most popular being that of Osgood (1949). In general, these hypotheses predict the following.

1. There are more likely to be negative transfer effects between two tasks when the stimulus elements are similar and the responses are different. For example, many people have difficulty changing from a floorboard gearshift in a car to a gearshift that is on the steering column. The stimulus display or regulatory cues from the view of the road remain the same, but the motor response of shifting gears is different.

2. Negative transfer is less likely when the stimulus elements of two tasks differ, but the responses remain the same. For example, if a batter is going to bunt, it should make little difference whether the pitch is a fast ball or a curve. However, the more the stimulus is changed, the less positive the transfer. A batter with experience only in slow-pitch baseball should expect that learning to hit in regular baseball may prove difficult.

3. If the stimulus and response elements of two tasks are obviously dissimilar, we would not expect transfer (either positive or negative) to occur.

4. Only when the stimulus and response elements of two tasks are identical can we reliably predict positive transfer.

There is considerable question regarding the validity and usefulness of transfer predictions based on the surface models of Osgood and others. As Holding (1976) notes, "There are, in fact, good reasons for viewing all transfer surfaces with mistrust" (p. 8). For this reason, it appears more desirable to view transfer in terms of specific situations encountered by the practitioner rather than in terms of transfer models.

SKILL-TO-SKILL TRANSFER

Most skill-to-skill transfer studies have failed to demonstrate positive transfer between skills that would appear highly similar. Nelson (1957), for example, studied transfer between three pairs of skills: a badminton volley and tennis stroking (against a wall); a volleyball tap and basketball tip for accuracy; and starting stances for track and football. What is striking about Nelson's study is that, despite the fact that the paired skills appear to be highly similar, the transfer effect was only slight. Skill specificity is the rule rather than the exception, and this finding is supported not only by the generally low correlations between skills but also by studies of skill-to-skill transfer.

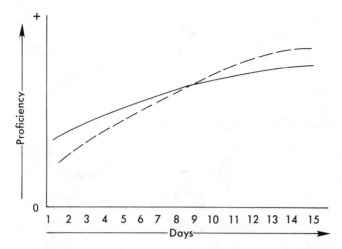

FIG. 9-5. Hypothesized performance curves during 3-week badminton clinic for participants with tennis experience (*solid line*), and without tennis experience (*dotted line*).

It is interesting to note that in Nelson's (1957) study the slight positive transfer found (e.g., between the basketball tip and the volleyball tap) may have been a function of the stage of learning. His subjects were given only three 30-minute trials. As you will recall from the discussion in the previous chapter, there is an increase in the specificity of a skill as an individual becomes more proficient. Had Nelson's subjects continued practice, the slight transfer that occurred may have been erased or may even have become negative transfer.

This raises an important issue in regard to the concept of transfer that is often overlooked. Although similar skills may show positive transfer in the early stages of learning, negative transfer may still occur in later stages. Fig. 9-5 may help to clarify this concept. The participants in a badminton clinic were divided into those who had a background in tennis (solid line) and those who did not (dotted line). A hypothetical plotting of their learning curves in badminton is shown in Fig. 9-5. Note that in the early stages of learning the players with tennis experience performed better than those without tennis experience, whereas the reverse was true in the later stages of learning. One might hypothesize that the similarities between tennis and badminton (both involving a court, net, racket, and aerial object) contributed to positive transfer for the players with tennis experience early in learning but that the specific differences (e.g., forearm rotation in badminton, size and trajectory of the bird in relation to the ball, and weight of the racket) hindered learning (negative transfer) in the later stages.

The concept of *differentiation* in learning was emphasized in the early chapters of this book and was seen to be a common consideration not only of the traditional learning theories but also of neurological theories. Although calling attention to the similarity of skills ("The tennis serve is like the overhand throw.") may assist the learner in quickly getting the idea of a movement ("chunking" in information-processing terms), unless at some point the differences are pointed out, we would expect negative transfer to interfere with learning (see solid line in Fig. 9-5).

In addition, we tend to generalize on the basis of our past experience. Learners, even without being told, assume, for example, that the badminton smash is like the tennis smash because the skills look alike. A simple drill that makes learners vividly aware of the major difference has been devised by Breen (1980). With badminton rackets in hand, learners place their elbow overhead and against a gymnasium mat hung on the wall; they then whip their rackets from back to front by forearm rotation (pronation) only. This movement allows them to differentiate between the tennis and badminton smash by the feeling of the strokes.

In view of the low transfer between skills, why are some tennis players also proficient at badminton? While there are undoubtedly some common perceptual and motor abilities involved, it is also likely that these people enjoy racket sports (squash may also be in their repertoire) and therefore are highly motivated. Most influential of all, however, is the fact that these individuals have mastered the specifics of each skill, that is, the subtle differences between the badminton smash and the tennis smash, the footwork and court placement, as well as the speed and trajectory of the badminton bird as compared with that of the tennis ball. The practitioner can assist the learner by pointing out differences and structuring practice so that the new skill can be learned with the least interference.

Reference to Fig. 9-5 may help clarify this important distinction. If instruction in the later stages of learning emphasized critical differences between tennis and badminton, we would expect that the tennis players might maintain the lead they demonstrated in early learning (e.g., the performance curves in Fig. 9-5 would not intersect).

PRACTICE-TO-PERFORMANCE TRANSFER

It should now be clear that the extent to which positive or negative transfer will occur depends to a large extent on the way the practitioner designs instruction. This is true whether we are considering skill-to-skill transfer or whether we are concerned with transfer from practice to the actual performance or game situation.

Obviously, practitioners plan practice sessions with the assumption that the practice will improve game performance. Yet we often fail to take into account the limitations of transfer, namely, environmental specificity. Whenever a skill is removed from the game situation for purposes of practice, it becomes a different skill that is subject to all the limitations of skill-to-skill transfer already mentioned.

What does this imply in terms of designing instruction? The one most important guideline should be: practice should *simulate* the game or performance situation as closely as possible. Because game situations vary, a corollary guideline is also implied: practice should be variable, encompassing as many of the game situations as possible. Let's look at each of these implications in turn.

Simulated performance conditions—A motor learning expert once commented to a group of Olympic paddlers: "If you really want to mix up the timing of a team of rowers, put an extra coat of varnish on their oars the night before an important competition" (Darden, 1978, p. 55). Despite this demonstrated specificity, we often devise practice drills that violate the principle of specificity. Cratty (1973) gives the example of the use of "tip-in" drills in basketball.

> One player positions himself on one side of the basketball backboard and attempts to tip the ball back to the board and make it rebound to the other side, over the basket, to the second participant who jumps up and attempts to duplicate the action in the other direction. Such a drill is supposedly preparatory for the game situation in which the task is usually to tip a rebound into the basket, scoring a goal (pp. 112-113).

As Cratty notes, such practice is likely to produce negative rather than positive transfer to the game situation.

Variable practice—Practitioners and coaches often concentrate on a few favorite drills. Even when these drills simulate realistic game situations, it is unlikely that a few drills will encompass the many specific conditions encountered in a game. Fig. 9-6 illustrates this principle. In traditional practice drills (Fig. 9-6, A) not all game situations are included. Thus we would expect this type of practice to be less effective than that provided by variable drills (Fig. 9-6, B).

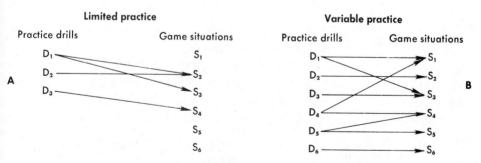

FIG. 9-6. Comparison of **A,** limited practice, and **B,** variable practice, in drill-to-game skill relationships. (Modified from Cratty, B.J. *Teaching motor skills.* Englewood Cliffs, N.J.: Prentice-Hall, 1973.)

Cratty (1973) gives an example of a comprehensive drill for defensive linemen in football.

> Instead of the foot-crossing drill, football coaches should carefully analyze the positions taken by the feet as defensive linemen move across the field, retreating backward to the left and right, rapidly changing position, moving forward, turning and running to the side, running forward to the left or right. . . . At the same time care should be taken not to limit the number of drills, thus excluding some of the game movements from the drill movements (p. 118).

Thus, presumably, drills should be included that simulate the various stimuli or regulatory cues (opponents) that determine where, when, and how the lineman moves.

Psychological similarity—Suinn (1978) very correctly emphasizes that in our consideration of transfer from practice to competition we must take into account not only physical similarities to game conditions but also psychological similarities.

> The rule is that practice makes perfect, if the practice demands are similar to the game demands. Some professional tennis players do not simply practice their serves; instead they practice serving to Nastase with the imaginal score of "30-40." If the event is such that the athlete has no control over adverse conditions, then practice should take place under adverse weather or course conditions. Basketball players are never asked in a game to shoot a free throw after a five minute rest; hence they [should] practice free throws *after* a full afternoon of running, and not while fresh and rested (p. 21).

Obviously, there are many variables operating in the actual performance situation that need to be considered by the practitioner when designing instruction. Preseason games may be one way by which the coach can help performers adjust to these variables, but the practitioner must also consider how drill practice can be made comprehensive and realistic rather than depending on preseason competition.

There is, of course, the problem of instructional design at early stages of learning. To subject the beginner to all of the variables of the game situation at once could have the effect of overloading the information-handling capacity of the learner. Our discussion of the transfer effects during early and later learning (Fig. 9-5) suggests that early practice need not be quite as specific as that during later learning. Darden (1978) gives an example in racketball.

> At first, hitting any type ball with a racquet will probably help his skill more than it will hurt it. Initially, there's some generality involved in skill training. As he becomes more proficient, however, the practice should become more and more specific . . . so specific, in fact, that many professional racquetball players can actually tell the difference between new and slightly used balls and racquets.

This is not to say that the practitioner need not be concerned with specificity of practice in the early learning period. Indeed our knowledge of specificity of training suggests that the principles implied—simulation of game situations and variable practice—be instituted progressively as soon as the learner can handle the increased information load. The best way of determining this would appear to be to try it. Only if the realistic practice conditions appear to confuse (overload) the learner should a simpler practice situation be considered. Singer (1975) cites a study by Briggs and Waters (1958) in which the authors recommend that for the greatest transfer effectiveness we should simplify the task as a whole rather than fractionalize the skill (p. 444). For example, maintain the gamelike setting, but decrease complexity of the situation (e.g., one-on-one prior to half-court scrimmage).

ABILITIES-TO-SKILL TRANSFER

Much has been said throughout this book in regard to the ability-skill concept (see, for example, Chapters 7 and 8). In essence, Fleishman's (1962) ability-skill paradigm assumes that the extent to which an individual has the perceptual and motor abilities required by a skill will determine in part both the rate at which the skill is learned and the proficiency attained.

This is not to say, however, that the performance or learning of skills requiring the same abilities will be correlated. Bachman (1961), for example, found little more than zero correlation between performance (and learning) on the stabilometer and a free-standing vertical ladder climb, two skills that appear to have a balance requirement in common. The specificity of abilities was discussed in Chapter 7, and the need to adapt ability training to each specific skill was emphasized.

This is not to say, however, that basic abilities do not transfer (facilitate learning or performance) to skills requiring that ability. For example, if we assume that only 30% of an individual's maximal leg power transfers to a specific skill requiring leg power, that 30% is not to be underestimated. Fig. 8-2 in Chapter 8 should help to clarify this point. The basic abilities involved in the performance of a particular motor skill are only one of many contributing elements. Thus, while recognizing that abilities do not transfer in toto to the performance of a specific skill, they certainly contribute to that performance.

Given the basic perceptual and motor abilities required by a skill, practice time can be devoted to adapting these abilities to the skill, to mastering its specifics, and to providing the time for overlearning the skill. As was emphasized earlier in this chapter, overlearning enhances retention.

In addition, mention should be made of the contribution of abilities to so-called fitness, in general. Although this is a reverse of abilities-to-skill transfer (skill-to-abilities), individuals often engage in specific skills (e.g., jogging), not for the sake of the skill itself but to increase fitness. However, participation in a specific skill will not develop an individual's maximal muscular power, flexibility, or endurance. There is still a place for general fitness or conditioning programs.

LIMB-TO-LIMB (BILATERAL) TRANSFER

The term *bilateral transfer, cross-training,* or *cross-education* is used to refer to the effect that the practice or training of one limb can have on the same limb on the other side of the body. The initial studies were undertaken at about the turn of the century when it was observed that the practice of a skill with one hand had a positive transfer effect on the opposite hand. Since then the phenomenon has been studied in relation to both rehabilitation and physical education activities.

The use of cross-training in rehabilitation was the subject of studies by Hellebrandt (1951) and her colleagues and by Walters (1955). As a result of training one limb, they found improvement in muscular power and endurance, as well as skill, in the contralateral limb. Although the improvement in the untrained limb was less marked than if it had been trained directly, Hellebrandt, Parrish, and Houtz (1947) suggested that cross-training might serve as a useful therapeutic method in cases where contralateral muscle groups are inaccessible to direct training due to temporary immobilization. For example, an individual in a limb cast could be expected to maintain residual strength (and to avoid muscular atrophy) in the immobilized limb by exercising the symmetrical muscles of the other side. The greatest transfer effects Walters (1955) found are obtained with overload training.

The value of bilateral transfer in physical education appears to be in the development of ambidexterity, that is, the ability to perform a skill on both sides. For example, it seems advantageous to be able to execute a basketball dribble with either hand and to kick a soccerball with either foot. In addition, some skills (diving, receiving a football pass) require the ability to turn or "break" in either direction equally well.

There seems to be general agreement that, in such cases, the effective use of bilateral transfer could save practice time. Although there is some conflicting evidence (Hellebrandt, 1951) on whether an individual should begin practice with the preferred or nonpreferred side, Ammons (1958) concludes that greater transfer could be expected from the preferred to the nonpreferred limb.

Unfortunately, we are not yet certain as to how such bilateral transfer effects come about. The answers, when we get them, will be important not only to our knowledge of nervous system functioning but also to the practical application of bilateral transfer to skill learning. For example, the two most often cited speculations regarding the bilateral transfer are (1) that it is the result of overflow of motor impulses (deVries, 1980; Hellebrandt, et al., 1947) and (2) that it is the result of mental, ideational, or cognitive elements (Cratty, 1973). The differing practical implications of each of these hypotheses are discussed briefly here, and a third alternative is offered.

Overflow hypothesis—Moritani and deVries (1979) have demonstrated that the bilateral transfer of strength training, at least, results entirely from nervous system activity and not from an increase in the size of the muscle (e.g., there was no muscular hypertrophy on the unpracticed side). deVries (1980) suggests that this transfer may be brought about by an overflow in the motor cortex of the brain (from the crossed to the uncrossed fibers). He sees this overflow as occurring only under overload conditions (progressive increase in work load) on the trained side (p. 101). This implies that the task of the practitioner in bringing about bilateral transfer is to design practice so that overload occurs (see Fig. 7-5).

Cognitive hypothesis—Cratty (1973) reports a study that would seem to confirm a cognitive explanation.

> One group of subjects practiced a one-handed task and then attempted to perform the task with the opposite hand, evidencing the expected positive transfer; a second group of subjects, however, was permitted only to observe practice in the one-handed task before attempting it with one of their hands. That the skill level evidenced by the second group was similar to that of the first group, which had prior physical practice, makes a strong case that the mental components of the task indeed caused the transfer effects seen in both groups (p. 109).

Cratty concludes that thinking about a skill may be productive in bringing about positive bilateral transfer.

An alternative hypothesis—That the study reported by Moritani and deVries (1979) involved bilateral transfer of strength and the study cited by Cratty (1973) involved the bilateral transfer of a skill may have important implications for the practitioner. Obviously, most motor skills involve elements (e.g., spatial-temporal patterning) that are similar whether performed on the right or left side, and, presumably, if an individual has learned these elements on one side, transferring them to performance on the other side should be facilitated. For example, a switch-hitter usually learns to bat on one side. To learn to bat on the other side takes less time, since common elements of the skill such as the stance, the stride, and eye focus do not need to be relearned cognitively. However, if we accept the overflow hypothesis for bilateral transfer of strength, this transfer will be facilitated if initial practice on the preferred side is conducted on an overload basis. This implies that to enhance an individual's ability to perform a skill on both sides, initial instruction on the preferred side should emphasize the understanding of the essential aspects of the skill cognitively and should also provide for overload practice.

At this point it seems desirable to suggest some practical guidelines that may assist you in helping learners develop bilateral skill proficiency:

1. Initial practice should be on the preferred side. Few individuals are naturally ambidexterous, and they are apt to learn faster and achieve success more rapidly by beginning on their preferred side.

2. This initial practice should emphasize a cognitive understanding of the essential aspects of a skill (e.g., stance, stride, and eye focus, in batting).

3. Practice should be on an overload basis (see Fig. 7-5).

4. Direct practice on the nonpreferred side must be provided. Learners tend to avoid this not only because it feels less comfortable (most of us have a preferred side that affects all of our movements) but also because they have less success. Observe, for example, the beginning tennis player who shifts court position so that all strokes can be made on the right side of the body. Practice must be structured to force performance of the skill on or to the nonpreferred side.

However, equal practice time will usually not be necessary. This is the value of the bilateral transfer phenomenon. Skill acquisition on the nonpreferred side should be relatively rapid if the previous guidelines have been followed.

PRINCIPLES-TO-SKILL TRANSFER

In recent years there has been an increasing emphasis on a conceptual approach in education. The rationale is that the individual who understands the concept or principle will be able to use it to solve many different problems. For example, the information-processing model, described in Chapter 4, consists of a number of interrelated concepts that are assumed to be generally applicable to solve a variety of learning and teaching problems. Similarly, there is the inverted U concept of optimal arousal. However, the expectation that principles will be used (transferred) is an assumption; the conditions under which the principles are taught and practiced determine whether or not they will be transferred.

Experimental support for a general principles theory of transfer was initially drawn from Judd's (1908) classical study. Two groups of fifth- and sixth-grade boys were asked to hit a small target placed under the water with a dart. The group that had been taught the principle of light refraction prior to performance was significantly better than the group that was not taught the principle. Hendrickson and Schroeder (1941) confirmed these findings with the added conclusion that the thoroughness of understanding of the principle is important in the level of transfer that can be expected.

However, other attempts to evaluate the effectiveness of the knowledge of principles on motor skill learning have been conflicting. For example, Nessler (1961), in a study of the effect of teaching mechanical principles of movement to low-skilled college women, concluded the following.

Skill learning for the poorly skilled is not analytical. A knowledge of mechanical principles may be helpful in analyzing the completed act, but does not seem to aid the poorly skilled in their performance. Poorly skilled students are interested in mechanical principles related to skill learning, but are unable to incorporate this theoretical knowledge into their performance of these motor skills (p. 79).

We need to be cautious in generalizing this finding. Researchers who have attempted to evaluate the effect of knowledge of mechanical principles on motor skill learning have used a variety of methods to present the principles to learners. For example, if the principle of "center of gravity" is presented in the language of physics or even in our own professional jargon, we can hardly expect the learner to be able to apply it to performance. Oxendine (1968) points out two important limitations of principles-to-skill transfer: (1) If the principle is not understood by the learner, it can hardly be expected to transfer. (2) Even when the principle is understood, it will not necessarily be applied to a second situation involving the principle (p. 83). In addition, as Lawther (1968) notes, "If much time is spent on theoretical explanation with consequent loss of physical practice time, the teaching procedures might well be questioned" (p. 101).

One of the most obvious assumptions of this book is that, under the proper conditions, principles and concepts are transferable. Because of the great potential of a principles approach to motor skill learning, the following guidelines, while speculative, suggest some of the ways the practitioner might enhance principles-to-skill transfer.

1. PRESENT THE PRINCIPLE IN TERMS FAMILIAR TO THE LEARNER. Recall that individuals perceptually filter information in terms of their past experience. By using the learner's everyday language, you are apt to be more successful. For example, rebound angles can be demonstrated by showing the effect of the angle at which the ball strikes a surface and its type of spin.

2. PROVIDE MANY VARIED EXAMPLES OF THE OPERATION OF THE PRINCIPLE. For example, the rebound principle can be demonstrated with a basketball against a backboard, in dribbling or bounce-passing a basketball, in a tennis serve or drive, in table tennis—the opportunities are almost limitless.

3. KEEP IN MIND THE LIMITED CONCENTRATION CHANNEL (LCC). We should not expect principles to be immediately applied to performance, particularly by the beginner who is concentrating on other aspects of performance such as motor control. This does not mean that we should not teach principles to the beginner. Our concern is not whether they are immediately usable but whether they can contribute to future performance and learning.

4. CONSIDER THE SEQUENCING OF A PRINCIPLE. Just as we sequence the learning of a skill, it is likely that principles would profit from sequencing. We first may be able to elicit only a reiteration of the principle by the learner, then a restatement

in his own words, followed by his ability to give examples. Finally, the learner should be able to use the principle across a range of motor skills, if the other guidelines have been followed.

STAGE-TO-STAGE DEVELOPMENT*

The development of motor skills is a continuous process. Lawther (1969), in fact, has defined motor skill learning as "the purposive putting together of movements, already in one's repertoire, into an organized pattern."

> At each successive stage of motor learning, the new learning is built on previous learning. The crawling, the reaching and grasping, the balancing, the walking, the climbing form bases on which to build more complex skills. Skills advance in hierarchies of increasing complexity (p. 14).

Viewed this way, motor skill development is a stage-to-stage transfer; that is, the extent to which the individual can learn a new skill is dependent in part on what has gone on before. Although this principle appears to be obvious, the fact remains that we too often assume that slow learners have some innate limitations. A more probable assumption might be that they lack experience.

This tendency to underrate the impact of experience is particularly apparent in the early stages of motor skill development. Some elementary school programs appear to be based on a concept of rather rigid age-determined movement patterns. That this should occur is not surprising, since early studies in child development emphasized the preeminence of maturation in the development of motor skills. However, a substantial body of evidence is accumulating to support the contention that so-called maturational processes are profoundly influenced by experience. This is consistent with Hunt's (1961) suggestion that the maturation-learning dichotomy may well be artificial and with Gerard's (1960) concept of cycles of development in which learning feeds back to change structure as well as function (see Fig. 1-2).

This is not to say that there are not traceable patterns of development. As Kay (1969) notes, "The rate of development varies from child to child so that one may sit or walk before another, but a child who cannot sit will not stand or walk" (p. 39). Similarly, the first stage toward walking is control of head movements, followed by the development of postural stability. In addition, it is becoming increasingly apparent that perceptual motor experiences during early childhood underlie adult skills. As Kay (1969) notes of a film analysis of children (ages 2, 5, and 15) catching a ball,

---

*I am grateful to Dr. Jeanne E. Snodgrass, Professor of Motor Development at The George Washington University, for her review of this section.

The striking feature lay in the contrast between the performances. It was difficult to imagine the beginnings of the highly coordinated, anticipatory, high speed but smooth action of the 15 year old in the performance of the two year old. But appearances are deceptive, and it was quite clear that at the intermediate age the foundations of the adult performance were being laid (p. 52).

Although a discussion of theories of motor development and specific developmental stages is beyond the scope of this book, its importance to a comprehensive understanding of motor skill learning and teaching cannot be overlooked. Fortunately, the study of motor development is becoming a recognized part of the professional preparation of practitioners (Brooks, 1979), and a number of motor development texts are available.

Since the concept of motor skill development as a transfer phenomenon is so crucial to the practitioner, an attempt has been made in the boxed material below to highlight some of the major characteristics of motor behavior and learning at various developmental stages. The point of interest here is not in chronological ages of specific details but in the development of motor skills from stage to stage. There is a great deal of overlap between the sequential stages.

Major characteristics of motor behavior during various developmental stages

Infancy	Reflexive action Developing postural stability Beginning upright locomotion
Early childhood	Prehension and handedness Speech Basic skill patterns: walking, jumping, throwing, kicking, etc.
Late childhood	Increasing proficiency in basic abilities and basic skills Beginning application to games and sports
Adolescence	Refinement of specific skills Cultural expectations influence type and intensity of activity
Adulthood	Peak proficiency dependent on the nature of the skill Less inclined to take up new activities
Old age	Proficiency depends on experience Modified skills for fitness, mobility, and enjoyment

---

Modified from Snodgrass, J.E. Personal communication, December 1980.

Obviously, all of us must be concerned with the sequential development of motor skills throughout the individual's life span. The high school teacher can no longer ignore the elementary school program, and the elementary school teacher must provide sufficient variety of activity so as to ensure the adult a broad repertoire of participation possibilities. In addition, we cannot confine our concerns to the arbitrary limits of school-aged individuals. Motor learning begins in infancy, and the preschool years provide the basis on which future learning is built. In addition, adulthood and aging can be enriched if we can overcome stereotyping and convince learners (of any age) that motor skill learning is a lifelong ability.

Teaching for transfer

A major assumption of this book is that the extent to which positive transfer will occur depends in large part on how the practitioner designs instruction and practice. Ellis (1965) refers to this as "teaching for transfer." Although he is concerned with the application of transfer principles in classroom settings, his guidelines are useful in highlighting some of the implications of transfer discussed in this chapter. These guidelines are paraphrased here for use by the physical educator or coach.

1. Maximize the similarity between the learning and performance situations.
2. Provide adequate experience with the original task.
3. Provide a variety of examples when teaching principles.
4. Identify for the learner the essential similarities and differences.

However, if there were to be one guideline overriding all others, it would be to keep in mind the specificity of transfer. This is true whether we are considering skill-to-skill transfer, practice-to-performance transfer, abilities-to-skill transfer, or limb-to-limb (bilateral) transfer. Unfortunately, the old adage "transfer is roughly proportionate to the degree of similarity between skills" has misled many practitioners. "Teaching for transfer" has too often been interpreted as "point out similarities" without consideration of critical differences.

Recall that in the traditional cognitive learning theories (Chapter 2) differentiation or discrimination was assumed under the law of similarity. The gestaltists perceived similarities as occurring at different levels of completeness and considered differentiation, as well as generalization, to be a crucial aspect of this. The importance of this view to the practitioner was stated by Hartmann (1942).

> Educationally, one task of teaching that assumes greater significance in the light of this discussion is the function of enabling pupils to see differences where formerly they saw only likeness or to perceive likeness where others discern naught but differences (p. 203).

Teaching, including instruction and practice, needs to be thought of as the "original task" that must be made transferable to other situations. Thus *transfer principles must be a continuous consideration in the design of instruction.* Instructional tasks are the subject of the following and final chapter of this book.

Sample thought sheet

1. Select a specific motor skill; describe how you would plan for overlearning. Be specific with regard to
   a. Criterion for learning (point B in Fig. 9-3)
   b. Criterion for overlearning (point C in Fig. 9-3)
2. Give a specific example (observed rather than hypothetical, if possible) of each of the following types of transfer.
   a. Skill-to-skill
   b. Practice-to-performance
   c. Abilities-to-skill
   d. Limb-to-limb
   e. Principles-to-skill
   f. Developmental stages
3. Select two motor skills that appear similar. List the following.
   a. Transferable similarities
   b. The critical differences
4. Select two motor skills that appear similar. Assuming that a learner has experience in one of these,
   a. Describe how you would teach the other to maximize positive transfer.
   b. Come prepared to demonstrate, if possible.

References

Ammons, R.B. Le mouvement. In G.H. Steward & J.P. Steward (Eds.), *Current psychological issues.* New York: Holt, Rinehart and Winston, 1958.

Bachman, J.C. Specificity versus generality in learning and performing two large motor tasks. *Research Quarterly*, 1961, 32, 3-11.

Breen, J.L. Personal communication, September 1980.

Briggs, G.E., & Waters, L.K. Training and transfer as a function of component interaction. *Journal of Experimental Psychology*, 1958, 56, 492-500.

Brooks, D. Survey of current status of motor development. *Journal of Physical Education and Recreation*, October 1979, pp. 79-80.

Cratty, B.J. *Teaching motor skills.* Englewood Cliffs, N.J.: Prentice-Hall, 1973.

Darden, E. Do tennis and racquetball go together? *Racquetball Illustrated*, December 1978, pp. 54-55.

deVries, H.A. *Physiology of exercise.* Dubuque, Iowa: William C. Brown, 1980.

Ellis, H.C. *The transfer of training.* New York: MacMillan, 1965.

Fitts, P.M. Factors in complex skill training. In R. Glaser (Ed.), *Training research and education.* Pittsburgh: University of Pittsburgh Press, 1962.

Fleishman, E.A. The description and prediction of perceptual-motor skill learning. In R. Glaser (Ed.), *Training research and education.* Pittsburgh: University of Pittsburgh Press, 1962.

Fleishman, E.A., & Parker, J.F., Jr. Factors in the retention and relearning of perceptual-motor skill. *Journal of Experimental Psychology*, 1962, 64, 215-226.

Gerard, R.W. Neurophysiology: an integration (molecules, neurons and behavior). In J. Field (Ed.), *Handbook of physiology: section 1, neurophysiology, vol. 3.* Washington, D.C.: American Physiological Society, 1960.

Hartmann, G.W. The field theory of learning and its educational consequences. In N.B. Henry (Ed.), *Forty-first yearbook of the National Society for the Study of Education: part 2: the psychology of learning.* Chicago: University of Chicago Press, 1942.

Hellebrandt, F.A. Cross education: ipsilateral and contralateral effects of unimanual training. *Journal of Applied Psychology,* 1951, *4,* 136-143.

Hellebrandt, F.A., Parrish, A.M., & Houtz, S.J. Cross-education: the influence of unilateral exercise on the contralateral limb. *Archives of Physical Medicine,* 1947, *28,* 76-84.

Hendrickson, G., & Schroeder, W.H. Transfer of training in learning to hit a submerged target. *Journal of Educational Psychology,* 1941, *32,* 205-213.

Holding, D.H. An approximate transfer surface. *Journal of Motor Behavior,* 1976, *8,* 1-9.

Hunt, J. McV. *Intelligence and experience.* New York: Ronald Press, 1961.

Judd, C.H. The relation of special training to special intelligence. *Educational Review,* 1908, *36,* 28-42.

Kay, H. The development of motor skills from birth to adolescence. In E.A. Bilodeau (Ed.), *Principles of skill acquisition.* New York: Academic Press, 1969.

Krueger, W.C. The effect of overlearning on retention. *Journal of Experimental Psychology,* 1929, *12,* 71-78.

Lawther, J.D. *The learning of physical skills.* Englewood Cliffs, N.J.: Prentice-Hall, 1968.

Lawther, J.D. Movement education and skill learning. *Gymnasion,* 1969, *1,* 13-16.

Melnick, M.J. Effects of overlearning on the retention of a gross motor skill. *Research Quarterly,* 1971, *42,* 60-69.

Moritani, T., & deVries, H.A. Neural factors vs. hypertrophy in the time course of muscle strength gain. *American Journal of Physical Medicine,* 1979, *58,* 115-130.

Nelson, D.O. Studies of transfer of learning in gross motor skills. *Research Quarterly,* 1957, *28,* 364-373.

Nessler, J. *An experimental study of methods adapted to teaching low-skilled freshman women in physical education.* Unpublished doctoral dissertation, Pennsylvania State University, 1961.

Osgood, C.E. The similarity paradox in human learning: a resolution. *Psychological Review,* 1949, *56,* 132-143.

Oxendine, J.B. *Psychology of motor learning.* New York: Appleton-Century-Crofts, 1968.

Purdy, B.J., & Lockhart, A. Retention and relearning of gross motor skills after long periods of no practice. *Research Quarterly,* 1962, *33,* 265-272.

Sale, D.G. *Chronic plasticity in reflex pathways: effects of training and disuse.* Paper presented at 27th Annual Meeting of the American College of Sports Medicine, Las Vegas, Nevada, May 1980.

Salmela, J.H. Psychology and sport: fear of applying. In P. Klavora & J.V. Daniel (Eds.), *Coach, athlete, and the sport psychologist.* Toronto: University of Toronto School of Physical and Health Education, 1979.

Singer, R.N. *Motor learning and human performance* (2nd ed.). New York: MacMillan, 1975.

Singer, R.N. *Motor learning and human performance* (3rd ed.). New York: MacMillan, 1980.

Snodgrass, J.E. Personal communication, December 1980.

Suinn, R.M. Psychology and sports performance: principles and applications. In W.F. Straub (Ed.), *Sport psychology: an analysis of athlete behavior* (2nd ed.). Ithaca, N.Y.: Mouvement Publications, 1978.

Walters, C.E. The effect of overload on bilateral transfer of motor skill. *Physical Therapy Review,* 1955, *35,* 567-569.

10 INSTRUCTIONAL TASKS

The focus throughout this book has been on the role of the practitioner in enhancing motor skill learning and performance. In Part One we looked at the practical implications of various learning theories. In Part Two three factors contributing to learning and performance were emphasized: the state of the learner, the nature of the skill, and the methods of instruction.

The purpose of this chapter is to pull together the major concepts presented in this book into a systematic framework that can help you apply the concepts in practice. This framework is organized into a system of instructional tasks or responsibilities: (1) analyzing the skill, (2) assessing the state of the learner and establishing proficiency goals, (3) designing instruction, and (4) evaluating and revising instruction. Each of these is broken down into subtasks to facilitate application. However, it is not the intent of this chapter to provide specific details on each of the tasks. Rather, you should refer to previous sections of this book as each of the tasks is highlighted.

Obviously, the instructional tasks presented here do not include all of a practitioner's responsibilities. For example, kinesiological or biomechanical analysis of a skill is an essential task. In addition, the organization of students for instruction (e.g., group, stations, or a combination of organizational methods) is important to effective communication and practice. Moreover, there are other outcomes besides motor skill learning that the teacher must be concerned with, such as social interaction and affective development. However, as long as we recognize the limitations of the tasks presented here, the framework proposed can be of assistance in bridging the gap between learning theory and instructional practice.

In Chapter 1 the importance of preplanning instruction was emphasized (see Fig. 1-4). This is certainly not a new concept; as practitioners, we have always been concerned with skill analysis and lesson plans. However, we have all too often failed to be systematic and inclusive. For example, skill analysis has generally been limited to the motor or movement aspects of a skill, and the traditional lesson plan has failed to take into consideration specific plans for structuring the

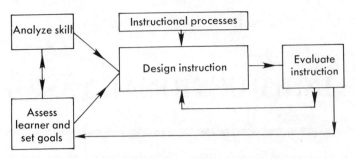

FIG. 10-1. A system of instructional tasks.

learning and practice environment and prearranged plans for improving performance. Singer (1977) states the problem very well.

> A traditionally taught physical activity class can be designated, for a start, with a series of "nots." Instructional objectives are not specified. Entry characteristics are not evaluated. Learning research and theory is usually not known by the instructor to any reasonable extent and is thus not put into operation within the instructional period (p. 120).

In addition, we have been notably negligent in preplanning a systematic means for evaluating and modifying our own performance as practitioners. We must be concerned not only with improving the performance of our students but also with improving our own performance, because the two are interdependent. Only as we continue to improve our instructional proficiency can we expect to help students reach their highest level of motor skill proficiency.

Therefore a major contention of this chapter is that we need to preplan, not only for instruction, but also for the evaluation of that instruction. Fig. 10-1 suggests a system of instructional tasks that need to be preplanned. Each of these tasks and the subtasks involved are discussed in the remainder of this chapter.

Analyze the skill

Fig. 10-1 emphasizes that the design of instruction should be based on the nature of the skill to be learned, on the status of the learner, and on what we know about the learning process. Only in this way can we systematically design instruction to fit both the specific skill and the individual learner.

However, there is some difference of opinion as to whether the practitioner should begin with an analysis of the skill or with a consideration of the learner's capacities. The assumption made in Chapter 8 was that we are more likely to analyze a skill realistically if we begin by studying the skill as it is executed in the performance situation.

In addition, if we begin by considering the learner's status first, we often underestimate the capacity of the learner. Consider, for example, the case of the archery student described in Chapter 1. The assumption that the student would not be able to participate in archery because she was handicapped by the absence of a forearm might have been avoided if the objective of the skill had been the primary consideration.

The problem of whether to consider the skill or the learner first can be solved by selecting a method of skill analysis, such as that suggested by Billing (1980), in which a skill is analyzed in terms of its perceptual, decision-making, movement, and feedback components (see Fig. 8-5). When this kind of analysis is followed by the assessment of the learner, the practitioner has a sound basis for simplifying the skill and for sequencing instruction so as to attain higher levels of proficiency.

A worksheet for skill analysis is on p. 222, which can help you achieve the objective of fitting instruction both to the skill and to the learner. Not all of the questions asked will be applicable to every skill, but each question should be considered. After answering each question, you should list specific implications for instruction. Obviously, you will want to refer to previous sections of this book, since each of the questions can only be highlighted here.

WHAT IS THE OBJECTIVE OF THE SKILL?

Recall that the objective of the skill refers to the purpose of an act (e.g., intercept the ball, stand on your head, put the arrow in the gold). In most skills the particular movement employed is only a means to an end. Although a few skills, such as diving, figure skating, and gymnastics, are judged in terms of their movement form, this is not true of all so-called closed skills. For example, the objective of a racing start is speed, and instruction should therefore be designed with this objective in mind. Thus the form of the start should be the movement that gives that individual the greatest speed (within the confines of the official rules, of course). In addition, the terminal proficiency goal should be in terms of speed. The most effective feedback would involve a comparison of knowledge of results (KR [speed]) and knowledge of performance (KP [movement]).

WHAT ARE THE RELEVANT (REGULATORY) STIMULI?

The relevant (regulatory) stimuli are the stimuli the performer must concentrate on to execute the skill successfully. At this point in our analysis we want to consider attention demands at high proficiency levels. For example, in any skill involving the tracking of a moving object (ball, bird, puck), attention must be on the object.

Number and priority?—There is seldom only one regulatory cue in open

Worksheet for skill analysis

Analysis of the skill	Implications for instruction
1. What is the objective of the skill?	
2. What are the relevant stimuli? Number and priority? Duration and intensity? Conflicting stimuli?	
3. What are the decision-making requirements? Criteria? Sequence? Speed?	
4. What are the movement requirements? Consistency? Coherence? Precision? Continuity? Conflicting reflexes?	
5. What intrinsic feedback is available? Type? Amount? Quality?	
6. What are the major ability requirements?	
7. What is the optimal arousal level?	

skills. In a volleyball spike, for example, the spiker needs to consider the position of opposing players. This suggests that we need to prioritize the regulatory cues for a specific skill. In the volleyball spike the primary regulatory cues would be the setup to the spiker and the net; a secondary cue might be the position and movement of opposing players. The important implication for instruction is that regulatory cues need to be present in the practice situation. Primary cues should be present from the beginning; secondary and tertiary cues, if not present at the beginning, need to be introduced as soon as possible.

Duration and intensity?—Billing (1980) has emphasized the desirability of analyzing not only the number of regulatory cues but also their duration and intensity (see Fig. 8-5). By increasing the duration of a regulatory stimulus or its intensity, we can simplify a skill for the beginner. Some of Billing's (1980) suggestions are noted in Chapter 8. For example, we can slow a ball down to give learners time to think about their response.

Confusing stimuli?—In addition, Billing (1980) suggests that we should include in our analysis of the perceptual requirements of a skill the confusing stimuli that may be present. This would appear to be worthwhile when these confusing or conflicting stimuli are an inherent part of the performance situation (e.g., the banter of the catcher or the "hiding" of the ball by the quarterback in football). Such confusing stimuli also need to be introduced into the practice situation as soon as possible so that the individual can learn to adapt to them.

WHAT ARE THE DECISION-MAKING REQUIREMENTS?

Criteria?—Let's return briefly to our example of the volleyball spiker. Obviously, the particular action plan of the spiker will depend on the setup; that is, of course, what makes the setup a regulatory cue. However, the spiker may decide to "dink" the ball rather than spike it. What determines such a decision? A "dink" may be used as an element of surprise to confuse the opponent; it may be used when the spiker perceives the movement of the opponent to be an effective block. The point being made here is that at some point in instruction, the learner must be taught the criteria for choosing one strategy over another.

Sequence?—As Billing (1980) notes, some skills, such as the standing broad jump, require little in the way of decision making, while others, such as the three-on-two fast break in basketball, require several decisions—Dribble or pass? To whom? When to shoot? What shot? The task for the performer becomes more feasible if the sequence for making such decisions is learned.

Speed or reaction time?—Although it is conceivable that the decision-making requirements of a skill might be simplified by setting up controlled drill situations in which the number of decisions to be made and the number of alternatives are reduced, a more effective approach would seem to be reducing the speed at which the decisions must be made. This allows the performer the opportunity to learn the criteria and sequencing of decisions. As this learning is achieved, the drill can be gradually speeded up until it simulates the choice reaction time (CRT) typical of the game situation.

WHAT ARE THE MOVEMENT REQUIREMENTS?

One of the most productive methods of analyzing the movement requirements of a skill would appear to be the use of scales or continuums such as those described in Chapter 8. The following movement considerations are recommended: consistency, coherence, accuracy, and continuity. Each is reiterated briefly here.

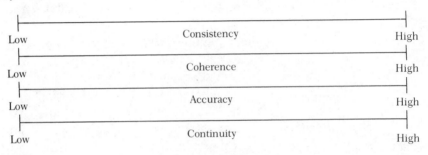

Consistency?—Closed skills such as diving, gymnastics, and synchronized swimming may be seen to require consistency of movement, that is, little variability from one performance to the next. Open skills, conversely, require the capacity to vary movements to adapt to the game situation at any particular moment in time. The instructional implications of the open-closed skill dichotomy have been emphasized repeatedly throughout this book. Suffice it to note here that there is considerable danger in extended isolated drill in open skills, such as a tennis drive, since this tends to "set" the movement through overlearning (e.g., make it more fixed rather than variable). Conversely, a tennis serve, which requires a relatively consistent movement, may, like diving, profit from extended drill. However, even in these cases, practice must also encompass actual performance conditions, as our discussion of practice-to-performance transfer in Chapter 9 emphasized. Incidentally, consistency of movement does not imply that everyone must use the same movement, only that the movement for any one individual needs to become more consistent. For example, in high jumping individuals should use the movement that is the most biomechanically efficient for them. Only when a skill is judged on the basis of a specific form would we dictate one set form for all.

Coherence?—Recall that in highly coherent skills (walking, skating, diving) one part of the movement is dependent on the previous part. Thus the more coherent a skill, the less likely we can break it down into parts for the purpose of instruction and, at the same time, maintain its integrity as a specific skill. As physical educators, we have been notoriously guilty of splitting a skill into very arbitrary parts. Johnson (1972) notes, for example, that one authority views the tennis forehand as being composed of more than a dozen distinct parts (p. 29). There are many reasons for avoiding part practice (e.g., Johnson, 1972), and more will be said later in this chapter of the controversy of whole versus part. Suffice it to note here that the practice of breaking a skill down into so-called subskills must take into consideration the coherence of the skill. Only when the subskill is a functional skill in its own right (e.g., sculling in a synchronized swimming stunt) should it be considered a desirable candidate for independent practice.

Accuracy?—Some skills, such as archery, require that the end result of the performance of the skill (e.g., putting the arrow in the gold) be highly accurate. Although somewhat less precision is required of a basketball player taking a free throw (the ball may hit the backboard or rim and still go through the basket), the free throw would still fall in the upper half of the accuracy continuum. Decreasing the accuracy requirement of a skill is a common method of simplifying a skill for the beginner. However, this might better be achieved by decreasing proficiency goals than by increasing the size of the target. For example, rather than enlarging the size of the basketball hoop, as some recommend, gradually increase the proficiency expectation from 2 out of 10 to 5 out of 10, and so on.

Continuity?—In the scale at the top of p. 183 several skills were placed on a scale from continuous to discrete, depending on the extent to which the movements of the skill are repetitive. Thus bicycling was seen to fall at the high end of the scale and the tennis serve (used only to start a point) at its lower end. Obviously, highly repetitive skills are usually learned (and overlearned) more rapidly than discrete skills. There are at least two major implications for instruction. First, more practice time needs to be devoted to discrete skills to bring them to the overlearning point. Second, erroneous practice of repetitive skills, for even short periods of time, runs the risk of "setting" incorrect patterns. Thus highly continuous skills need to be monitored closely so that errors are not overlearned.

There is at least one other aspect of the movement requirements of a skill that needs to be considered, and that is the extent to which the movement involves specific neuromuscular reflexes (head-righting, equilibrium, etc.) that might interfere with performance. These were discussed in some detail in Chapter 3, and you may want to review them at this time. Suffice it to note here that it is the practitioner's responsibility to be aware of these reflexes and to help the learner inhibit them, if need be.

WHAT INTRINSIC FEEDBACK IS AVAILABLE?

The importance of feedback to learning has been a recurring theme throughout this book. However, there are several facets of feedback that need to be considered in the analysis of a skill: the type of intrinsic feedback available, the amount, and its quality.

Type?—The suggestion has been made that KR is more useful in open skills and KP in closed skills. However, this is a generalization that has exceptions; we must consider the objective of the skill. For example, the objective of a racing start is speed. Therefore we should ask ourselves to what extent is feedback relative to speed intrinsic in the performance of the start itself. Unfortunately, little if any intrinsic KR regarding speed is available in a racing start. Obviously, then, this information must be provided by the practitioner (supplementary feedback). In addition, there appear to be few skills that provide KP intrinsically, since performers cannot usually view their own movements (and kinesthetic feedback has limitations, as noted in Chapter 5). Obviously, the supplementary provision for mirrors, videotape, and so on, becomes a major task of the practitioner.

Amount?—Some skills have a great deal of intrinsic feedback. Other skills have very little, and the learner must depend on supplementary feedback provided by the practitioner. For example, in target archery the performer gets immediate and specific KR (the arrow went into the outer circle). The practitioner does not need to supply KR but rather must be concerned with providing information that will assist the learner in improving the next performance (KP). Conversely, in a racing start the objective is speed, and there is little if any intrinsic KR regarding speed available. The practitioner is faced with the task of providing not only KR (speed) but also the movement information (KP) to improve the speed of the next start.

Quality?—Even when there is a great deal of feedback intrinsic to the skill, its quality may be lacking. For example, compare a tennis drive with target archery. In target archery the performer receives very specific KR (the arrow was low and to the right), whereas the tennis drive, even when the ball falls within the court boundaries, does not indicate the precision with which the player can place the ball within the court. Obviously, supplementary feedback arrangements, such as dividing the tennis court into placement areas or providing points of aim within the court, might be useful supplementary KR in the tennis drive. Recall also that success is a powerful determinant of future performance. The extent to which an individual can succeed in a skill by using poor biomechanics increases the probability that the action plan will be repeated. Feedback that answers the question To what extent did I achieve the goal? would appear to be more valuable than that which merely answers the question Did I succeed, or not? Although the latter provides reinforcement, little information is available.

WHAT ABILITIES ARE REQUIRED?

Chapter 7 discussed specific perceptual and motor abilities, and the importance of analyzing the ability requirements of a skill was emphasized in Chapter 8 on skill analysis. To reiterate briefly here, knowledge of the ability requirements of a skill can be used to (1) help identify individuals' performance problems (e.g., dynamic visual acuity or flexibility), (2) structure individualized training programs to meet the performers' deficiencies, and (3) provide performers with advance information so that they will make use of the ability in the game situation (e.g., peripheral vision).

If individuals lack a basic ability required by a skill, continued failure leads to frustration and, often, dislike of the activity. We need to know where the problem is and how to alleviate it. The problem may not be apparent in the earliest stages of learning, however. Recall that there may be a change in the ability requirements of a skill as practice continues and proficiency increases.

Thus we must continually monitor performance, and when there is an indication that the individual is failing to improve, despite his desire to do so, a screening for ability problems may be in order. At that point it may be necessary to design a detour ability training program until the individual is ready to reenter the originally designed program.

WHAT IS THE OPTIMAL AROUSAL LEVEL?

Although the optimal arousal level for peak performance on a particular skill is unlikely to be the best arousal level for learning that skill, it should be kept in mind. As learners increase in proficiency they should also be increasing their ability to control their own arousal in accord with the nature of the various skills involved in the activity. For example, the tennis player who maintains the same level of arousal (tension) for all strokes will tend to become a less efficient player than the one who has learned to change pace (e.g., ease up on drop shots).

Arousal control (and change of pace) is an important ability contributing to performance, and although general arousal control training programs (e.g., relaxation training) are useful, the principle of specificity of skills suggests that the pattern of arousal required in one activity (tennis) may be quite different from that required in another (basketball). By knowing the optimal arousal levels for the various tennis skills (volley, lob, smash), we have some basis for establishing a basic arousal pattern for that activity.

Determine the learner's proficiency goals

The instructional system shown in Fig. 10-1 emphasizes the need to establish proficiency goals. Only when we know what we are trying to accomplish can we effectively design instruction or evaluate the student's progress (or our own).

However, to effectively sequence instruction, we need to establish proficiency goals in a systematic way. The practitioner needs to consider (1) the terminal goal desired, (2) the learner's current level of proficiency, and (3) a set of intermediate goals that will allow learners to progress from their current proficiency to desired proficiency in the time allowable.

TERMINAL GOALS

Table 6 depicts a relatively simple, individualized program for a golf drive. In this case the terminal goal was established on the basis of the learner's current proficiency on that skill. However, it is often desirable or necessary to establish the terminal objective first. For example, in rehabilitation, a therapist may determine that for the patient to carry out necessary daily activities, a specific terminal proficiency is required. In this case, the terminal goal is established first, then the patient's current proficiency.

However, the assumption made in this chapter is that physical education in the schools is usually time-bound; that is, the practitioner and the learner have an allotted time frame (e.g., a semester) within which instruction must be "fitted." In this case, it seems more appropriate to begin by assessing the learner's current level of proficiency and then to establish a realistic terminal goal that both the practitioner and the learner deem achievable within the time allotted. Thus the terminal goal stated in Table 6—using a No. 1 wood, the learner can drive 8 out of 10 balls off the tee for a distance of 175 yards—was determined as a realistic goal for six half-hour sessions, based on the learner's starting (current) proficiency, which was 1 out of 3 balls for 70 yards.

Note that all of the proficiency goals in Table 6 (current, terminal, and intermediate) are stated in measurable or observable terms. Only by stating goals in observable terms can we effectively (1) design instruction, (2) evaluate the progress of a student, and (3) evaluate our own instructional performance. There are two major considerations in stating such goals:

1. What is it that the learner must do to demonstrate the achievement of the goal?
2. To what extent will the learner be able to do it?

The following examples of some terminal proficiency statements should help to clarify this important task:

1. The learner can drive a golf ball from a tee, using a No. 1 wood, 8 out of 10 times to a point 175 yards from the point it is hit.
2. The learner, using a 3-point partial weight-bearing gait (PWB) of the right lower extremity (RLE), demonstrates independence in (a) getting in and out of a wheelchair and (b) going up and down stairs. (*Independence* is defined as success in 2 out of 4 trials.)

Table 6 □ *Sample worksheet for proficiency goals (golf drive)**

	Proficiency goals	Demonstrated proficiency	Problems and solutions
T	Drive 8 out of 10 balls to a distance of 175 yd off the tee, using a No. 1 wood.	7 balls at 175 yd; 3 balls at 150 yd	
5	7 out of 10 balls at 175 yd	6 balls at 175 yd; 3 balls at 150 yd	
4	5 out of 10 balls at 175 yd	5 balls at 175 yd; 3 balls at 150 yd	
3	3 out of 10 balls at 175 yd	2 balls at 175 yd; 4 balls at 150 yd	
2	5 out of 10 balls at 150 yd	3 balls at 140 yd	Head-shoulder linkage; practice with imagery?
1	3 out of 10 balls at 150 yd	2 balls at 140 yd	
C		1 out of 3 balls at 70 yd	

*T, Terminal goal; C, current proficiency; 1-5, intermediate goals.

3. The child can, without assistance, dial a telephone number correctly 5 times in succession without error.

It should be noted that terminal goals may be stated in terms of a set of proficiencies for a unit of instruction (e.g., a semester of badminton). However, the skills encompassed (e.g., serve, clear, smash) should also be stated in proficiency terms.

CURRENT PROFICIENCIES

Although much lip service has been given in education regarding the desirability of fitting instruction to the learner's level, seldom do we actually know what students are already able to do when they come to us. Often, we assume that they have no background, and we proceed to teach beginning tennis, which we may view as consisting of instruction in forehand, backhand, and serve. As Singer (1977) notes, "Although in all of education the importance of measuring and considering entry behaviors is acknowledged in the learning process, apparently little research and practice proceeds along these lines" (p. 116).

This does not mean that the practitioner is not familiar with the practice of pretesting. Too often pretesting is done together with posttesting at the end of instruction to provide a means for measuring improvement and for grading. This is a very limited use of pretesting. Assessing current proficiency is necessary to allow us not only to set challenging but realistic terminal proficiency goals but also to give direction to the content and sequencing of instruction.

Pretesting is, of course, one method of assessing current proficiency. For example, a battery of tests for various badminton skills can be administered that can give us some indication of where we need to begin instruction and of how far we can expect to go within a given period of time.

However, pretesting in its formal sense is not the only way to assess current proficiency; I may demonstrate a skill and ask the learner to try it. In Table 6, for example, the learner, after seeing the golf drive demonstrated, was asked to drive 3 balls, and the results were recorded.

However, there are other considerations in regard to a learner's background that the practitioner may want to consider. Because of the specificity of skills, the learner's background of experience in other skills may be relevant to the design of instruction. For example, knowing that a badminton student has experience in tennis can provide a basis for "chunking" information in the early stages of learning. In addition, such knowledge suggests that an important task of the practitioner, especially in the later stages of instruction, will be to design instruction so that differences are pointed out.

INTERMEDIATE GOALS

The establishment of intermediate goals leading to the desired terminal proficiency serves the following purposes.

1. INTERMEDIATE GOALS PROVIDE A BASIS FOR ESTIMATING THE PROGRESS OF THE LEARNER. Rather than depending solely on evaluation at the end of instruction, progress can be monitored continually and problems identified while there is still time to do something about them. In Table 6, for example, expected improvement in the golf drive did not occur. The learner was allowing his head to rotate with his shoulders (head-shoulder linkage). In this case, mental imagery was sufficient to solve the problem; the individual was asked to continue looking at an imaginary ball on the tee during the follow-through.

2. INTERMEDIATE GOALS, BEING INDIVIDUALIZED, ALLOW LEARNERS TO CONCENTRATE ON THOSE SKILLS IN WHICH THEY NEED THE MOST WORK.

3. INTERMEDIATE GOALS TEND TO BE HIGHLY MOTIVATING. Such short-term goals provide reinforcement that increases the probability of achieving higher levels of proficiency. Thus the Law of Effect is operating throughout the period of instruction.

Intermediate goals and, indeed, terminal goals should be flexible. At best, they are an estimate of the rate at which an individual can progress. If demonstrated proficiency exceeds the established goals, the goals should be revised upward.

The desirability of writing down proficiency goals should be obvious. However, we also need to emphasize that demonstrated proficiency needs to be recorded. This is a task that can be handled by each learner. For example, proficiency goals, as shown in Table 6, can be entered on a 3 × 5 card that learners carry with them. They can then record their results. Discrepancies would signal to learners that they should check with their teacher to help resolve the difficulty.

An important aspect of goal setting, if it is to achieve all of its purposes, is that learners should have a part in establishing and revising their goals. Obviously, the practitioner has the experience, both with the skill and with teaching it, that is necessary to set challenging but realistic goals. However, learners must see themselves as being able to achieve these goals. Since the goals are flexible, nothing is lost by considering the learner's point of view.

Design instruction

The instructional system diagramed in Fig. 10-1 emphasizes that the design of instruction must include not only the nature of the skill and the status of the learner but also what we know about the learning process. These processes were discussed in Part One of this book and most conspicuously in Chapter 4 on information processing. Although we are far from having a science of learning at this point, learning theorists are beginning to unravel some of the mysteries of learning. As a result, several models of skill acquisition have been formulated that provide the practitioner with a framework for the design of instruction.

One of the most popular models has been that of Gentile (1972). She suggests that, regardless of the particular skill to be learned, all learners go through essentially the same processes. As paraphrased by Pease (1977), Gentile's (1972) model of skill acquisition involves the following sequence of events.

The learner:
(1) Perceives what is to be learned and desires to try it
(2) Identifies the relevant stimuli in the environment
(3) Formulates a motor [action] plan
(4) Emits a response
(5) Attends to the results
(6) Revises the motor [action] plan
(7) Emits another response (and repeats steps 5, 6 and 7) (p. 105)

This particular model of skill acquisition appears to have special usefulness for the practitioner because it can be translated into a sequence of instructional tasks. Pease (1977), in fact, has formulated a teaching model based on Gentile's learning model, which you may want to study.

The worksheet on p. 232 suggests a different framework for designing instruction that appears to be consistent with Gentile's learning model while, at the same time, allowing for consideration of some of the major concepts presented in this book. It should be noted, however, that the tasks enumerated on the worksheet constitute only a tentative framework for designing instruction. At best, this

Instructional processes □ *Worksheet for design of instruction*

1. *Structure the environment*
   _____ Provide appropriate regulatory cues
   _____ Control noise sources
   _____ Arrange for supplementary feedback

2. *Establish a concept of purpose*
   _____ Clarify the objective of the skill
   _____ Demonstrate the skill
   _____ Determine the learner's level

3. *Emphasize essentials of the skill*
   _____ Identify regulatory cues
   _____ Suggest an action plan
   _____ Identify focus of concentration

4. *Enhance retention of instruction*
   _____ Use appropriate sensory modality
   _____ "Chunk" instruction
   _____ Provide immediate practice

5. *Provide practice opportunities*
   _____ Provide realistic practice conditions
   _____ Stress whole practice
   _____ Individualize practice

6. *Improve performance*
   _____ Compare outcome with proficiency goal or action plan
   _____ Provide feedback to improve next performance
   _____ Update proficiency goals

framework must be flexible, to be changed as a learner's needs and new evidence dictate. In addition, there are undoubtedly instructional considerations that have not been included. You are encouraged to revise and refine the checklist so that it becomes, for you, a more useful guide for designing instruction.

Each of the tasks and subtasks listed on the worksheet is discussed only briefly here to clarify the nature of the task. You will want to refer to previous sections of this book for more detailed information. Moreover, in using the checklist to design instruction for a specific skill, you must keep in front of you your analysis of the skill (worksheet on p. 222) and the learner's proficiency goals (Table 6).

STRUCTURE THE ENVIRONMENT

The purpose of preplanning the learning environment is to help ensure that the essentials for learning a particular skill are present. The importance of providing the necessary regulatory cues and a feasible arrangement for effective information feedback can hardly be overstressed. The fact remains that we tend to assume that these can be provided off the cuff during teaching. Not so. They must be given creative consideration beforehand to ensure their effectiveness.

In addition, since the most appropriate learning environment (including regulatory cues and feedback) may be somewhat different as a learner's proficiency increases, restructuring the learning environment is a continuous process. The problem is basically one of providing the appropriate regulatory cues and feedback while at the same time controlling noise.

Provide appropriate regulatory cues—The importance of providing a realistic practice situation has been emphasized throughout this book. Recall that regulatory cues were defined as relevant stimuli required for effective performance. However, since all the perceptual cues essential to high proficiency may prove to be an overload for the beginner, the practitioner needs to establish a priority for introducing regulatory cues into the practice situation. For example, in learning to bat, a pitched ball (or simulated pitch from a ball machine) would appear to be a requisite regulatory cue even for the beginner. However, pitching variations, opposing fielders, and baserunners are also regulatory cues and should be introduced as soon as possible. The point being made here is that the practitioner must plan ahead so as to ensure that the appropriate regulatory cues will be included at some point.

Control noise sources—We commonly think of noise as environmental stimuli that interfere with attention and concentration. However, *noise* was defined earlier as the overload of any of the information-handling processes of the individual, from either external or internal sources. Noise may be visual (lack of figure-ground clarity), auditory (spectators' comments), or tactile (poor steering or brake mechanisms in a car or poorly fitting sports equipment). However, when distracting stimuli are an inherent part of the performance situation, the practitioner must gradually introduce them into the practice situation so that the individual can learn to adapt to them, or filter them out. In addition, since the learner is progressively able to filter out irrelevant stimuli, what constitutes noise for the beginner may be quite different from that affecting a more advanced performer. The practitioner must therefore plan ahead to structure the learning environment in terms of both the stage of learning and the nature of the specific skill.

Arrange for appropriate supplementary feedback—Arranging for appropriate supplementary feedback is such an essential element in learning that the practitioner must give it creative thought beforehand. Too often we wait until the individual has performed, and rely on correction, usually verbal, after the fact. By making arrangements beforehand for the most appropriate type of feedback (depending on the level of the learner and the nature of the skill), we can greatly enhance the effectiveness of supplementary feedback (e.g., the provision for mirrors in dance and points of aim in accuracy skills). By making arrangements for such feedback tools to be used by the learners in the practice situation, practitioners can also extend their help to all students rather than just the few they may be able to view directly at any one point in time. Such self-evaluation methods also give the learner more immediate feedback. In addition, if progressive goals are established in connection with such self-evaluation techniques, the practitioner's time can be spent with those learners who are not progressing. But self-evaluative feedback methods take creative thought and time to set them up. Skill analysis, including the objective of the skill and its status on the open-closed scale, can help the practitioner focus on the most appropriate type of supplementary feedback (worksheet on p. 222).

ESTABLISH A CONCEPT OF PURPOSE

Despite the fact that learning can occur unconsciously, the point of view taken here is that it is apt to occur more rapidly if learners know what they are supposed to accomplish. Thus the practitioner needs to (1) clarify the objective of the skill, (2) demonstrate the skill, and (3) determine the learner's level.

Clarify the objective of the skill—Analyzing the objective of the skill (hit the ball, stand on your head, put the arrow in the gold) has been stressed throughout this book. Unfortunately, although we usually know what the objective is, we often fail to communicate it to the learner. For example, what is the objective of an offensive volley in tennis? Too often we assume that the objective of a skill is so obvious that there is no need to clarify it, and we proceed immediately to teaching the movement form for the stroke. If, instead, the learner is shown the objective of the offensive volley (to decrease the time the opponent has to react efficiently), the movements will make sense to him. Similarly, the learner should be made aware that the objective of a badminton clear is to "clear" the racket reach of the opponent and thus force the opponent into the backcourt.

Demonstrate the skill—Generally, the most effective way to help a learner get the idea of a skill is to demonstrate it, without concurrent verbalization, if possible. However, there is some need for caution. For example, if a complex routine on the trampoline is demonstrated, some learners may say (at least to themselves), "No way!"; that is, the perceived degree of difficulty is such that they cannot see themselves as being capable of learning it. Imagine, for example, a demonstration of juggling 5 balls. Obviously, lower proficiency levels (e.g., juggling 2 balls) can be demonstrated initially while communicating the idea of how the skill is done at the same time. Note that a demonstration may be given by videotape or film, if necessary. In addition, some learners may get the idea of the skill through tactile or verbal means.

Determine the learner's level—A great deal of instruction time could be saved (and motivation enhanced) if we would let learners try the skill following the demonstration. Some may have identified the regulatory cues and come up with an effective, if not perfect, action plan from the initial presentation. If so, it may be desirable to have these individuals move directly into practice on the skill (with prearranged, self-evaluative feedback). Those who have not achieved an effective action plan are ready to learn the essentials of the skill.

EMPHASIZE ESSENTIALS OF THE SKILL

At this point, learners know the purpose of the skill and are aware that they need help in learning. Thus they are apt to be motivated to attend to instructions designed to help them improve.

However, instruction at this point should convey only that information which is necessary to approximate the performance of the skill, either in terms of results or movement, depending on the nature of the skill and the stage of learning. There are several reasons practitioners should not dwell on details in the early stages of learning. First and foremost, however, is that learning, as viewed in this book, is a process of gradual differentiation, both perceptually and motorically. Therefore the practitioner should begin at the learner's demonstrated level by (1) calling attention to the regulatory cues appropriate to the stage of learning, (2) gradually refining the action or movement plan (gross framework idea), and (3) identifying the focus of concentration.

Identify relevant regulatory cues—Even if we assume that learners have the desire to learn and have a clear idea of the outcome to be produced, they must learn to attend to the relevant stimuli that regulate that performance. For example, the skier must note the configurations of the terrain, the presence of ice patches, and the position of other skiers, including their direction and speed. By analyzing the skill beforehand, the practitioner has already prioritized the regulatory cues and can decrease or increase the difficulty of the skill according to the learner's level. For example, a relatively flat terrain with relatively few skiers may be more appropriate for the beginner. The word relative is important. The absence of all regulatory cues should be avoided, if possible.

Suggest an action plan—While, traditionally, we have emphasized learning the correct form of movement, there are several reasons for believing that the learner's attention should be directed more to the objective of the movement than to its precise form, except in those skills where the success is judged in terms of form. As you recall, much movement integration occurs below the level of conscious awareness, and concentration on isolated parts can result in ineffective movement. In addition, individuals differ in their structural characteristics. Although there are biomechanical principles that should be applied, what is effective form for one individual is not necessarily so for another. Lawther (1968) suggests that the "gross framework" approach has the advantage of being adaptable to individual structural characteristics. "If the learner gets the general idea and is motivated to practice, he will gradually adjust his performance to his own individuality as a result of his feedback from practice results" (p. 155). However, the practitioner can speed up this process by getting individuals into a biomechanically efficient position and by gradually inhibiting unneeded (extraneous) movements.

Identify focus of concentration—Recall from our discussion of the limited concentration channel (LCC) in Chapter 4 (see Fig. 4-7) that learners cannot effectively concentrate on more than one thing at a time (e.g., regulatory cues and motor control). However, the answer does not necessarily lie in eliminating regulatory cues (a moving ball in batting) to concentrate on the action plan (swinging the bat). Rather, the practitioner should study the skill analysis (worksheet on p. 222) to find ways of simplifying the concentration demands while maintaining the essentials of the skill. For example, tennis players often have a great deal of difficulty in executing an effective smash in badminton because the tennis smash has been overlearned. By manipulating the regulatory cues (e.g., setting the bird up higher), the tennis player has time to think about the action plan for the badminton smash. At times it is necessary or desirable to remove the regulatory cue briefly (e.g., get the feel of the badminton smash as compared to the tennis smash), but this should be of brief duration. In any case, the practitioner needs to identify the focus of concentration for the learner, and this will change, depending on the stage of learning and the nature of the skill. The practitioner, in addition, should already have determined where concentration needs to be focused for high proficiency and work toward achieving this focus.

Some guidelines for sensory modes of instruction

Verbal	Manual	Visual
Keep explanation to a minimum in early stages of learning.	Give feel of spatial pattern or point of force.	Demonstrate correctly; learners will differ in what they see.
Increase verbalization only as skill understanding increases.	Use only when learner has positive attitude toward it.	Maintain normal speed, if possible.
Avoid excessive analysis of movement of body parts.	Use only briefly so that individual kinesthesis can occur.	Present more than once, especially for beginners.

ENHANCE RETENTION OF INSTRUCTION

The information-processing model (see Fig. 4-2) emphasizes that between the reception of input (instruction, in this case) and the use of it by the learner, there are at least two major intervening processes that influence what "gets through" to the individual: the perceptual filter (PF) and the short-term store (STS). There are at least three things the practitioner should do to ensure that these processes do not interfere with instruction: (1) use the appropriate sensory modality, (2) "chunk" instruction, and (3) provide immediate practice.

Use appropriate sensory modality—Instruction, including feedback, can be visual, verbal, or manual (tactile), but the effectiveness of any one means depends on the nature of the skill, the stage of learning, and the capacities of the individual learner. In general, however, visual demonstration, rather than verbalization, appears to be more effective in the early stages of learning. The use of explanation may be useful in the later stages of learning as the individual becomes more proficient in the skill and more familiar with its terminology. The use of manual guidance (moving a part of the learner's body or providing resistance to movement) has been successful in teaching the deaf and blind, and there is some basis for believing that more extensive use of tactile methods could be productive. It appears to be especially useful in giving the learner an idea of the spatial pattern of a skill (e.g., drawing a bow) or of the site of force application (e.g., resistance on the soles of the feet in a crawl kick). However, since the feel of being moved is not the same as the individual's kinesthetic perception of his own movement, manual guidance should be relatively brief. An attempt is made in the boxed material at the top of this page to summarize some of Lockhart's (1966) suggestions. However, as she notes, "In practice, the good instructor uses all means of communication which are available to him. If one approach does not work, he tries another" (p. 66).

"Chunk" instruction—Recall that STS is limited by the amount of information it can hold. Instruction that contains a number of steps to be followed or items to be remembered is apt to be forgotten by the learner before it can be used. Often, however, the same information can be communicated to the learner by "chunking" the items into one or two phrases. Another way of "chunking" is to use analogies, drawing on the individual's transferable memory (e.g., "Crouch as though sitting in a chair"). Often, single cue words (e.g., "reach," "sweep") are useful. However, to be effective, "chunking" must be in terms familiar to the learner. Do not underestimate the importance of this task. Someone recently made a comment relative to the proposed 9-digit postal zip codes: "If we load the short-term memory bank with too many items, the bottom falls out and all is lost."

Provide immediate practice—STS, as you recall, is limited not only by the amount of information it can hold, but also by time. Unless put to use immediately, it is lost within seconds. Thus immediate practice is crucial. However, occasionally it is not feasible to practice immediately (e.g., waiting for space to practice or moving from one place to another). In this case, it behooves the practitioner to repeat the instruction (be it visual or verbal) again at the practice site. An alternative is to have students mentally rehearse the instruction (see Fig. 4-6). However, since individuals, through the PF, tend to transform (add, delete, or change) information (see Fig. 4-5), the practitioner needs to be cautious in his use of mental rehearsal in the early stages of learning. An exception to this is vocalized rehearsal. For example, Lockhart (1966) reports one study in which verbal rehearsal consisted of listening to instructions and then repeating them to a partner. In another study learners reported their interpretations of what they were to do. (Incidentally, colorful words such as *racket swishes* were best retained.) However, the investigator found that students often had not received the instruction as given. Vocalized rehearsal thus has the advantage of indicating the extent to which the learner has perceived instruction correctly. Whatever means is used, the practitioner has the responsibility of seeing that instruction is not lost by providing immediate practice, either physically or mentally.

PROVIDE PRACTICE OPPORTUNITIES

To reiterate a critical concept emphasized in this book, improvement in proficiency (learning) depends on the conditions of practice, not repetition. The old adages "practice makes perfect" or "the more practice, the better" are so misleading that they are best laid to rest. The question to be addressed should be What conditions of practice will yield the greatest returns in the least amount of time? The answers to this question have in fact been the focus of this book, and not all of them can be readdressed here. Certainly, the role of feedback is a crucial consideration and should not be thought of as being separate from practice. In addition, consideration of the amount of practice was addressed in some detail in Chapter 9 on retention and transfer. Therefore the focus in this short summary of instructional considerations is on those aspects of practice that are often over-looked by the practitioner: (1) the specificity of practice, (2) whole part practice, and (3) the role of proficiency goals in practice.

Provide realistic practice conditions—The specificity of learning has been stressed throughout this book, and in Chapter 9 practice was viewed as an original task that needed to be made transferable to the actual performance situation. The practice-to-performance transfer concept emphasizes that practice may enhance, have no effect, or even be detrimental to performance, depending on the extent to which the practice environment simulates the performance conditions. This includes providing not only the appropriate regulatory cues but also the psychological conditions typical of the performance situation. Thus, while open skills may be seen to require practice that provides the opportunity for developing variable responses (e.g., Arnold, 1978), closed skills, which should build toward a consistency of movement, also need to be practiced in realistic environments (e.g., wind, audience, judging). Obviously, there has to be some progression for introducing the realistic elements into the practice situation so that the beginner will not be overloaded. Unfortunately, there is little research to guide us in such sequencing. The possibility remains that we may be much too pessimistic regarding the ability of learners to adapt rapidly to extraneous stimuli. Let's try realistic practice situations early and do some field testing. We may be pleasantly surprised.

Stress whole practice—The evidence in favor of whole skill practice is substantial (Johnson, 1972). Unfortunately, part practice continues to be the dominant method used. For example, swimming is assumed to be a difficult task for a beginner, and each stroke is broken down into parts (kick, arm stroke, breathing), which are then practiced as isolated entities. There are at least three advantages to whole skill practice. First, the integration or coherence of the skill is maintained. Johnson (1972) notes, for example, that in basketball a pivot and reverse dribbling move is meaningless unless an opponent has forced the move by the defensive action (p. 31). Second, whole skill practice is more time efficient; that is, the learner does not have to spend time putting parts together. As a result, more time is available for overlearning, which, as you recall, is the major factor influencing retention. Third, whole skill practice is more motivating to the learner. Obviously, both the nature of the skill and level of the learner are important considerations, but the practitioner who uses part methods may be handicapping rather than helping the learner (Johnson, 1972, p. 31). However, brief practice of functional subskills (e.g., sculling in synchronized swimming) may be beneficial at times, especially for the more proficient who have already experienced the whole skill.

Individualize practice—The desirability of individualized proficiency goals has already been noted, and this assumes individualized practice. However, the task of individualizing practice need not be overwhelming. A station approach is, of course, one way of accomplishing this. For example, students may go to those stations that are set up for practicing the particular skills that they need the most work on. Students may have their own proficiency goals in hand, or a sequence of proficiency levels may be posted at each station. However, it is also possible to individualize practice within a group setting. The important provision in this case is that learners focus on that aspect of the skill on which they need work and recognize that they may be performing at a different level than that of another learner. Obviously, the task becomes more feasible if sequenced proficiency goals are available. Learners also need to be encouraged to seek help (information feedback [IF]) from the teacher when they find themselves having difficulty progressing to the next level.

IMPROVE PERFORMANCE

IF has been defined in this book as sensory input that makes possible an improvement in performance. This is different from traditional definitions of feedback in that it does not readily distinguish between instruction and IF. The assumption here is that all instruction should be IF, that is, information to improve performance based on the individuals' current proficiencies. While there are undoubtedly valid exceptions to this view of IF, it would appear to be a useful one for our purposes. It emphasizes that learners usually have some background on which we can begin to build, and the importance of determining the learner's current proficiencies has already been noted.

The questions remains, however, as to what kind of feedback is best for improving performance. Recall that a differentiation was made in Chapter 4 between feedback and IF. Learners are always receiving comments about their performance, from other students and even from themselves. Not all this feedback leads to improvement; in fact, it can be detrimental.

In addition, although KR and KP or even the comparison between them (evaluative feedback) may be useful components of IF, they do not automatically improve proficiency. For example, in target archery the performer receives immediate KR (the arrow hit the outer circle), but this does not necessarily help the individual improve, even when compared with KP (the movement felt right). Obviously, most skills are going to require supplementary IF (e.g., modification of movement or change in point of aim), and this is a primary task of the practitioner.

Despite the fact that supplementary feedback is one of the most important factors in the learning of motor skills, it appears that, as practitioners, we have been notably negligent in our consideration of this task. Fishman and Tobey (1978), following a comprehensive study of the types of supplementary feedback actually used by teachers, state the problem very well.

As this study progressed, it became evident that many of the differences in ways that feedback was administered were due to practical limitations and to what seemed to be a less difficult approach for the teacher. There was very little theoretical basis for variations in approach. In fact, individual teachers varied their approach very little. For a given teacher, the feedback tended to be stereotyped and habitual (p. 61).

For example, the types of feedback used most often were positive reinforcement ("Good girl") and concurrent movement correction ("No, point your toes more").

There are, however, no "cookie-cutter" answers to the problem. Fishman and Tobey (1978) suggest that, for a start, practitioners become cognizant of the many ways in which supplementary feedback can be given.

There appear to be at least two major steps in effecting improvement in proficiency: (1) a comparison of performance outcome with the proficiency goal or plan of action and (2) feedback that will improve the next performance. Both of these, it should be noted, imply the need to individualize IF.

Compare outcome with proficiency goal or action plan—The importance of evaluative feedback was discussed in Chapter 4 (see Fig. 4-9), and you may want to review that discussion at this point. However, the practitioner should continually review the analysis of a skill (p. 222) to determine the outcome (KR, KP, or both) that should be observed at any particular stage of learning. Needless to say, in the final analysis it is the objective of the skill that is the critical outcome. For example, in target archery, success is finally measured in terms of score. However, at an earlier stage, outcome information regarding the precision of results may be more useful. By itself, score does not tell us how much consistency the individual is achieving (an important requirement in target archery, since we want six arrows clustered in the center circle). By recording the dispersion of arrows on the target (Fig. 10-2), the teacher has some basis for determining how best to help the learner improve the next performance.

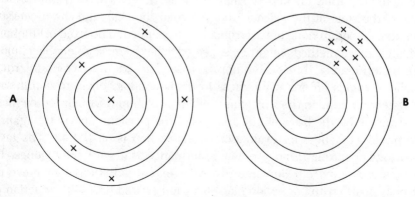

FIG. 10-2. A scattergram in archery. **A,** High variability. **B,** Low variability.

Provide feedback to improve next performance—If, in the scattergram shown in Fig. 10-2, the arrows show wide dispersion (Fig. 10-2, *A*), the teacher would look for variability in the movement form of the learner. Conversely, if the arrows are clustered on the target (Fig. 10-2, *B*) but off center, the teacher would look for a consistent error in form or a visual or point-of-aim problem. Kerr and Smoll (1977) note the desirability of observing this "intraindividual variability." However, it should not be thought of as limited in usefulness to skills requiring accuracy. In tennis serving, for example, we want to be able to vary the placement of the ball within the service court. Kerr and Smoll (1977) also point out the desirability of recording outcome results. Although in archery the student can readily see the dispersion of arrows in the target, other skills (e.g., placement of volleyball serves during a game or scrimmage) are widely spaced in time and require that a written record be kept.

Update proficiency goals—As Kerr and Smoll (1977) note, proficiency goals that are too high may create frustration, while those set too low may cause a lack of incentive to develop capabilities to their fullest extent. The importance of maintaining a record of performance outcome has been stressed. When this demonstrated proficiency deviates too far from preplanned proficiency goals (Table 6), the teacher and learner should jointly review the proficiency goals and increase or decrease them accordingly. This does not mean that the desired terminal proficiency goal need be changed, although it may. Rather, additional, intermediate short-term goals may be set up (e.g., "Cluster 6 consecutive arrows on the target within a 1-foot radius"). However, standards of achievement and expectations (proficiency goals) will not be the same for all; they must be adjusted to the individual learner.

Evaluate and revise instruction

Three factors contributing to performance and learning have been emphasized in this book: the state of the learner, the nature of the skill, and the processes of instruction. Although none of these should be assumed to be fixed or unchangeable, instructional methods might be expected to be the most amenable to modification. Unfortunately, this is often not the case. The extent to which instruction is flexible depends on our willingness to try new approaches; to determine in some systematic fashion the why of our results, which may be failure; to redesign our instruction on the basis of our analysis of the problem; and to try again.

A sample worksheet for evaluation of instruction is on p. 243. The task is basically one of getting IF on our own performance as teachers or coaches. Thus it involves evaluating our outcome (To what extent did students achieve their proficiency goal?) with our action plan (instruction) and revising our action plan for the next instructional period.

Instructional processes □ *Worksheet for evaluation of instruction*

	Evaluation (problem)	Revision (solution)
1. *Best environment?* _____ _____ Regulatory cues provided? _____ "Noise" controlled? _____ Arranged feedback? 2. *Purpose clear?* _____ _____ Objective clear? _____ Skill demonstrated? _____ Assessed learner? 3. *Essentials emphasized?* _____ _____ Identified cues? _____ Gross framework? _____ Concentration focused? 4. *Retention enhanced?* _____ _____ Best modality? _____ Chunked instruction? _____ Immediate practice? 5. *Best practice?* _____ _____ Realistic practice? _____ Whole practice? _____ Individualized practice? 6. *Best feedback?* _____ _____ Led to improvement? _____ Reached proficiency goal?		
7. Could goal have been reached sooner? _____ How? _____ _____ _____ _____ _____		

Since our concern is not just good teaching but better teaching, it may be more useful to begin our evaluation with the questions, Could students have achieved their goals sooner? and How? The answers to these questions are more likely to generate an active search for more effective instructional techniques.

However, we must realize that even the most promising technique is seldom successful until we have practiced it. Recognition of the fact that teaching itself is a continual learning endeavor should help to alleviate the dissatisfaction that so often occurs in the early stages of learning a new teaching skill.

An appendix to this book suggests a sequence of practice opportunities that can help you in your task of moving from theory to practice. I hope it will continue to be an exciting journey for you.

Sample thought sheet

1. Select a specific motor skill. Using the worksheet for skill analysis on p. 222, analyze the skill in terms of high proficiency requirements.
2. Describe how you might simplify the skill for a beginner, keeping in mind the objective of the skill and its perceptual, decision-making, and movement requirements (No. 1 above).
3. Using the worksheet for evaluation of instruction on p. 243,
   a. Observe and rate (+ and 0) an actual sports teaching situation.
   b. Following your observation, record your comments (e.g., the basis for your ratings).
   c. Where possible, make suggestions on how you might solve the instructional problem.
   d. Star (*) those tasks that you found difficult to interpret.
4. As a final project, select an individual of any age and
   a. Design instruction for teaching this individual a skill in which he has not previously participated.
   b. Teach the skill.
   c. Evaluate your instruction.

References

Arnold, R.K. Optimizing skill learning: moving to match the environment. *Journal of Physical Education and Recreation*, November-December 1978, pp. 84-86.

Billing, J. An overview of task complexity. *Motor Skills: Theory into Practice*, 1980, 4(1), 18-23.

Fishman, S. & Tobey, C. Augmented feedback. In W.G. Anderson & G.T. Barrett, *What's going on in gym: descriptive studies of physical education classes*. Monograph 1, Motor Skills: Theory into Practice, 1978. (Available from 24 Tauton Lake Dr., Newtown, Conn. 06470.)

Gentile, A.M. A working model of skill acquisition with application to teaching. *Quest*, 1972, 17, 3-23.

Johnson, M.L. A case for using large motor tasks. *Journal of Health, Physical Education, and Recreation*, March 1972, pp. 29-31.

Kerr, B., & Smoll, F.L. Variability in individual student performance: implications for teachers. *Motor Skills: Theory into Practice*, 1977, 1(2), 75-86.

Lawther, J.D. *The learning of physical skills*. Englewood Cliffs, N.J.: Prentice-Hall, 1968.

Lockhart, A. Communicating with the learner. *Quest*, 1966, 6, 57-67.

Pease, D.A. A teaching model for motor skill acquisition. *Motor Skills: Theory into Practice*, 1977, 1(2), 104-112.

Singer, R.N. The learning systems approach to instruction in psychomotor activities. *Motor Skills: Theory into Practice*, 1977, 1(2), 113-122.

Appendix

OPPORTUNITIES FOR PRACTICE

If the objective of moving from theory to practice is to be fully met, it is necessary to go beyond the material that can be presented in any book. Knowledge, even knowledge of the implications of learning theories for instruction, does not ensure the application of that knowledge. Considerable time must be devoted to the practice side of the objective. The purpose of this appendix, therefore, is to suggest a sequence of practice experiences that can help individuals in applying learning concepts to instructional situations.

Briefly, the sequence of practice experiences includes (1) the use of thought sheets, such as those provided at the end of each chapter, prior to class meetings; (2) discussions between students and between students and instructors that are aimed at clarifying the concepts and attaining a wider diversity of implications for instruction; (3) guided observation and evaluation of teaching and coaching situations; (4) guided practice in using the concepts in instructional situations; and (5) independent teaching projects that use a systematic model such as that described in Chapter 10 (see Fig. 10-1).

Obviously, not all of these opportunities are feasible within a particular course or class setting, since course objectives, student needs, time, and available facilities differ greatly. However, many of the opportunities suggested can be found at other sites within a school, university, or clinical setting, and these practice opportunities need to be sought out by individual students or groups of students.

It does seem desirable, however, that such practice experiences be sequenced in such a way as to enhance rather than frustrate the individual's ability to apply the concepts to the practical situation. First, a basic understanding of the concept is essential. This can be accomplished through reading the text, using the thought sheets, and engaging in clarifying discussions with other students and instructors. Even at this level, however, observation of actual practical situations is important. The best way to understand a principle or concept is to see it in operation, preferably in a variety of situations. In the final analysis, of course, we must practice applying the concept ourselves, that is, put it to use in our own teaching or coaching.

The particular sequence of practice experiences suggested here should be thought of as only one example of possible learning opportunities. Other learning experiences can be devised to meet the particular needs of specific courses, students, instructors, and settings. The important concept is that we need to seek practice opportunities and that we should use them in a reasonable sequential order.

Thought sheets

Thought sheets, such as those used in this book, were conceived to save class time for clarification and application of the concepts emphasized in the text. When used following the reading and prior to class, they have been quite useful in helping students reach a level of understanding of particular concepts beyond that of simple recall.

Since many students have not previously been exposed to the concepts (or even, in some cases, to the terminology), it was assumed that the depth of understanding necessary to apply the concepts in practice takes time. The reading of the text and the answering of the thought sheets provide for only the initial levels of understanding of the concepts. However, when followed up with clarifying discussions, the thought sheets have been deemed by students using them to be one of the most useful tools in moving from theory to practice.

It should be noted, however, that it is often necessary to dispel the notion, early in the use of thought sheets, that the answers given are right or wrong. Rather, they should be thought of as incomplete and should be used as indications of where clarification is needed.

However, the specific thought sheets provided in this book are samples only. Instructors and students can best construct thought sheets of their own that are specifically relevant to their particular needs.

In addition, students should be cautioned not to let the thought sheets direct their reading. There is much to be gained from reading the text material that is not specifically addressed in the very limited thought sheets provided.

Clarifying discussions

The use of the thought sheets before class allows the time spent in class to be devoted to clarifying the concepts so that students can reach a higher level of understanding of the concepts. However, students should not limit their sources for clarification to a specific course or class. As will be noted in the next section, observation is an important tool in the theory-to-practice journey. In like manner, sharing examples of application with other students and instructors, in and out of class, is useful, as long as we recognize that the result of such sharing can lead to two quite different, but equally productive, results. First, the sharing of interpretations or examples of application may lead to the "Aha" or "Now I see" reaction. Second, and conversely, it may lead a person to exclaim, "I *thought* I understood it!" Note that the latter reaction serves a useful purpose (e.g., the need for additional clarification to reach a higher level of understanding).

The clarifying discussions should have as their objective the goal not only of making the concept more generalized (e.g., usable in a variety of situations) but also of making it more particularized (e.g., usable in certain specified situations but not in others). One way this might be accomplished is to seek clarifying discussions with individuals having varied backgrounds. For example, discussions among students with dissimilar occupational backgrounds (e.g., physical education, physical or occupational therapy, and dance) or activity experiences (e.g., basketball, baseball, and fencing) provide a diversity of examples of application. Discussions with those whose experience and expertise are similar (e.g., basketball) often can provide more particularization, that is, specificity of application.

Guided observations

Prior to actually using a concept in practice, observation is useful in achieving ever higher levels of understanding. It is hoped that a habit of observation as a method of learning will already have been established.

Observation can be used at almost any level of understanding. For example, some of the sample thought sheets used in this book call on students to give an example. It is much more useful to give an actual example from observation than to give a hypothetical one.

At higher levels, students can make extended observations of teaching and coaching situations. This is most useful if these observations are in some way directed or guided and if they call for specific evaluations rather than general criticisms or reactions. For example, the sample thought sheet for Chapter 10 calls on students to evaluate a teaching or coaching situation using the checklist shown on p. 243. For each item evaluated, the student records not only the rating but also the suggested solution to the problem observed.

Guided practice

As in the case of observation, actual practice in applying concepts to instruction can occur at various levels of understanding. At initial levels, students can demonstrate the operation of a particular concept (e.g., head-righting reflex) or its implications (e.g., inhibiting the head-righting reflex in a specific skill). At higher levels of understanding, students can demonstrate how they might actually apply a concept in a teaching or coaching situation, for example, "Demonstrate how your approach to teaching a closed skill and an open skill would differ" or "Demonstrate how you would teach this skill to ensure positive transfer." Finally, it would seem desirable to have students actually teach a skill to an individual or group in a situation in which they can receive feedback both from those they teach and from the course instructor (e.g., using the worksheet on p. 243).

One of the most useful comments received from students who have participated in this kind of experience is that they derive additional benefits from being a learner. In addition, the feedback to a student from the learners has tended to be as useful and complete as that given by the course instructor when it is guided by a specific evaluation form, such as that on p. 243. Obviously, the feasibility of such an approach may be limited in many classroom settings, but, as much as possible, students should seek opportunities to practice in real situations.

Independent projects

Ideally, the culminating learning experience should be an independent teaching project in which students use their knowledge to teach a skill and evaluate their own teaching. Such an experience should encompass all of the instructional tasks shown in Fig. 10-1: (1) an analysis of the skill (worksheet on p. 222), (2) an assessment of the learner and statement of proficiency goals (Table 6), (3) the design of instruction (worksheet on p. 232), and (4) the evaluation of that instruction (worksheet on p. 243). The projects are most useful if carried out over a period of time (e.g., a minimum of four daily sessions) for the learner or learners to progress beyond the early learning stages and to offset daily performance variability.

Obviously, a single teaching project is not going to provide the amount of practice necessary for overlearning and retention. If, however, students keep in mind that learning a new teaching skill is really not that different from learning a new sports skill, then they will not expect immediate success. It is hoped that with the end in view, more effective teaching and coaching will suffice to encourage student practitioners to continue past the early learning stages.

NAME INDEX

249

SUBJECT INDEX

---

*Boldface numbers indicate pages on which figures are found; t indicates pages on which tables appear.